펼쳐 보면 느껴집니다

단 한 줄도 배움의 공백이 생기지 않도록
문장 한 줄마다 20년이 넘는
해커스의 영어교육 노하우를 담았음을

덮고 나면 확신합니다

수많은 선생님의 목소리와
정확한 출제 데이터 분석으로 꽉 찬
교재 한 권이면 충분함을

해커스북 중·고등
HackersBook.com

WHY
HACKERS
GRAMMAR SMART?

Completely master English grammar

누구나 쉽게
이해할 수 있는

실생활에서 그대로
사용할 수 있는

Smart Check → Practice →
Writing Exercise →
Chapter Test로 이어지는

간결한 문법 설명

유용한 표현과 예문

단계별 문제 풀이

HACKERS
Grammar Smart

Starter

HACKERS
Grammar Smart

Level 1

HACKERS
Grammar Smart

Level 2

HACKERS
Grammar Smart

Level 3

Effectively prepare for middle school English exams

학교 시험 기출경향을
완벽 반영한 문제로

서술형 포함 내신 완벽 대비

풍부한 문제의 Workbook과
다양한 부가 학습 자료로

학습효과 Up Up!

Hackers Grammar Smart 시리즈를 검토해주신 선생님들

경기

강무정	광교EIE고려대학교어학원
강민정	김진성의 열정어학원
김민성	빨리강해지는학원
윤혜영	이루다영수학학원
이창석	정현영어학원
이창헌	더블원영어학원
정필두	시흥배곧 정상어학원
조은혜	이든영수학원

최희정	SJ클쌤영어
탁은영	EiE고려대학교어학원 태전퍼스트캠퍼스
한지수	위드유어학원
홍영숙	솔로몬학원
황정민	한수위학원

부산

배미경	삼정아카데미학원
이미영	수영학원

서울

신봉철	강북세일학원
양세희	양세희수능영어학원
이현아	이은재어학원
채가희	대성세그루학원
최세아	씨앤씨학원

인천

송인택	변화와도전학원

해커스 어학연구소 자문위원단 3기

강원

박정선	잉글리쉬클럽
최현주	최샘영어

경기

강민정	김진성열정어학원
강상훈	평촌RTS학원
강지인	강지인영어학원
권계미	A&T+ 영어
김미아	김쌤영어학원
김설화	업라이트잉글리쉬
김성재	스윗스터디학원
김세훈	모두의학원
김수아	더스터디(The STUDY)
김영아	백송고등학교
김유경	벨트학원
김유경	포시즌스학원
김유동	이스턴영어학원
김지숙	위디벨럽학원
김지현	이지프레임영어학원
김해빈	해빛영어학원
김현지	지앤비영어학원
박가영	한민고등학교
박영서	스윗스터디학원
박은별	더킹영수학원
박재홍	록키어학원
성승민	SDH어학원 불당캠퍼스
신소연	Ashley English
오귀연	루나영어학원
유신애	에듀포커스학원
윤소정	ILP이화어학원
이동진	이룸학원
이상미	버밍엄영어교습소
이연경	명품M비욘드수학영어학원
이은수	광주세종학원
이지혜	리케이온
이진희	이엠원영수학원
이충기	영어나무
이효명	갈매리드앤톡영어독서학원
임한글	Apsun앞선영어학원
장광명	엠케이영어학원
전상호	평촌이지어학원
전성훈	훈선생영어교실
정선영	코어플러스영어학원
정준	고양외국어고등학교
조연아	카이트학원
채기림	고려대학교EIE영어학원
최지영	다른영어학원
최한나	석사영수전문
최희정	SJ클쌤영어학원
현지환	모두의학원
홍태경	공감국어영어전문학원

경남

강다훤	더(the)오르다영어학원
라승희	아이작잉글리쉬
박주언	유니크학원
배송현	두잇영어교습소
안윤서	어썸영어학원
임진희	어썸영어학원

경북

권현민	삼성영어석적우방교실
김으뜸	EIE영어학원 옥계캠퍼스
배세왕	비케이영수전문고등관학원
유영선	아이비티어학원

광주

김유희	김유희영어학원
서희연	SDL영어수학학원
오진우	SLT어학원수학원
정영철	정영철영어전문학원
최경옥	봉선중학교

대구

권익재	제이슨영어
김명일	독학인학원
김보곤	베스트영어
김연정	달서고등학교
김혜란	김혜란영어학원
문애주	프렌즈입시학원
박정근	공부의힘pnk학원
박희숙	열공열강영수학학원
신동기	신통외국어학원
위영선	위영선영어학원
윤창원	공터영어학원 상인센터
이승현	학문당입시학원
이주현	이주현영어학원
이헌욱	이헌욱영어학원
장준현	장쌤독해종결영어학원
주현아	민샘영어학원
최윤정	최강영어학원

대전

곽선영	위드유학원
김지운	더포스둔산학원
박미현	라시움영어대동학원
박세리	EM101학원

부산

김건희	레지나잉글리쉬 영어학원
김미나	위드중고등영어학원
박수진	정모클영어국어학원
박수진	지니잉글리쉬
박인숙	리더스영어전문학원
옥지윤	더센텀영어학원
윤진희	위니드영어전문교습소
이종혁	진수학원
정혜인	엠티엔영어학원
조정래	알파카의영어농장
주태양	솔라영어학원

서울

Erica Sull	하버드브레인영어학원
강고은	케이앤학원
강신아	교우학원
공현미	이은재어학원
권영진	경동고등학교
김나영	프라임클래스영어학원
김달수	대일외국어고등학교
김대니	채움학원
김문영	창문여자고등학교
김정은	강북뉴스터디학원
김혜경	대동세무고등학교
남혜원	함영원입시전문학원
노시은	케이앤학원
박선정	강북세일학원
박수진	이은재어학원
박지수	이플러스영수학원
서승희	함영원입시전문학원
양세희	양세희수능영어학원
우정용	제임스영어앤드학원
이박원	이박원어학원
이승혜	스텔라영어
이정욱	이은재어학원
이지연	중계케이트영어학원
임예찬	학습컨설턴트
장지희	고려대학교사범대학부속고등학교
정미라	미라정영어학원
조민규	조민규영어
채가희	대성세그루영수학원

울산

김기태	그라티아어학원
이민주	로이아카데미
홍영민	더이안영어전문학원

인천

강재민	스터디위드제이쌤
고현순	정상학원
권효진	Genie's English
김솔	전문과외
김정아	밀턴영어학원
서상천	최정서학원
이윤주	트리플원
최예영	영웅아카데미

전남

강희진	강희진영어학원
김두환	해남맨체스터영수학원
송승연	송승연영수학원
윤세광	비상구영어학원

전북

김길자	맨투맨학원
김미영	링크영어학원
김효성	연세입시학원
노빈나	노빈나영어전문학원
라성남	하포드어학원
박재훈	위니드수학지앤비영어학원
박향숙	STA영어전문학원
서종원	서종원영어학원
이상훈	나는학원
장지원	링컨더글라스학원
지근영	한솔영어수학학원
최성령	연세입시학원
최혜영	이든영어수학학원

제주

김랑	KLS어학원
박자은	KLS어학원

충남

김예지	더배움프라임영수학원
김철홍	청경학원
노태겸	최상위학원

충북

라은경	이화윤스영어교습소
신유정	비타민영어클리닉학원

HACKERS
GRAMMAR
SMART
LEVEL 3

HACKERS

Contents

Preview

명쾌한 설명과 실용적인 문장으로 Smart하게 학습

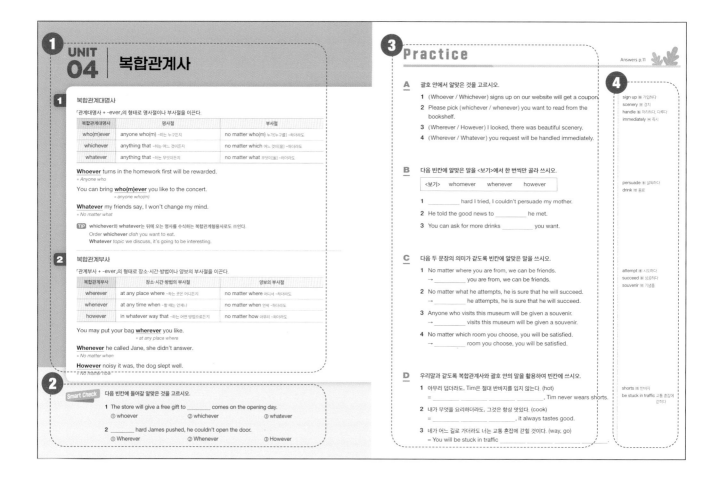

각 레벨에 딱 맞는
Essential Grammar Units

① Grammar Lesson
해당 레벨에서 익혀야 할 문법 개념을 명쾌한 설명과 실용적인 예문을 통해 정확하게 이해할 수 있습니다. TIP을 통해 내신 시험에서 출제되는 심화 문법까지 학습하여 고난도 문제에도 대비할 수 있습니다.

③ Practice
다양한 유형의 풍부한 연습문제를 통해 문법 개념을 자연스럽게 이해할 수 있습니다.

② Smart Check
간단한 문제를 통해 위에서 배운 문법 개념을 잘 이해했는지 바로바로 확인할 수 있습니다.

④ Vocabulary
연습문제에 쓰인 주요 어휘를 추가로 학습하여 어휘력까지 높일 수 있습니다.

*어휘 정리에 사용된 약호
명 명사 동 동사 형 형용사 부 부사 전 전치사 접 접속사

기초부터 실전까지 Perfect하게 완성

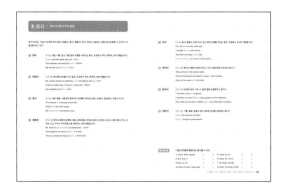

기초를 탄탄히 다지는
기초 문법

중학영문법을 이해하기 위해 꼭 알아야 하는 기초 문법이 정리되어 있어, 문법 실력이 부족한 학생들도 기초를 탄탄히 다지고 본학습을 시작할 수 있습니다.

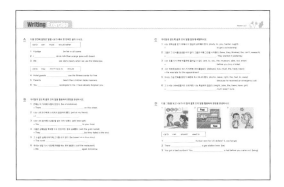

쓰기 활동으로 문법을 체득하는
Writing Exercise

다양한 유형의 서술형 문제를 풀어보며 쓰기 연습을 충분히 할 수 있습니다. 이를 통해 서술형을 강조하는 최근 내신 평가 트렌드에 대비할 수 있습니다.

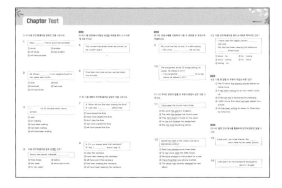

문제 풀이로 학습 내용을 확실히 점검하는
Chapter Test

전국 내신 기출문제 출제 유형을 기반으로 한 다양한 문제를 풀어보며 실제 시험에 대비할 수 있습니다. 서술형 주관식 문제 및 고난도 문제로 학습한 문법 개념에 대한 이해도를 점검할 수 있습니다.

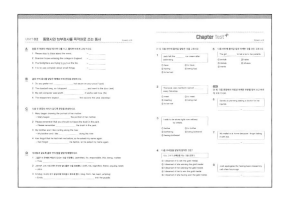

학습 효과를 더욱 높이는
Workbook

각 UNIT별, Chapter별로 풍부한 양의 추가 문제를 풀면서 본교재에서 익힌 문법 개념을 확실히 복습하고 부족한 부분은 보완할 수 있습니다.

해커스북 중·고등

www.HackersBook.com

기초 문법

영어 문법, 그 기초부터 알고 들어가자!

1 품사 | 영어 단어의 8가지 종류

영어 단어는 기능과 성격에 따라 **명사, 대명사, 동사, 형용사, 부사, 전치사, 접속사, 감탄사로** 분류할 수 있으며, 이를 **품사라고** 한다.

❶ 명사

명사는 **사람, 사물, 장소, 개념 등의 이름을 나타내는 말로,** 문장에서 **주어, 목적어, 보어 역할을** 한다.

Susan became taller than me. <주어>

The students will read the book. <목적어>

My favorite city is Seoul. <보어>

❷ 대명사

대명사는 **명사를 대신해서 쓰는 말로,** 문장에서 **주어, 목적어, 보어 역할을** 한다.

My cousin visited us yesterday. She had dinner with us. <주어>

I lost my teddy bear. I found it in the park. <목적어>

His question was this. <보어>

❸ 동사

동사는 **사람, 동물, 사물 등의 동작이나 상태를 나타내는 말로,** be동사, 일반동사, 조동사가 있다.

The woman is a famous movie star.

They liked the new house.

We must clean the kitchen now.

❹ 형용사

형용사는 **명사나 대명사의 형태, 성질, 상태 등을 나타내는 말로,** 문장에서 명사나 대명사를 꾸미는 **수식어,** 또는 주어나 목적어를 보충 설명하는 **보어 역할을** 한다.

Mr. Swan is a successful businessman. <수식어>

The dolphins are very playful. <주격 보어>

The air conditioner kept us cool. <목적격 보어>

⑤ 부사

부사는 동사, 형용사, 다른 부사, 또는 문장 전체를 꾸미는 말로, 문장에서 수식어 역할을 한다.

Eric did **well** on his math test.

I bought a **very** soft curtain.

The thief ran away **really** fast.

Unfortunately, our team lost the game.

⑥ 전치사

전치사는 명사나 대명사 앞에서 장소, 시간, 방법 등을 나타내는 말이다.

They arrived **at** the airport early.

Paul and Veronica promised to meet **in** the evening.

Dad cut the rope **with** the knife.

⑦ 접속사

접속사는 단어와 단어, 구와 구, 절과 절을 연결해주는 말이다.

I will take a bus **or** a subway.

Fred likes to watch TV **and** play games on the weekend.

You must put on warm clothes **when** you climb the mountain.

⑧ 감탄사

감탄사는 기쁨, 놀람, 슬픔과 같은 다양한 감정을 표현하는 말이다.

Wow, this pizza is so tasty!

Oops, I forgot my homework.

Check-up 다음 단어들에 해당되는 품사를 쓰시오.

1 nearly, often, quickly [   ]   **5** under, for, by [   ]

2 and, that, if [   ]   **6** Oops, Oh, Ouch [   ]

3 they, us, its [   ]   **7** sit, laugh, should [   ]

4 beauty, France, happiness [   ]   **8** sharp, amazing, lonely [   ]

정답 1 부사 2 접속사 3 대명사 4 명사 5 전치사 6 감탄사 7 동사 8 형용사

2 문장의 성분 | 영어 문장을 만드는 재료

영어 문장을 만드는 여러 가지 재료로 **주어, 동사, 목적어, 보어, 수식어**가 있으며, 이를 **문장의 성분**이라고 한다.

❶ 주어

주어는 **동작이나 상태의 주체가 되는 말**로, '누가, 무엇이'에 해당한다.

Nate wants to drink some tea.

Swimming in the sea is my hobby.

❷ 동사

동사는 **주어의 동작이나 상태를 나타내는 말**로, '~하다, ~이다'에 해당한다.

The boy has curly hairs.

They will watch the movie on TV.

❸ 목적어

목적어는 **동작의 대상이 되는 말**로, '~을/를, ~에게'에 해당한다.

Mr. Steven sold the house.

Amy asked the teacher a question.

❹ 보어

보어는 **주어나 목적어를 보충 설명하는 말**이다.

Rachel felt sad about the news. <주격 보어>

The neighbor asked us to be quiet. <목적격 보어>

❺ 수식어

수식어는 문장에 반드시 필요하지는 않지만 다양한 위치에서 **여러 가지 의미를 더해주는 말**이다.

That beautiful woman is my mother.

I left the classroom after the class.

Check-up 다음 밑줄 친 부분의 문장 성분을 쓰시오.

1 <u>Ms. Andrews</u> told the students a story. [   ]

2 I found <u>the cell phone</u> in the refrigerator. [   ]

3 Liam wrote his friend <u>a long letter</u>. [   ]

4 Charles <u>can play</u> the guitar very well. [   ]

5 The <u>brave</u> firefighters rescued many people. [   ]

6 The rain made my shoes <u>wet</u>. [   ]

정답 1 주어 2 목적어 3 목적어 4 동사 5 수식어 6 보어

3 문장의 형식 | 영어 문장의 5가지 형태

영어 문장은 크게 다음의 **다섯 가지 형식**으로 나눌 수 있다.

> 1형식: 주어 + 동사
> 2형식: 주어 + 동사 + 주격 보어
> 3형식: 주어 + 동사 + 목적어
> 4형식: 주어 + 동사 + 간접 목적어 + 직접 목적어
> 5형식: 주어 + 동사 + 목적어 + 목적격 보어

❶ 1형식

1형식은 **주어와 동사**만으로도 의미가 통하는 문장으로, **수식어구**가 함께 쓰이기도 한다.

Jake laughed.
주어 　동사

They are running in the park.
주어 　동사 　　수식어구

❷ 2형식

2형식은 **주어, 동사**와 주어를 보충 설명하는 **주격 보어**를 가지는 문장이다. 주격 보어 자리에는 **(대)명사**나 **형용사**가 올 수 있다.

Amy became the class president.
주어 　동사 　　주격 보어(명사)

The hamburger looks delicious.
　　주어 　　　동사 　주격 보어(형용사)

❸ 3형식

3형식은 **주어, 동사**와 동작의 대상이 되는 **목적어**를 가지는 문장이다. 목적어 자리에는 **(대)명사, 동명사, to부정사, 명사절** 등이 올 수 있다.

The photographer took the picture.
　　　주어 　　　동사 　목적어(명사)

Chris and I met her yesterday.
　　주어 　　동사 목적어(대명사)

④ 4형식

4형식은 주어, 동사와 간접 목적어, 직접 목적어를 가지는 문장이다. 4형식 문장은 「주어 + 동사 + 직접 목적어 + 전치사(to/for/of) + 간접 목적어」 형태의 3형식 문장으로 바꿔 쓸 수 있다.

Tina brought her friends some snacks.
　주어　　동사　　간접 목적어　　직접 목적어

→ Tina brought some snacks to her friends.
　주어　　동사　　직접 목적어　전치사　간접 목적어

The teacher asked the students a question.
　주어　　　동사　　간접 목적어　　직접 목적어

→ The teacher asked a question of the students.
　주어　　　동사　　직접 목적어　전치사　간접 목적어

⑤ 5형식

5형식은 주어, 동사, 목적어와 목적어를 보충 설명하는 **목적격 보어**를 가지는 문장이다. 목적격 보어 자리에는 동사에 따라 **명사, 형용사, to부정사, 동사원형, 분사**가 올 수 있다.

명사　　　Danny calls himself a genius.
　　　　　주어　　동사　　목적어　　목적격 보어

형용사　　The traffic jam made the driver angry.
　　　　　　　주어　　　　동사　　목적어　목적격 보어

to부정사　Shawn told his dog to sit.
　　　　　주어　　동사　　목적어　목적격 보어

동사원형　The doctor didn't let the patient leave.
　　　　　　　주어　　　　동사　　목적어　목적격 보어

분사　　　My brother had his laptop repaired.
　　　　　　주어　　　동사　　목적어　　목적격 보어

Check-up 다음 문장의 형식을 쓰시오.

1 This room is so hot. [　　　]

2 The coach advised the team to practice harder. [　　　]

3 Sam sent the gift to me from France. [　　　]

4 We grew some carrots in the farm. [　　　]

5 Erica arrived at the station. [　　　]

6 Ms. Trevor felt sad. [　　　]

7 Nate showed his sister a video. [　　　]

8 Reading old diaries made me laugh. [　　　]

정답 1 2형식 2 5형식 3 3형식 4 3형식 5 1형식 6 2형식 7 4형식 8 5형식

12 영어 실력을 높여주는 다양한 학습 자료 제공 HackersBook.com

4 구와 절 | 말 덩어리

두 개 이상의 단어가 모여 하나의 의미를 나타내는 말 덩어리를 **구**나 **절**이라고 하며, **구**는 「주어 + 동사」를 포함하지 않고 **절**은 「주어 + 동사」를 포함한다. 구와 절은 문장에서 **명사, 형용사, 부사 역할**을 할 수 있다.

❶ 명사 역할   명사 역할을 하는 명사구와 명사절은 문장 안에서 명사처럼 **주어, 목적어, 보어**로 쓰인다.

     명사구   The letter from England was written in 1789. <주어>

     명사절   I think that Mr. Brown is a kind neighbor. <목적어>

❷ 형용사 역할   형용사 역할을 하는 형용사구와 형용사절은 형용사처럼 **명사나 대명사를 꾸민다.**

     형용사구   The bridge built in 20th century is over the lake.

     형용사절   This is the movie which Mariah likes the most.

❸ 부사 역할   부사 역할을 하는 부사구와 부사절은 부사처럼 **동사, 형용사, 다른 부사, 또는 문장 전체를 꾸민다.**

     부사구   Tony cooked the steak to have dinner.

     부사절   We were excited because it was snowing outside.

Check-up   다음 문장의 밑줄 친 부분이 해당하는 것을 고르시오.

1 The bench next to the tree is very old.   (명사구 / 명사절)

2 Matt promised to keep my secret.   (명사구 / 명사절)

3 Did you see the ring which Kelly was wearing?   (형용사구 / 형용사절)

4 After you arrive at the airport, they will pick you up.   (부사구 / 부사절)

5 You can buy this cake at the Deboa bakery.   (명사구 / 부사구)

6 The problem is that he doesn't have his passport.   (명사절 / 형용사절)

7 These oranges are too sour.   (형용사구 / 부사구)

8 Brian checked the address before he sent the package.   (형용사절 / 부사절)

Chapter

01

시제

시제는 동사의 형태를 바꿔 행동이나 사건이 발생한 시점을 표현하는 것이다.

UNIT 01 | 현재완료시제

1 현재완료시제(have + p.p.)

과거에 일어난 일이 현재까지 영향을 미칠 때 쓴다.

She **has played** the violin for 20 years.

> **TIP** 현재완료시제는 특정한 과거 시점을 나타내는 표현(**yesterday, last, ago, when** 등)과 함께 쓸 수 없다.
> Irene (~~has visited~~, **visited**) Busan two months *ago*.

❶ 완료(~했다): 과거에 일어난 일이 현재에 완료되었음을 나타내며, just, already, yet, lately, recently 등과 주로 함께 쓴다.

I **have** *already* **finished** my science project.

❷ 경험(~해본 적이 있다): 과거부터 현재까지의 경험을 나타내며, once, ~ times, ever, never, before 등과 주로 함께 쓴다.

Samantha **has seen** this movie *three times*.

❸ 계속(~해왔다, ~했다): 과거부터 현재까지 계속되는 일을 나타내며, 「for(~ 동안) + 지속 기간」, 「since(~ 이후로) + 시작 시점」, how long 등과 주로 함께 쓴다.

Liam **has stayed** in Seoul *for* a year.
Liam **has stayed** in Seoul *since* last year.

❹ 결과(~했다 (지금은 ~이다)): 과거에 일어난 일의 결과가 현재까지 영향을 미치고 있음을 나타낸다.

He **has lost** his favorite watch. (He doesn't have it now.)

> **TIP** **have been to**는 경험을 나타내고, **have gone to**는 결과를 나타낸다.
> Jane **has been to** Russia. <경험: ~에 가본 적이 있다>
> Jane **has gone to** Russia. <결과: ~에 갔다 (지금은 여기에 없다)>

---

2 현재완료진행시제(have been + V-ing)

과거에 일어난 일이 현재에도 계속 진행되고 있음을 나타낼 때 쓴다.

Tom **has been playing** computer games for an hour.
(= Tom started to play computer games an hour ago. He is still playing computer games.)

Smart Check 다음 빈칸에 들어갈 알맞은 것을 고르시오.

1 Hannah _____ yoga classes for three weeks.
① takes   ② has taken   ③ taken

2 The students _____ together since 6 o'clock.
① study   ② are studying   ③ have been studying

Practice

A 괄호 안에서 알맞은 것을 고르시오.

1 The company (rents / has rented) this office building since 2015.

2 Luke (never hear / has never heard) the singer's song before.

3 I (met / have met) my friends at the IT exhibition yesterday.

4 Emily (is trying / has been trying) to make doughnuts for two hours.

rent 통 (사용료를 내고) 빌리다
IT 명 정보통신 기술
    (information technology)
exhibition 명 박람회

B 괄호 안의 동사를 현재완료시제나 과거시제 형태로 바꿔 문장을 완성하시오.

1 My father _____ as a teacher for 15 years. (work)

2 Victoria _____ the musical ticket last week. (buy)

3 Tim's family _____ a family photo a few days ago. (take)

4 The milk _____ in the fridge for weeks already. (be)

fridge 명 냉장고

C 현재완료진행시제를 이용하여 다음 두 문장을 한 문장으로 연결하시오.

1 I started to wait for my mother an hour ago. I'm still waiting for her.
→ I _____ _____ _____ for my mother for an hour.

2 Eva began to practice basketball this morning. She's still practicing it.
→ Eva _____ _____ _____ basketball since this morning.

3 The artist began to draw a picture two days ago. He's still drawing it.
→ The artist _____ _____ _____ a picture for two days.

4 We started to discuss the issue at 10:30. We're still discussing it.
→ We _____ _____ _____ the issue since 10:30.

discuss 통 논의하다
issue 명 문제, 사안

D 우리말과 같도록 괄호 안의 말을 활용하여 빈칸에 쓰시오.

1 그 조각상은 이곳에 20년 동안 있어왔다. (be)
= The statue _____ _____ here for 20 years.

2 그들은 이미 가게에 있는 모든 꽃들을 팔았다. (already, sell)
= They _____ _____ _____ all the flowers in the shop.

3 너는 전에 뉴질랜드에 가본 적이 있니? (ever, be)
= Have you _____ _____ _____ New Zealand before?

4 사람들은 실종된 아이를 다섯 시간 동안 찾고 있다. (search for)
= People _____ _____ _____ _____ the missing child
for five hours.

statue 명 조각상
search for ~을 찾다
missing 형 실종된, 없어진

UNIT 02 | 과거완료시제와 미래완료시제

1 과거완료시제(had + p.p.)

과거의 특정 시점 이전에 발생한 일이 그 시점까지 영향을 미칠 때 쓴다.

The play **had** just **ended** when I returned from the restroom. <완료>
She **had** never **seen** kangaroos before she came to Australia. <경험>
Nate **had waited** outside for 15 minutes before his friends joined. <계속>
Mr. Jones couldn't buy anything because he **had lost** his wallet. <결과>

> **TIP** 「had + p.p.」는 과거에 일어난 두 개의 일 중 먼저 일어난 일을 나타내기 위해 쓰기도 하며, 이때 먼저 일어난 일을 대과거라고 한다.
> I *broke* the watch that my friend **had given** to me.
> ('내가 시계를 망가뜨린 일'보다 '나의 친구가 나에게 시계를 준 일'이 먼저 일어남)

2 과거완료진행시제(had been + V-ing)

과거의 특정 시점 이전에 발생한 일이 그 시점에도 계속 진행되고 있었음을 나타낼 때 쓴다.

He **had been sleeping** for two hours when his mom woke him up.
We **had been swimming** for a long time before we had lunch.

3 미래완료시제(will have + p.p.)

미래의 특정 시점까지 완료되거나 계속될 일을 나타낼 때 쓴다.

I **will have left** home by the time my sister arrives.
Amy **will have lived** in New York for 14 years next month.

4 미래완료진행시제(will have been + V-ing)

미래의 특정 시점에도 계속 진행될 일을 나타낼 때 쓴다.

Peter **will have been reading** the novel for hours by midnight.
My aunt **will have been working** at the bank for six years next month.

Smart Check 다음 빈칸에 들어갈 알맞은 것을 고르시오.

1 Ms. Moore _____ an actress before she became a director.
① has been ② had been ③ will have been

2 It _____ for a week when I came to Seattle.
① has rained ② had been raining ③ will have been raining

3 If I travel to London one more time, I _____ that city three times.
① have visited ② had visited ③ will have visited

Practice

Answers p.2

A 괄호 안에서 알맞은 것을 고르시오.

1 I (had submitted / will have submitted) my homework by tomorrow.

2 They (have never ridden / had never ridden) a plane before they visited Japan.

3 When I was born, my family (has been / had been) living in Seoul for eight months.

4 Sofia (had been / will have been) taking ballet classes for five years next year.

submit 图 제출하다
ride 图 타다
take a class 수업을 듣다

B 괄호 안의 동사를 활용하여 완료시제 문장을 완성하시오.

1 The party _____ when I got into the room. (end)

2 If he tells me the story once more, I _____ it five times. (hear)

3 Justin _____ by the time the baseball game begins. (arrive)

4 Before I ate dinner, I _____ for 50 minutes. (exercise)

get into ~에 들어가다
once more 한 번 더

C 다음 문장을 완료진행시제를 이용한 문장으로 바꿔 쓰시오.

1 I called them an hour after they started talking about the schedule.
→ They _____ _____ _____ about the schedule for an hour when I called them.

2 It started snowing two days ago. Tomorrow will be the third day.
→ It _____ _____ _____ _____ for three days tomorrow.

3 She decided to enter the contest a year after she started practicing dancing.
→ She _____ _____ _____ dancing for a year when she decided to enter the contest.

schedule 图 일정
enter 图 참가하다

D 우리말과 같도록 괄호 안의 말을 활용하여 완료시제 문장을 완성하시오.

1 비록 그는 충분한 수면을 취했었지만 여전히 피곤했다. (get enough sleep)
= Although he _____, he was still tired.

2 저녁 여섯 시면 Emma는 피아노를 두 시간째 치고 있을 것이다. (play the piano)
= Emma _____ for two hours by 6 P.M.

3 경찰관들이 도착할 때쯤 도둑은 달아났을 것이다. (run away)
= The thief _____ by the time the police officers arrive.

run away 달아나다

Writing Exercise

A 괄호 안의 동사를 활용하여 다음 두 문장을 한 문장으로 연결하시오. (단, 완료시제와 완료진행시제만 사용하시오.)

1 I was in Dubai last month. I just returned to Korea. (be)

→ I _____ _____ _____ _____ before.

2 Mr. Ford started dancing in 1990. He retired from dancing 15 years later. (dance)

→ Mr. Ford _____ _____ for 15 years before he retired.

3 The little girl lost her doll. She still can't find it. (lose)

→ The little girl _____ _____ _____ _____.

4 Betty started to take drawing classes in 2019. She's still taking them. (take)

→ Betty _____ _____ _____ _____ _____ since 2019.

5 Ms. Baker opened an Italian restaurant in 1998. She still owns it. (own)

→ Ms. Baker _____ _____ _____ _____ since 1998.

6 They started to do the research on penguins five years ago. They're still doing it. (do)

→ They _____ _____ _____ _____ _____ _____ _____ for five years.

7 I've read this comic book nine times so far. I'll read it again tonight. (read)

→ I _____ _____ _____ this comic book ten times if I read it again tonight.

B 우리말과 같도록 괄호 안의 말을 활용하여 문장을 완성하시오.

1 Henry는 조심하지 않았었기 때문에 칼에 베였다. (not, be careful)

= Henry cut himself with the knife because _____.

2 우리는 아주 오랜 시간 동안 태양 에너지를 사용해왔다. (use solar energy)

= _____ for a very long time.

3 그녀는 초등학교 이후로 그녀의 영어 실력을 향상시켜왔다. (improve her English skills)

= _____ since elementary school.

4 나는 기차를 놓쳤었기 때문에 또 다른 표를 예매했다. (miss the train)

= I booked another ticket because _____.

5 네가 그에게 전화할 때쯤 그는 도서관에 갔을 것이다. (go to the library)

= _____ by the time you call him.

6 Natalie는 그녀의 팔을 다쳤을 때 한 시간 동안 테니스를 하고 있었다. (play tennis)

= _____ for an hour when she hurt her arm.

C 우리말과 같도록 괄호 안의 말을 알맞게 배열하시오.

1 너의 전화기는 5분 동안 울리고 있다. (has, your, ringing, phone, been)

= _____ for five minutes.

2 나는 점심으로 무엇을 먹을지 이미 결정했다. (have, decided, I, already)

= _____ what I'm going to eat for lunch.

3 내가 카페에서 그녀를 봤을 때 Hill씨는 커피를 마시고 있었다. (coffee, had, drinking, Ms. Hill, been)

= _____ when I saw her at the café.

4 다음 달이면 그는 체육관을 6개월째 운영하고 있을 것이다. (running, will, he, gym, have, been, the)

= _____ for six months next month.

5 내가 알아차리기 전에 그 개는 나의 안경을 망가뜨렸다. (my, dog, broken, glasses, the, had)

= _____ before I noticed.

6 그녀는 2010년부터 그 독서 클럽의 회원이었다. (a, has, member, of, she, book, the, club, been)

= _____ since 2010.

D 다음 그림을 보고 괄호 안의 말을 활용하여 완료시제 문장을 완성하시오.

1

2

1 Ellie felt happy because she _____. (win the math competition)

2 Robert and Tyler _____ for ten years next year. (be friends)

Chapter Test

[1-3] 다음 빈칸에 들어갈 알맞은 것을 고르시오.

1

> Mary _____ French since last semester.

① study　　　　② studies
③ will study　　④ has studied
⑤ will have studied

2

> Mr. Brown _____ in our neighborhood for two years next month.

① lives　　　　② lived
③ has lived　　④ had lived
⑤ will have lived

3

> I _____ for 30 minutes when Jimmy arrived.

① wait
② am waiting
③ have been waiting
④ had been waiting
⑤ will have been waiting

4 다음 빈칸에 들어갈 말로 <u>어색한</u> 것은?

> Benny has played volleyball _____.

① three times　　② before
③ last week　　　④ since last month
⑤ for two years

[5-6] 다음 문장에서 어법상 <u>어색한</u> 부분을 찾아 <u>쓰고</u> 바르게 고쳐 쓰시오.

5

> The concert has ended when we arrived, so we couldn't see it.

_____ → _____

6

> If we take one more picture, we had taken five pictures.

_____ → _____

[7-8] 다음 대화의 빈칸에 들어갈 알맞은 것을 고르시오.

7

> A: When did you first start playing the flute?
> B: Last year. I _____ before then.

① have played the flute
② have never played the flute
③ don't play the flute
④ had never played the flute
⑤ will have played the flute

8

> A: Do you always wear that necklace?
> B: Yes. I _____ since I was 13.

① wear this necklace
② have been wearing this necklace
③ will have worn this necklace
④ had been wearing this necklace
⑤ will have been wearing this necklace

서술형

[9-10] 완료시제를 이용하여 다음 두 문장을 한 문장으로 연결하시오.

9

My uncle lost his car key. It is still missing.
→ My uncle _____ his car key.

10

The songwriter wrote 50 songs during his career. He retired in 2017.
→ The songwriter _____ 50 songs before he retired in 2017.

[11-12] 주어진 문장의 밑줄 친 부분과 용법이 같은 것을 고르시오.

11

I have seen the movie many times.

① My uncle has gone to England.
② The child has broken her mom's vase.
③ They have lived in Korea for five years.
④ He has just finished his assignment.
⑤ She has tried skydiving before.

12

Daniel has been in the chess club since elementary school.

① Betty has planted some trees lately.
② He has never seen the Eiffel Tower.
③ We have worked on this project for a year.
④ I have forgotten your phone number.
⑤ The singer has recently released her new album.

13 다음 빈칸에 들어갈 말이 순서대로 짝지어진 것은?

• I have used this digital camera _____ last year.
• My dad has been cleaning the bathroom _____ three hours.

① since – for
② for – during
③ since – during
④ for – since
⑤ during – for

고난도

14 다음 중 밑줄 친 부분이 어법상 바른 것은?

① The TV show has already started before we came home.
② It had been raining for an hour when I woke up.
③ Emily has had a stomachache yesterday.
④ I didn't know that Jane has been absent from school.
⑤ He has been writing an essay for three days by tomorrow.

서술형

[15-16] 괄호 안의 동사를 활용하여 빈칸에 알맞은 말을 쓰시오.

15

Kayla and I are close friends. We _____ _____ each other for ten years. (know)

16

Josh didn't do his homework because he _____ _____ about it. (forget)

[17-18] 다음 중 어법상 <u>어색한</u> 것을 고르시오.

17 ① I have taken cooking classes since 2018.
② The summer festival has already begun.
③ Kelly has visited the art museum last week.
④ How long have you been practicing the speech?
⑤ The cat has been sleeping for more than an hour.

18 ① Mr. Wright had been a firefighter before he became a soldier.
② I have never seen such clear water until I visited this beach.
③ Mark will have been learning skating for four years by next year.
④ The girl had been playing outside for three hours when her mom called her.
⑤ By the time the printer is fixed, I will have finished writing the document by hand.

서술형

[19-20] 우리말과 같도록 괄호 안의 말을 알맞게 배열하시오.

19
내일이면 Sarah는 여행을 위해 그녀의 가방을 쌌을 것이다. (her, packed, will, bag, have, Sarah)

= By tomorrow, _____
for the trip.

20
너는 호랑이를 본 적이 있니? (tiger, have, seen, you, ever, a)

= _____?

고난도

21 다음 중 어법상 바른 것의 개수는?

ⓐ I haven't gotten the message from him yet.
ⓑ Aaron will be the class president for six months by next week.
ⓒ Laura had bought a new shirt, so she decided not to buy another one.
ⓓ Jeff has been playing the drums since this morning.
ⓔ She has been talking about the news for an hour when I entered the class.

① 1개   ② 2개   ③ 3개
④ 4개   ⑤ 5개

서술형

[22-24] 우리말과 같도록 괄호 안의 말을 활용하여 완료시제나 완료진행시제 문장을 완성하시오.

22
과학자들은 그 문제를 최근에 논의했다. (discuss the issue)

= The scientists _____
lately.

23
내가 집에 돌아왔을 때 나의 남동생은 낮잠을 오랫동안 자고 있었다. (take a nap)

= My brother _____
for a long time when I came back home.

24
다음 주면 Emily는 세계를 3개월째 여행하고 있을 것이다. (travel around the world)

= Emily _____
_____ for three months by next week.

Chapter

02

조동사

조동사는 be동사나 일반동사와 함께 쓰여 여러 가지 의미를 더하는 말이다.

UNIT 01 | can, may, must, should

1 can

능력·가능, 허가, 요청, 추측을 나타낸다.

Jane **can**(= **is able to**) play more than three instruments. <능력·가능: ~할 수 있다>
You **can** leave early if you don't feel well. <허가: ~해도 된다>
Can you lend me the book for the weekend? <요청: ~해주겠니?>
My answer for this question **could** be wrong. <약한 추측: ~일 수도 있다>
The puppies **can't** be hungry already. I just fed them. <강한 부정의 추측: ~일 리가 없다>

> **TIP** 조동사는 두 개를 연속해서 쓸 수 없으므로 다른 조동사와 함께 쓸 때는 **can** 대신 **be able to**를 쓴다.
> I (~~will can~~, **will be able to**) help you clean your room.

2 may

허가, 약한 추측을 나타낸다.

May I take a look at this photo album? <허가: ~해도 된다>
The hotel **may** be fully booked this weekend. <약한 추측: ~일지도 모른다>

3 must

의무, 강한 추측을 나타낸다.

We **must**(= **have to**) turn in the essay by tomorrow. <의무: ~해야 한다>
The players **must** be upset because they lost the game. <강한 추측: ~임이 틀림없다>

> **TIP** **must not**은 강한 금지(~하면 안 된다)를 나타내며, **don't have to**는 불필요(~할 필요가 없다)를 나타낸다.
> Passengers **must not** move around while the bus is moving.
> You **don't have to**(= **don't need to/need not**) tell me anything.

4 should

충고·의무(~해야 한다)를 나타낸다.

You **should**(= **ought to**) save money for the future.
We **should not**(= **ought not to**) leave any trash in the park.

Smart Check 다음 빈칸에 들어갈 알맞은 것을 고르시오.

1 All of the guests will _____ arrive on time.
　① can　　　　　　　　② be able to　　　　　③ may

2 This mushroom is poisonous, so you _____ eat it.
　① must not　　　　　② don't have to　　　③ ought to

Practice

Answers p.3

A 괄호 안에서 알맞은 것을 고르시오.

1 You (may / may not) borrow my pen, but make sure to return it.

2 Lucas (is able to / must) be nervous because of his final exam.

3 That (can't / could) be Victoria. She has gone overseas.

4 I will (can / be able to) look after your cats while you are away.

5 Children (don't have to / must not) use this device without the teacher's permission.

make sure 반드시 (~하도록) 하다
overseas ⏵ 해외로
look after ~을 돌보다
permission ⏵ 허락, 허가

B 다음 빈칸에 알맞은 말을 <보기>에서 한 번씩만 골라 쓰시오.

<보기>	can	may	should

1 You _____ be careful not to fall off the ladder.

2 He _____ run 100 meters in eleven seconds.

3 I'm not sure, but the hospital _____ open at 9 A.M.

fall off 떨어지다
ladder ⏵ 사다리

C 다음 두 문장의 의미가 같도록 빈칸에 알맞은 말을 쓰시오.

1 The floor is slippery. You should not run here.
→ The floor is slippery. You _____ _____ _____ run here.

2 My dad can drive a bus. He has the license.
→ My dad _____ _____ _____ drive a bus. He has the license.

3 We must hurry since the train is about to leave.
→ We _____ _____ hurry since the train is about to leave.

slippery ⏵ 미끄러운
license ⏵ 면허
be about to 막 ~하려고 하다

D 우리말과 같도록 괄호 안의 말을 활용하여 빈칸에 쓰시오.

1 Nancy는 수학에서 A를 받았기 때문에 추가 수업을 들을 필요가 없다. (take)
= As Nancy got an A in math, she _____ _____ _____ _____ an extra class.

2 네가 떠나기 전에 모든 짐이 점검되어야 한다. (be checked)
= All of the luggage _____ _____ _____ before you leave.

3 문 앞에 누군가가 있는 것이 틀림없다. (be)
= There _____ _____ someone in front of the door.

4 David는 그의 과학 프로젝트에 어떠한 도움도 필요하지 않을지도 모른다. (need)
= David _____ _____ _____ any help with his science project.

extra ⏵ 추가의
luggage ⏵ 짐, 수하물

UNIT 02 | had better, would rather, used to, may as well

1 **had better + 동사원형**: ~하는 것이 낫다

We **had**[We'**d**] **better** wear something warm.
You'**d better not** spread rumors about others.
→ had better의 부정형은 had better not이다.

2 **would rather + 동사원형**: (차라리) ~하겠다

I **would**[I'**d**] **rather** go to the mall alone.
I'**d rather not** eat out tonight.
→ would rather의 부정형은 would rather not이다.

TIP would rather A than B: B하느니 차라리 A하겠다
I **would rather** *walk* there **than** *take* the subway.
Would you **rather** play *basketball* **than** *soccer*?

3 **used to + 동사원형**: ~하곤 했다, 전에는 ~이었다

Mark **used to**(= **would**) go hiking with his dad. <과거의 반복적인 습관>
There **used to** be a huge library across the street. <과거의 상태>
→ 과거의 상태를 나타내는 used to는 would로 바꿔 쓸 수 없다.

4 **may as well + 동사원형**: ~하는 편이 좋다

You look pale. You **may as well** get some rest.
I don't know where the station is. We **may as well** ask someone.

Smart Check 다음 빈칸에 들어갈 알맞은 것을 고르시오.

1 My sister's hair _____ be much shorter last year.
① had better　　　　　② would　　　　　③ used to

2 I _____ buy the green dress than the black one.
① would rather　　　　② rather　　　　　③ used to

3 The store is closed today, so we _____ come again when it's open.
① had better not　　　② may as well　　　③ used to

4 You _____ forget to take an umbrella because it will rain in the afternoon.
① hadn't better　　　　② had better not　　③ not had better

Practice

Answers p.3

A 괄호 안에서 알맞은 것을 고르시오.

1 We (had better / used to) report the accident to the police now.

2 Amanda used to (take / taking) the bus to school every day.

3 Paul would rather read books (than / to) watch TV.

4 You (had not better / had better not) tell a lie to your friends.

5 There (used to / would) be an old temple near my house.

6 My computer is broken. I (used to / may as well) call the repairman.

report 图 알리다, 전하다
accident 명 사고
temple 명 사원, 절
repairman 명 수리공

B 다음 빈칸에 알맞은 말을 <보기>에서 한 번씩만 골라 쓰시오.

<보기>	had better	would rather	used to

1 A: There _____ be a supermarket here.
  B: I know. I often went there to buy snacks.

2 A: It is really hot and humid today.
  B: Yes, it is. I _____ stay home than go outside.

3 A: You _____ avoid eating junk food.
  B: OK. I'll try not to eat it.

humid 형 습한
avoid 图 피하다
junk food 명 정크 푸드

C 우리말과 같도록 괄호 안의 동사를 활용하여 빈칸에 쓰시오.

1 나의 삼촌은 내게 장난감을 사주곤 했다. (buy)
  = My uncle _____ _____ _____ me toys.

2 나는 차라리 너의 질문에 대답하지 않겠다. (answer)
  = I _____ _____ _____ _____ your question.

3 너는 아침을 거르지 않는 것이 낫겠다. (skip)
  = You _____ _____ _____ _____ breakfast.

4 우리는 과거에 우리의 조부모님을 매년 방문하곤 했다. (visit)
  = We _____ _____ our grandparents every year in the past.

5 그 호텔은 인기 있기 때문에, 너는 빨리 방을 예약하는 편이 좋겠다. (reserve)
  = Because the hotel is popular, you _____ _____ _____
  _____ a room quickly.

skip 图 거르다, 건너뛰다
reserve 图 예약하다

UNIT 03 | 조동사 + have + p.p.

「조동사 + have + p.p.」는 과거 사실에 대한 추측, 후회·유감, 가능성을 나타낸다.

1

can't + have + p.p.: ~했을 리가 없다 (강한 추측)

Tim **can't have arrived** here earlier than me.
The girl **can't have ridden** the roller coaster. She is too short.

2

must + have + p.p.: ~했음이 틀림없다 (강한 추측)

He is disappointed. He **must have failed** the test.
Jane **must have lived** in Korea before.

3

may[might] + have + p.p.: ~했을지도 모른다 (약한 추측)

Luke **may have stayed** up all night. He looks tired.
I **might have left** my wallet on the bus.

4

should + have + p.p.: ~했어야 했다(하지만 하지 않았다) (후회나 유감)

You **should have listened** to Paul's advice.
I **should** not **have lied** to my parents.

5

could + have + p.p.: ~했을 수도 있었다 (후회나 가능성)

You should not run. You **could have spilled** the water.
We **could have cooked** dinner, but we ate out.

Smart Check 다음 빈칸에 들어갈 알맞은 것을 고르시오.

1 She _____ this book. It's written in Russian.
　① can't have read　　　② must have read　　　③ may have read

2 The tourists look exhausted. They _____ too many places.
　① can have visited　　　② may have visited　　　③ should have visited

3 Liam's leg is broken. He _____ it while he was playing soccer.
　① can't have broken　　　② must have broken　　　③ should have broken

4 He _____ there, but he decided to just walk.
　① must have driven　　　② can have driven　　　③ could have driven

Practice

Answers p.3

A 괄호 안에서 알맞은 것을 고르시오.

1 Lucy (could / must) have returned the small shirt, but she didn't.

2 They're not here. They (may / may have) left already.

3 John won the dance contest. He (can't / must) have been happy.

4 I got hurt while ice skating. I (may / should) have been more careful.

return 통 반품하다
already 분 이미

B <보기>의 조동사와 괄호 안의 말을 활용하여 빈칸에 쓰시오.

<보기>	can't	must	should

1 Amy is healthy. She _____ _____ _____ hard. (exercise)

2 Henry _____ _____ _____ his mother's birthday. He even bought a present for her. (forget)

3 I got a poor grade on the exam. I _____ _____ _____ _____ too much time on mobile games. (not, spend)

poor 형 좋지 못한
spend 통 (시간을) 보내다

C 우리말과 같도록 다음 문장에서 틀린 부분을 바르게 고쳐 완전한 문장을 쓰시오.

1 그들은 비행기를 놓친 것이 틀림없다.
= They may have missed the plane.
→ _____.

2 Tyler는 어제 학교에 갔을 리가 없다.
= Tyler can't go to school yesterday.
→ _____.

3 그녀는 그 충격적인 이야기를 들었을지도 모른다.
= She should have heard the shocking story.
→ _____.

miss 통 놓치다
shocking 형 충격적인

D 우리말과 같도록 괄호 안의 말을 활용하여 빈칸에 쓰시오.

1 나는 같은 실수를 하지 말았어야 했다. (make)
= I _____ _____ _____ _____ the same mistake.

2 그의 농담은 몇몇 사람들을 당황하게 했을지도 모른다. (upset)
= His joke _____ _____ _____ some people.

3 싱가포르는 너무 더웠다. 그곳은 섭씨 30도 이상이었던 것이 틀림없다. (be)
= It was too hot in Singapore. It _____ _____ _____ over 30°C there.

mistake 명 실수
upset 통 당황하게 하다

Writing Exercise

A 다음 빈칸에 알맞은 말을 <보기>에서 한 번씩만 골라 쓰시오.

> <보기>　　can　　must　　would rather

1 A judge _____ be fair in all cases.

2 I _____ drink milk than orange juice with bread.

3 We _____ see stars clearly when we use the telescope.

> <보기>　　may　　don't have to　　should

4 Hotel guests _____ use the fitness center for free.

5 Parents _____ teach their children table manners.

6 You _____ apologize to me. I have already forgiven you.

B 우리말과 같도록 괄호 안의 말을 활용하여 문장을 완성하시오.

1 전에는 이 거리에 서점이 있었다. (be a bookstore)
= There _____ on this street.

2 나는 나의 친구에게 소리치지 말았어야 했다. (yell at my friend)
= I _____ .

3 너는 너의 음식에 소금을 덜 넣는 것이 낫겠다. (add less salt)
= You _____ to your food.

4 그들은 금메달을 획득할 수도 있었지만, 결국 실패했다. (win the gold medal)
= They _____ , but they failed in the end.

5 그 소설은 실제 이야기에 근거할 리가 없다. (be based on a true story)
= The novel _____ .

6 우리는 내일 다시 식당에 전화를 하는 편이 좋겠다. (call the restaurant)
= We _____ again tomorrow.

C 우리말과 같도록 괄호 안의 말을 알맞게 배열하시오.

1 너는 장학금을 받기 위해서 더 열심히 공부해야 한다. (study, to, you, harder, ought)
= _____ to get a scholarship.

2 그들은 그 조사를 끝냈을 리가 없다. 그들은 어제 그것을 시작했다. (have, they, finished, the, can't, research)
= _____ . They started it yesterday.

3 너는 표를 사기 전에 박물관에 들어갈 수 없다. (are, to, you, the, museum, able, not, enter)
= _____ before you buy a ticket.

4 그는 약속에 늦었다. 버스가 지연된 것이 틀림없다. (delayed, bus, must, the, have, been)
= He was late for the appointment. _____ .

5 의사는 긴급 전화를 받았기 때문에 즉시 떠나야 했다. (doctor, leave, right, the, had, to, away)
= _____ because he received an emergency call.

6 그 소녀는 Julie였을지도 모르지만, 나는 확실하지 않았다. (might, Julie, the, been, have, girl)
= _____ , but I wasn't sure.

D 다음 그림을 보고 <보기>의 말과 괄호 안의 말을 활용하여 문장을 완성하시오.

1

2
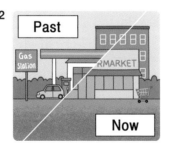

3

<보기>	can	should	used to

1 _____ Korean won for US dollars? (I, exchange)

2 There _____ a gas station here. (be)

3 You got a bad sunburn! You _____ a hat before you came out. (bring)

Chapter Test

[1-3] 다음 빈칸에 들어갈 알맞은 것을 고르시오.

1

We _____ have a swing in the garden, but we removed it last year.

① must
② should
③ had better
④ would rather
⑤ used to

2

That person _____ be Julia. She left this town a year ago.

① must not
② can't
③ should not
④ doesn't have to
⑤ would rather not

3

Tom hasn't answered the phone all day. He _____ his phone.

① must turn off
② should turn off
③ had better turn off
④ must have turned off
⑤ should have turned off

4 다음 우리말을 영작할 때 빈칸에 들어갈 알맞은 것은?

Scott은 집 전체를 청소한 이후 피곤할지도 모른다.
= Scott _____ be tired after cleaning the whole house.

① can't
② shouldn't
③ may
④ may as well
⑤ had better

서술형
5 다음 두 문장의 의미가 같도록 빈칸에 알맞은 말을 쓰시오.

Anne can speak French and English.
→ Anne _____ _____ _____ _____ French and English.

6 주어진 문장의 밑줄 친 부분과 의미가 같은 것은?

People <u>must</u> have regular meals in order to take care of their health.

① may
② can
③ could
④ have to
⑤ used to

[7-8] 다음 중 어법상 <u>어색한</u> 것을 고르시오.

7 ① You should be honest with your friends.
② Peter must finish the task on his own.
③ We may as well going to the bookstore now.
④ I would rather wear glasses than lenses.
⑤ Janice used to swim well when she was a child.

8 ① I might have left my phone on the table.
② You should have brought an umbrella.
③ Can you pass me the water bottle?
④ We could have moved to Paris, but we stayed.
⑤ Mary must had been a good student.

[9-10] 주어진 문장의 밑줄 친 조동사와 의미가 <u>다른</u> 것을 고르시오.

9

> You <u>may</u> bring your pet to this café.

① Richard <u>may</u> be asleep now.
② You <u>may</u> invite many friends to the party.
③ <u>May</u> I go to the restroom now?
④ You <u>may</u> not touch the paintings on the wall.
⑤ Visitors with tickets <u>may</u> park their car outside the building.

10

> The students <u>must</u> prepare for the school festival.

① I <u>must</u> feed my goldfish every day.
② Sarah <u>must</u> practice the song for the contest.
③ You <u>must</u> recycle cans and bottles.
④ The tall and skinny boy <u>must</u> be Josh.
⑤ They <u>must</u> leave for the airport soon.

서술형

[11-12] 다음 빈칸에 공통으로 들어갈 알맞은 말을 쓰시오.

11

> • Aaron _____ _____ play badminton in the past.
> • There _____ _____ be many apple trees in my hometown, but not anymore.

12

> • Thomas _____ have been at the library yesterday. It was closed.
> • She _____ be sleepy. She went to bed early last night.

13 다음 우리말을 영작한 것 중 <u>어색한</u> 것은?

① 너는 전혀 서두를 필요가 없다.
= You need not hurry at all.
② 우리는 도움을 요청하는 편이 좋겠다.
= We may as well ask for help.
③ 사람들은 잔디 위를 걸으면 안 된다.
= People must not walk on the grass.
④ 그녀는 더 신중했을 수도 있었다.
= She could have been more cautious.
⑤ Jeremy는 주사를 맞았어야 했다.
= Jeremy must have gotten a shot.

서술형

[14-16] 우리말과 같도록 괄호 안의 말을 활용하여 빈칸에 쓰시오.

14

> Hill씨는 그 기술들을 쉽게 배울 수 있을 것이다. (learn)

= Mr. Hill _____ _____ _____ the skills easily.

15

> 그는 해결책을 알았던 것이 틀림없다. (know)

= He _____ _____ _____ the solution.

16

> 나는 샐러드를 먹느니 차라리 피자를 먹겠다. (eat, pizza, salad)

= I _____ _____ _____ _____ _____ .

17 다음 중 어법상 바른 것은?

① There would be a big market near my house.
② Mr. Green may have been late to the meeting.
③ I not would rather eat fast food for my health.
④ Kids should not to follow a stranger.
⑤ We ought to not be too disappointed.

[18-19] 다음 대화의 빈칸에 들어갈 알맞은 것을 고르시오.

18

A: Let's go to the movies after school.
B: Sorry. I _____ finish my assignment by tomorrow.

① can   ② could   ③ used to
④ ought to   ⑤ might

19

A: He is so good at Spanish.
B: I know. He _____ have lived in Spain before.

① must   ② can't   ③ would
④ should   ⑤ can

고난도
20 다음 중 짝지어진 두 문장의 의미가 <u>다른</u> 것은?

① You don't have to say sorry to me.
  → You don't need to say sorry to me.
② Matt can draw cartoons very well.
  → Matt is able to draw cartoons very well.
③ Karen may have bought a present for you.
  → Karen might have bought a present for you.
④ The kitten can't be thirsty already.
  → The kitten must not be thirsty already.
⑤ They used to dance in front of people.
  → They would dance in front of people.

서술형
[21-23] 다음 문장에서 어법상 <u>어색한</u> 부분을 찾아 쓰고 바르게 고쳐 쓰시오.

21

You may rather ask your homeroom teacher about the problem.

_____ → _____

22

She woke up too early. She has to be tired.

_____ → _____

23

Eric shouldn't have passed the exam. He didn't even take it.

_____ → _____

고난도
24 다음 중 어법상 바른 것끼리 묶인 것은?

ⓐ Dennis can join the orchestra if he wants.
ⓑ You could have be really hurt.
ⓒ People had better not look directly at the sun.
ⓓ I had rather go to the sea than the mountain.
ⓔ We will can play the drums well after many lessons.

① ⓐ, ⓑ   ② ⓐ, ⓒ   ③ ⓑ, ⓓ
④ ⓒ, ⓔ   ⑤ ⓓ, ⓔ

Chapter
03

수동태

수동태는 주어가 어떤 행위의 대상이 되는 것이다.

UNIT 01 | 수동태의 쓰임

1 수동태

「be동사 + p.p.(과거분사)」의 형태로 주어가 행위의 대상이 되는 것을 나타낸다.

The song **is loved** by many teenagers.
This tree **was planted** by my grandfather.

> **TIP** 목적어를 가지지 않는 동사(stay, appear, happen 등)나 목적어를 가지는 동사 중에서 소유나 상태를 나타내는 동사(have, belong to, resemble 등)는 수동태로 쓸 수 없다.
> Something strange (~~was happened~~, **happened**) last night.
> Helen (~~is resembled~~, **resembles**) her aunt.

2 행위자가 생략된 수동태

행위자가 일반인이거나 중요하지 않을 때는 「by + 행위자」를 생략할 수 있다.

This dish **is called** bulgogi.
Our classroom **was cleaned** yesterday.

3 수동태의 다양한 형태

❶ 미래시제: 「will be + p.p.」

Dinner **will be prepared** by Dad.
The movie **will be released** next month.

❷ 진행시제: 「be동사 + being + p.p.」

The tower **is being built** in the city center.
The song **was being played** a few minutes ago.

❸ 완료시제: 「have/had been + p.p.」

Many items **have been stolen** from the store.
The window **had been broken** when I saw it.

❹ 조동사가 있는 수동태: 「조동사 + be + p.p.」

This restroom **can be used** by visitors.
Your belongings **should not be put** on the floor.

Smart Check 다음 빈칸에 들어갈 알맞은 것을 고르시오.

1 The drowning man _____ by the lifeguard.
① save   ② saved   ③ was saved

2 The machine _____ by an expert.
① must operate   ② must be operated   ③ be must operated

Practice

A 괄호 안에서 알맞은 것을 고르시오.

1 North America was (discovered / discovering) by Columbus.

2 The history museum (belongs to / is belonged to) the state.

3 The paper will (recycle / be recycled) next Monday.

4 The broken chair has (repaired / been repaired) by my uncle.

5 Most mangoes (produced / are produced) in India.

6 A little cat suddenly (appeared / was appeared) in front of me.

discover ⑧ 발견하다
belong to ~에 속하다
state ⑨ 국가
recycle ⑧ 재활용하다
repair ⑧ 수리하다
produce ⑧ 생산하다
suddenly ⑨ 갑자기

B 다음 능동태 문장을 수동태로 바꿔 쓰시오.

1 I found Austin's dog on the street.
→ Austin's dog _____ on the street by me.

2 Kelly has read all of the books on the bookshelf.
→ All of the books on the bookshelf _____ by Kelly.

3 Ethan and his father are painting the fence.
→ The fence _____ by Ethan and his father.

4 People might see a rainbow after the rain.
→ A rainbow _____ after the rain.

5 The professor will present the research results tomorrow.
→ The research results _____ by the professor tomorrow.

present ⑧ 발표하다
research ⑨ 연구
result ⑨ 결과, 결실

C 우리말과 같도록 괄호 안의 말을 활용하여 빈칸에 쓰시오.

1 그녀의 카페는 식물과 꽃으로 장식되어 있다. (decorate)
= Her café _____ _____ with plants and flowers.

2 그 에세이는 금요일까지 제출되어야 한다. (should, hand)
= The essay _____ _____ _____ in by Friday.

3 이 건물에 있는 엘리베이터들은 일주일 동안 점검되어왔다. (inspect)
= The elevators in this building _____ _____ _____ for a week.

4 몇몇의 유용한 프로그램들이 나의 컴퓨터에 설치되고 있다. (install)
= Some useful programs _____ _____ _____ on my computer.

decorate ⑧ 장식하다
hand in 제출하다
inspect ⑧ 점검하다
install ⑧ 설치하다
useful ⑩ 유용한

UNIT 02 | 4형식/5형식 문장의 수동태

1 4형식 문장의 수동태

❶ 4형식 문장은 목적어가 두 개이므로 각 목적어를 주어로 하는 두 개의 수동태 문장을 만들 수 있다. 이때 직접 목적어가 주어인 수동태 문장은 간접 목적어 앞에 주로 전치사 to/for/of 중 하나를 쓴다.

Linda **told** *me a secret.* → *I* **was told** a secret by Linda. <간접 목적어가 주어>
→ *A secret* **was told to** me by Linda. <직접 목적어가 주어>

❷ 직접 목적어가 주어인 수동태 문장에서 간접 목적어 앞에 쓰는 전치사는 동사에 따라 다르다.

to를 쓰는 동사	give, send, pass, show, teach, tell 등	A picture *was shown* **to** her by Nate.
for를 쓰는 동사	buy, cook, make, get, build 등	A necklace *was made* **for** me by my mom.
of를 쓰는 동사	ask, inquire 등	Many questions *were asked* **of** the actor by her.

> **TIP** **buy, cook, make, get** 등의 동사가 쓰인 4형식 문장을 수동태로 바꿀 때는 주로 직접 목적어를 주어로 쓴다.
> Jim bought me a present. → **A present** was bought for me by Jim.
> I was bought a present by Jim. (×)

2 5형식 문장의 수동태

❶ 목적격 보어가 명사, 형용사, to부정사인 5형식 문장을 수동태로 바꿀 때는 목적격 보어를 그대로 쓴다.

The movie **made** us **sad.**
→ We **were made sad** by the movie.

The teacher **told** Bella **to be** quiet.
→ Bella **was told to be** quiet by the teacher.

❷ 사역동사가 쓰인 5형식 문장을 수동태로 바꿀 때는 목적격 보어로 쓰인 동사원형을 to부정사로 바꾼다.

My dad **made** me **do** the dishes.
→ I **was made to do** the dishes by my dad.

❸ 지각동사가 쓰인 5형식 문장을 수동태로 바꿀 때는 목적격 보어로 쓰인 동사원형을 V-ing형이나 to부정사로 바꾼다.

We **heard** Liam **give** a speech.
→ Liam **was heard giving[to give]** a speech by us.

Smart Check 다음 빈칸에 들어갈 알맞은 것을 고르시오.

1 The ball was passed _____ me by Edward.
  ① to ② for ③ of

2 The visitors were made _____ in a line.
  ① stand ② to stand ③ standing

Practice

Answers p.4

A 괄호 안에서 알맞은 것을 고르시오.

1 The library was built (for / of) kids by the government.

2 The man was made (stop / to stop) his car by the police officer.

3 Table manners were taught (to / for) me by my parents.

4 Many aircrafts were seen (fly / flying) in the sky.

government 명 정부
table manner 명 식사 예절
aircraft 명 항공기

B 다음 빈칸에 to, for, of 중 알맞은 것을 쓰시오.

1 A scholarship was given _____ Eric by the principal.

2 The way to the bus stop was inquired _____ me by a tourist.

3 A special dinner was cooked _____ the couple by the chef.

4 This shirt was bought _____ me by my best friend.

scholarship 명 장학금
principal 명 교장, 총장
tourist 명 관광객

C 다음 능동태 문장을 수동태로 바꿔 쓰시오.

1 The children call the cat Milo.

→ The cat _____ .

2 Some customers sent the store a complaint.

→ A complaint _____ .

3 Sandra heard someone knock on the door.

→ Someone _____ .

4 The doctor advised my grandfather to exercise regularly.

→ My grandfather _____ .

customer 명 손님
complaint 명 불평, 항의
regularly 부 규칙적으로

D 우리말과 같도록 괄호 안의 말을 활용하여 빈칸에 쓰시오.

1 지구 온난화는 지금보다 더 악화될 것으로 예상된다. (expect, be)

= Global warming _____ _____ _____ _____ worse than now.

2 침실들은 청소 직원에 의해 깔끔하게 유지된다. (keep, tidy)

= The bedrooms _____ _____ _____ by the cleaning staff.

3 모든 참가자들은 토론 중에 규칙들을 따르게 되었다. (make, follow)

= All participants_____ _____ _____ _____ the rules during the debate.

global warming 명 지구 온난화
tidy 형 깔끔한, 단정한
participant 명 참가자
during 전 ~ 중에, ~ 동안
debate 명 토론, 토의

UNIT 03 | 주의해야 할 수동태

1 목적어가 **that**절인 문장의 수동태

❶ that절 전체를 수동태 문장의 주어로 쓸 때 「It + be동사 + p.p. + that ~」의 형태로 쓴다.

People say that the novel is a masterpiece.
→ **It is said that** the novel is a masterpiece.

❷ say, think, believe, know, expect 등의 동사의 목적어로 쓰인 that절의 주어를 수동태 문장의 주어로 쓸 때 「that절의 주어 + be동사 + p.p. + to부정사 ~」의 형태로 쓴다.

People know that *spicy food* is bad for the stomach.
→ *Spicy food* **is known to be** bad for the stomach.

2 구동사의 수동태

두 개 이상의 단어로 이루어진 구동사를 수동태로 쓸 때 동사만 「be동사 + p.p.」의 형태로 쓰고, 나머지 부분은 동사 뒤에 그대로 쓴다.

put off ~을 미루다 → be put off ~이 미뤄지다	look after ~를 돌보다 → be looked after ~가 돌봐지다
deal with ~을 다루다 → be dealt with ~이 다뤄지다	take care of ~를 돌보다 → be taken care of ~가 돌봐지다
look up to ~를 존경하다 → be looked up to ~가 존경받다	look down on ~를 무시하다 → be looked down on ~가 무시되다

James **took care of** my dogs last night.
→ My dogs **were taken care of** by James last night.

3 **by** 이외의 전치사를 쓰는 수동태

수동태에서 행위자는 보통 by와 함께 사용하지만, by 이외의 전치사를 쓰는 경우도 있다.

be made of ~으로 만들어지다 (재료 성질이 변하지 않음)	be filled with ~으로 가득 차 있다
be made from ~으로 만들어지다 (재료 성질이 변함)	be covered with ~으로 덮여 있다
be interested in ~에 흥미가 있다	be satisfied with ~에 만족하다
be known to ~에게 알려져 있다	be crowded with ~으로 붐비다
be surprised at ~에 놀라다	be worried about ~에 대해 걱정하다

Benjamin **is interested in** classical music.
The building **was filled with** smoke because of the fire.

Smart Check 다음 빈칸에 들어갈 알맞은 것을 고르시오.

1 A four-leaf clover is believed _____ good luck.
① brings   ② to bring   ③ brought

2 The tourist site was crowded _____ travelers.
① by   ② with   ③ at

Practice

Answers p.5

A 괄호 안에서 알맞은 것을 고르시오.

1 The hotel is said (to have / having) a wonderful view of the sea.

2 The sky was completely covered (to / with) clouds in the morning.

3 My math teacher is (looked up / looked up to) by many students.

4 It (thinks / is thought) that a good beginning makes a good ending.

completely 🔳 완전히
beginning 🔳 시작
ending 🔳 결말

B 다음 빈칸에 알맞은 전치사를 <보기>에서 골라 쓰시오.

<보기>	to	with	in

1 This doughnut is filled _____ strawberry cream.

2 Lucy is interested _____ ancient history.

3 The director's action movie is known _____ most Koreans.

ancient 🔳 고대의
director 🔳 감독

C 다음 능동태 문장을 수동태로 바꿔 쓰시오.

1 Doctors and nurses take care of the patients.
→ The patients _____.

2 My family put off the trip until next year.
→ The trip _____ until next year.

3 We expect that Logan will be a successful businessman.
→ Logan _____.

4 The people at the meeting looked down on Mr. Brown's suggestion.
→ Mr. Brown's suggestion _____
at the meeting.

patient 🔳 환자
successful 🔳 성공한
businessman 🔳 사업가
suggestion 🔳 제안, 제의

D 우리말과 같도록 괄호 안의 말을 활용하여 문장을 완성하시오.

1 파리는 세계에서 가장 매력적인 도시들 중 하나라고 말해진다. (say)
= _____ Paris is one of the most attractive cities in
the world.

2 Jacob은 식물원의 크기에 놀랐다. (surprise)
= Jacob _____ the size of the botanical garden.

3 그 중대한 문제는 전문가들에 의해 직접 다뤄졌다. (deal with)
= The critical issue _____ by the experts themselves.

attractive 🔳 매력적인
botanical garden 🔳 식물원
critical 🔳 중대한, 중요한
issue 🔳 문제, 사안
expert 🔳 전문가

Writing Exercise

A   다음 능동태 문장을 수동태로 바꿔 쓰시오.

1 Harry broke the lamp on the table.
→ The lamp on the table _____ .

2 The company should take the pollution problem seriously.
→ The pollution problem _____ .

3 My uncle bought me some winter clothes.
→ Some winter clothes _____ .

4 The professor has explained the theory for 30 minutes.
→ The theory _____ for 30 minutes.

5 People say that the temple is worth visiting.
→ It _____ .
→ The temple _____ .

B   우리말과 같도록 괄호 안의 말을 활용하여 문장을 완성하시오.

1 그 소년은 나에 의해 벤치에 앉아있는 것이 보였다. (see, sit)
= The boy _____ on a bench by me.

2 많은 이용자들은 빠른 인터넷에 만족한다. (satisfy)
= Many users _____ the fast Internet.

3 호랑이들은 정글에서 발견될 수 없다. (can, find)
= Tigers _____ in the jungle.

4 비타민은 우리의 건강에 주요한 역할을 한다고 생각된다. (think)
= _____ vitamins play a major role in our health.

5 Sophia는 그 애니메이션 영화의 공주를 닮았다. (resemble)
= Sophia _____ the princess in the animation movie.

6 그 축구 선수는 그의 코치에 의해 무시당했다. (look down on)
= The soccer player _____ by his coach.

Chapter 03

수동태

Hackers Grammar Smart Level 3

C 우리말과 같도록 괄호 안의 말을 알맞게 배열하시오.

1 결정은 이번 주말에 내려질지도 모른다. (be, may, decision, a, made)

= _____ at the end of this week.

2 중국어는 요즘 많은 학생들에 의해 학습되고 있다. (learned, many, is, students, by, being)

= Chinese _____ these days.

3 정비공의 가방은 차를 수리하기 위한 도구들로 가득 차 있었다. (with, filled, was, tools)

= The mechanic's bag _____ for repairing the car.

4 말하기 대회의 승자는 진행자에 의해 곧 발표될 것이다. (announced, will, host, by, be, the)

= The winner of the speech contest _____ soon.

5 정원은 그 정원사에 의해 돌봐진다. (of, by, the, is, gardener, care, taken)

= The garden _____ .

6 용의자는 형사에 의해 자백하게 되었다. (detective, was, to, confess, made, by, the)

= The suspect _____ .

D 다음은 Emma의 일기이다. 밑줄 친 문장을 수동태로 바꿔 쓰시오.

Today was my sister's birthday.
1 My parents and I baked the birthday cake this morning. It tasted delicious, and my sister also loved it. Later, her friends came to our house.
2 They bought her some gifts. **3** The gifts made her feel happy. I hope today was one of the happiest days in her life.

1 The birthday cake _____ this morning.

2 Some gifts _____ .

3 She _____ .

Chapter Test

[1-3] 다음 빈칸에 들어갈 알맞은 것을 고르시오.

1

> The unique building _____ by a famous architect.

① designs ② designed
③ is designing ④ was designed
⑤ was designing

2

> This furniture can only _____ by strong people.

① move ② be moving
③ be moved ④ being moved
⑤ is moved

3

> The mayor _____ by the citizens for years.

① respects ② be respected
③ has respected ④ has been respecting
⑤ has been respected

4 다음 빈칸에 들어갈 말이 나머지 넷과 <u>다른</u> 것은?

① The students were made _____ finish their homework today.
② Eating fruit is known _____ be good for our health.
③ Science facts were taught _____ us by the teacher.
④ First prize was given _____ Jane.
⑤ Many questions were asked _____ the criminal by reporters.

서술형

[5-6] 다음 문장에서 어법상 <u>어색한</u> 부분을 찾아 쓰고 바르게 고쳐 쓰시오.

5

> Fairy tales were told the kid by her parents.

_____ → _____

6

> Dishes are washing by the dishwasher now.

_____ → _____

7 다음 중 어법상 바른 것은?

① Thomas is resembled his mother.
② The plants watered by Jim yesterday.
③ Our dog is called to Max by us.
④ My nephew was looked after by me.
⑤ I was surprised in his thoughtful remarks.

8 다음 대화의 빈칸에 들어갈 말이 순서대로 짝지어진 것은?

> A: Do you know the writer of this book?
> B: Of course. She is said _____ the writer of best-selling books.
> A: Did you get her latest novel?
> B: No. The bookstore was crowded _____ too many people. They all wanted her new book.

① being – with ② being – of
③ to be – with ④ to be – of
⑤ to being – with

[9-10] 다음 중 어법상 어색한 것을 고르시오.

9　① The song was sung by an unknown singer.
　② The secret must be kept between us.
　③ A number of spam mails have been sent to me.
　④ We were made to stay home after midnight.
　⑤ A tiger was appeared in the mountain.

10　① It is known that Einstein won the Nobel Prize.
　② He is interested of European history.
　③ Sharon is worried about making new friends.
　④ Hawaii is said to have beautiful beaches.
　⑤ Cheese is made from milk.

[11-12] 다음 빈칸에 공통으로 들어갈 알맞은 것을 고르시오.

11
- Mary was satisfied _____ the test result.
- The cars were covered _____ snow this morning.

① to　② for　③ of
④ with　⑤ at

12
- Kevin's house is made _____ wood.
- The babies were taken care _____ by their grandmother.

① to　② for　③ of
④ with　⑤ at

서술형

[13-15] 우리말과 같도록 괄호 안의 말을 활용하여 문장을 완성하시오.

13　내가 도착했을 때 저녁 식사는 준비되어 있었다. (prepare)

= The dinner _____ when I arrived.

14　빵이 오븐에서 데워지고 있다. (heat)

= Bread _____ in the oven.

15　그 고객의 요청은 관리자에 의해 다루어질 것이다. (will, deal with)

= The customer's request _____ by the manager.

16 다음 우리말을 알맞게 영작한 것을 모두 고르시오.

그 새는 우리에 의해 노래하는 것이 들렸다.

① The bird is heard to singing by us.
② The bird was heard to sing by us.
③ The bird was heard to singing by us.
④ The bird was heard singing by us.
⑤ The bird was heard sing by us.

17 우리말과 같도록 주어진 <조건>에 맞게 영작하시오.

> 그는 최고의 배우라고 말해진다.

> <조건>　1. He를 주어로 쓰시오.
> 　　　　2. say, the best, actor를 활용하시오.
> 　　　　3. 8단어로 쓰시오.

= _____ .

18 다음 중 문장의 태를 잘못 바꾼 것은?

① People know that eating junk food is bad.
　→ Eating junk food is known to be bad.
② Some members looked down on her opinion.
　→ Her opinion was looked down by some members.
③ The cook made the visitors nice dishes.
　→ Nice dishes were made for the visitors by the cook.
④ Dad told me to turn off the TV.
　→ I was told to turn off the TV by Dad.
⑤ I saw Ron run down the stairs.
　→ Ron was seen running down the stairs by me.

19 다음 문장을 수동태로 바꿔 쓰시오.

> The children look up to the grandparents.
> → The grandparents _____
> _____ by the children.

[20-21] 괄호 안의 말을 활용하여 빈칸에 알맞은 말을 쓰시오.

20
> The meeting _____ _____
> _____ by the leader last week. (put off)

21
> Chocolate cakes _____ _____
> _____ in the bakery right now. (bake)

22 다음 글의 빈칸에 들어갈 말이 순서대로 짝지어진 것은?

> I _____ some good news by Laura.
> She said that she had started singing in a
> school band, and her band _____ to
> give a performance at the upcoming school
> festival.

① told – had allowed
② told – had been allowed
③ was told – had allowed
④ was told – had been allowed
⑤ was telling – had been allowed

23 다음 능동태를 수동태로 바꾼 문장에서 어법상 어색한 부분을 찾아 쓰고 바르게 고쳐 쓰시오.

> My mom made me organize my desk.
> → I was made organize my desk by my mom.

_____ → _____

Chapter

04

부정사

부정사는 문장 안에서 명사·형용사·부사 역할을 할 수 있으며,
인칭이나 수에 따라 형태가 변하지 않는다. 부정사에는 「to + 동사원형」
형태의 to부정사와 to 없이 동사원형만 쓰는 원형부정사가 있다.

UNIT 01 | to부정사의 명사적 용법

1 주어/목적어/보어

to부정사는 명사 역할을 할 때 문장 안에서 주어, 목적어, 보어로 쓰인다.

To watch basketball games is exciting. <주어>
Jake promised **not to make** the same mistake. <목적어>
Her goal is **to learn** a new musical instrument. <보어>

2 가주어/가목적어 it

❶ to부정사가 주어로 쓰일 때는 주로 주어 자리에 가주어 it을 쓰고 진주어 to부정사(구)를 뒤로 보낸다.

It is impossible **to live** without oxygen.
It is dangerous **to drive** when it's raining heavily.

❷ to부정사가 5형식 문장의 목적어로 쓰일 때는 목적어 자리에 가목적어 it을 쓰고 진목적어 to부정사(구)를 뒤로 보낸다.

I found **it** difficult **to raise** three cats.
These shoes make **it** easier **to climb** mountains.

3 의문사 + to부정사

「의문사 + to부정사」는 문장 안에서 명사처럼 쓰이며, 「의문사 + 주어 + should + 동사원형」으로 바꿔 쓸 수 있다.

what + to부정사	무엇을 ~할지	where + to부정사	어디에(서)/어디로 ~할지
who(m) + to부정사	누구를/누구에게 ~할지	when + to부정사	언제 ~할지
which + to부정사	어느 것을 ~할지	how + to부정사	어떻게 ~할지

I decided **what to eat** for dinner.
→ I decided **what I should eat** for dinner.

Liam doesn't know **how to operate** the machine.
→ Liam doesn't know **how he should operate** the machine.

Smart Check 다음 빈칸에 들어갈 알맞은 것을 고르시오.

1 A doctor's duty is _____ care of patients.
① takes ② took ③ to take

2 Smartphones made _____ convenient to search for information.
① it ② them ③ this

3 The server told the guests where _____.
① sit ② to sit ③ sitting

Practice

Answers p.6

A   <보기>의 동사를 활용하여 문장을 완성하시오.

<보기>	build	hold	use	find

1 The explorers hoped _____ the hidden treasure.

2 I found it confusing _____ this application.

3 Jacob's dream is _____ a house for his family.

4 The company decided where _____ the launch event.

hold 통 개최하다
explorer 명 탐험가
hidden 형 숨겨진
treasure 명 보물
confusing 형 혼란스러운
application 명 응용 프로그램
launch event 출시 행사

B   다음 문장을 가주어 it을 사용한 문장으로 바꿔 쓰시오.

1 To see the stars in cities is not easy.

→ It _____ .

2 To assemble a computer is complicated.

→ It _____ .

3 To camp in the forest is thrilling.

→ It _____ .

assemble 통 조립하다, 모으다
complicated 형 복잡한
thrilling 형 아주 신나는, 흥분되는

C   다음 두 문장의 의미가 같도록 빈칸에 알맞은 말을 쓰시오.

1 My mother taught me how I should deal with unexpected challenges.

→ My mother taught me _____ _____ _____ _____ unexpected challenges.

2 To spend summer in Europe is my plan.

→ _____ is my plan _____ _____ summer in Europe.

3 Did Ms. Dean tell us when we should hand in the homework?

→ Did Ms. Dean tell us _____ _____ _____ _____ the homework?

deal with ~을 다루다
unexpected 형 예기치 않은
challenge 명 문제, 난제
hand in 제출하다

D   우리말과 같도록 괄호 안의 말을 활용하여 빈칸에 쓰시오.

1 우리는 세상을 더 좋은 곳으로 만들기를 바란다. (wish, make)

= We _____ _____ _____ the world a better place.

2 Porter씨의 직업은 자동차를 설계하는 것이다. (design)

= Mr. Porter's job _____ _____ _____ cars.

3 나는 다른 사람들을 존중하는 것이 중요하다는 것을 알게 되었다. (respect)

= I found _____ important _____ _____ others.

design 통 설계하다
respect 통 존중하다

1 to부정사의 형용사적 용법

명사나 대명사를 수식하거나 「be동사 + to부정사」의 형태로 주어를 설명한다.

❶ (대)명사 수식: '~할, ~하는'의 의미이다.

She doesn't have *any time* **to relax**.

I'm going to bring *something* **to read** on the plane.

> **TIP** 「to부정사 + 전치사」가 수식하는 명사나 대명사는 to부정사 뒤에 있는 전치사의 목적어이다. 이때, 전치사를 반드시 쓴다.
> Can you lend me *a pencil* **to write with**? (← write with a pencil)

❷ 「be동사 + to부정사」: 예정, 가능, 의무, 운명, 의도를 나타낸다.

Ben **is to arrive** earlier than I expected. <예정: ~할 예정이다>

The thief **was** not **to be found** anywhere. <가능: ~할 수 있다>

You **are to wear** a uniform in school. <의무: ~해야 한다>

Hannah **was to become** a popular singer. <운명: ~할 운명이다>

If we **are to succeed**, we have to try our best. <의도: ~하려고 하다>

2 to부정사의 부사적 용법

동사, 형용사, 부사, 문장 전체를 수식하며, 다양한 의미를 나타낸다.

Jim exercises regularly **to lose** weight. <목적: ~하기 위해>
> → 목적의 의미를 강조하기 위해 to 대신 in order to나 so as to를 쓸 수 있다.

I was pleased **to hear** the good news. <감정의 원인: ~해서, ~하니>

The child must be a genius **to solve** the puzzle. <판단의 근거: ~하다니>

Mr. Davis lived **to be** 101 years old. <결과: (…해서 결국) ~하다>

To hear him speak English, you'd think he is an American. <조건: ~한다면>

Sea water isn't safe **to drink**. <형용사 수식: ~하기에>

Smart Check 다음 빈칸에 들어갈 알맞은 것을 고르시오.

1 My family is looking for a house _____.
   ① live   ② to live   ③ to live in

2 The city _____ a new public library next year.
   ① be to build   ② is to build   ③ is build

3 Let's wake up early tomorrow _____ the sunrise.
   ① watches   ② watched   ③ to watch

Practice

Answers p.6

A 다음 문장의 밑줄 친 부분을 바르게 고쳐 쓰시오.

1 Josh brought a cup of hot chocolate <u>to drinking</u>. → _____

2 This T-shirt is very comfortable <u>wear</u> at home. → _____

3 Each student was given a piece of paper <u>to write</u>. → _____

4 The president <u>is to visiting</u> India next month. → _____

comfortable 〚형〛 편한
president 〚명〛 대통령

B <보기>의 말을 활용하여 문장을 완성하시오.

<보기>	take	open	sing	talk with

1 You need your ID _____ a bank account.

2 The band selected songs _____ at the concert.

3 We need someone _____ about this issue.

4 All students are _____ the exam at the end of the semester.

ID 〚명〛 신분증(=identification)
bank account 은행 계좌
semester 〚명〛 학기

C 주어진 문장을 우리말로 해석하시오.

1 I know the fastest way to get to the airport.

= _____ .

2 If you are to avoid a traffic jam, you should leave earlier.

= _____ .

3 He was surprised to see a snake in the garden.

= _____ .

get to ~에 도착하다
avoid 〚동〛 피하다
traffic jam 〚명〛 교통 체증

D 우리말과 같도록 괄호 안의 말을 활용하여 빈칸에 쓰시오.

1 나는 식료품을 사기 위해 상점에 갔다. (buy)

= I went to the store _____ _____ _____ _____ groceries.

2 Linda는 그녀의 자유 시간 동안 할 어떤 것도 없었다. (anything, do)

= Linda didn't have _____ _____ _____ during her free time.

3 그 개에게 가지고 놀 몇몇의 장난감을 주자. (toys, play with)

= Let's give the dog some _____ _____ _____ .

grocery 〚명〛 식료품

UNIT 03 | 부정사를 목적격 보어로 쓰는 동사

1 to부정사를 목적격 보어로 쓰는 동사

| want   ask   tell   expect   allow
advise   order   encourage   … | + | 목적어 | + | to부정사 |

They *want* their daughter **to become** a lawyer.
He *advised* me **to apologize** to Cindy.

2 원형부정사를 목적격 보어로 쓰는 동사

❶ 사역동사

| make   have   let | + | 목적어 | + | 원형부정사 |

Mom *made* me **wash** the dishes.
The teacher *had* us **write** a ten-page essay.
Mary *let* her friend **borrow** her notes.

> **TIP** · **help**는 목적격 보어로 원형부정사와 **to**부정사를 둘 다 쓸 수 있다.
> We *helped* the little boy (**to**) **find** the way.
>
> · **get**은 사역의 의미를 갖지만 목적격 보어로 **to**부정사를 쓴다.
> The police officer *got* the man **to show** his driver's license.

❷ 지각동사

| see   watch   look at   hear
listen to   feel   … | + | 목적어 | + | 원형부정사 |

We *watched* the dancers **perform** on the stage.

> **TIP** 목적격 보어로 쓰이는 현재분사와 과거분사
> · 지각동사의 목적격 보어 자리에 현재분사를 써서 동작이 진행 중임을 강조할 수 있다.
> I *saw* a cat **crossing** the street.
>
> · 사역동사나 지각동사의 목적어와 목적격 보어의 관계가 수동이면 목적격 보어 자리에 과거분사를 쓴다.
> He had *his computer* **repaired**.
> Kelly heard *her name* **called**.

Smart Check 다음 빈칸에 들어갈 알맞은 것을 고르시오.

1 My parents allowed me _____ out until 11 P.M.
① stay   ② to stay   ③ staying

2 The ending of the novel made him _____.
① cry   ② to cry   ③ crying

Practice

Answers p.6

A 괄호 안에서 알맞은 것을 고르시오.

1 They made the moving company workers (load / to load) the boxes.

2 The parents didn't allow their son (talk / to talk) with food in his mouth.

3 The clerk told the customers (stand / to stand) in line.

4 The chef smelled something (to burn / burning) in the kitchen.

5 I had my eyes (testing / tested) before buying glasses.

6 Every neighbor heard the dog (bark / to bark) loudly.

moving company 이삿짐 운송 회사
load 동 싣다, 태우다
clerk 명 점원
customer 명 고객
stand in line 일렬로 나란히 서다

B 괄호 안의 말을 활용하여 문장을 완성하시오.

1 Alice wants someone _____ dinner for her. (cook)

2 The kids made me _____ the rules of the game. (explain)

3 She asked John _____ with the assignment. (help)

4 The tour guide advised us _____ outside at night. (not, go)

5 We saw Megan and Tom _____ with each other. (argue)

6 I didn't let my younger brother _____ my computer. (use)

explain 동 설명하다
assignment 명 과제, 숙제
tour guide 명 여행 가이드
argue 동 말다툼하다

C 우리말과 같도록 괄호 안의 말을 활용하여 문장을 완성하시오.

1 나의 어머니는 내가 집에 오자마자 나의 손을 씻게 하셨다. (have, wash)
= My mother _____ my hands as soon as I came home.

2 팀의 코치는 Kyle이 경쟁력 있는 선수가 되기를 기대한다. (expect, become)
= The team coach _____ a competitive player.

3 Henry는 무언가가 벽에 충돌하는 것을 들었다. (hear, crash into)
= Henry _____ the wall.

4 아로마 오일은 내가 스트레스를 완화하는 것을 도와준다. (help, relieve)
= The aroma oil _____ stress.

competitive 형 경쟁력 있는
crash into ~에 충돌하다
relieve 동 완화하다

UNIT 04 | to부정사의 의미상 주어, 시제, 태

1 to부정사의 의미상 주어

to부정사가 나타내는 행위의 주체가 문장의 주어와 다를 때 의미상 주어를 to부정사 앞에 쓴다.

❶ to부정사의 의미상 주어는 보통 「for + 목적격」의 형태로 쓴다.

It is difficult **for him** *to remember* others' names.
I ordered another sandwich **for you** *to eat*.

❷ to부정사의 의미상 주어가 사람의 성격·성질을 나타내는 형용사(kind, polite, rude, wise, honest, selfish, foolish, careless, generous 등) 뒤에 쓰일 때는 「of + 목적격」의 형태로 쓴다.

It is *wise* **of you** *to listen* to our advice.
It was *foolish* **of her** *to believe* the story.

2 to부정사의 시제

❶ 단순 부정사: 「to + 동사원형」의 형태로, to부정사의 시제가 주절의 시제와 같을 때 쓴다.

Nina **seems to be** upset.
(→ It *seems* that Nina *is* upset.)

❷ 완료 부정사: 「to have + p.p.」의 형태로, to부정사의 시제가 주절의 시제보다 앞설 때 쓴다.

Nina **seems to have been** upset.
(→ It *seems* that Nina *was* upset.)

3 to부정사의 수동태

❶ 단순형: 「to be + p.p.」의 형태로, to부정사가 수동의 의미이고 시제가 주절의 시제와 같을 때 쓴다.

The bill needs **to be paid** immediately.
I didn't expect **to be given** such a nice present.

❷ 완료형: 「to have been + p.p.」의 형태로, to부정사가 수동의 의미이고 시제가 주절의 시제보다 앞설 때 쓴다.

Ken is lucky **to have been chosen** as the winner.
Mr. Jones was glad **to have been elected** a president.

Smart Check 다음 빈칸에 들어갈 알맞은 것을 고르시오.

1 It is impossible _____ to sing better than my sister.
① for me   ② of me   ③ me

2 He seems _____ hard last weekend.
① studied   ② to be studied   ③ to have studied

Practice

Answers p.7

A 괄호 안에서 알맞은 것을 고르시오.

1 It is not easy (for / of) me to speak in front of a large crowd.

2 Fred seems (to live / to have lived) in Spain before.

3 I want (to invite / to be invited) to Victoria's farewell party.

4 It was rude (for / of) him to keep looking at his phone during the meal.

> crowd 몡 사람들, 군중
> farewell party 몡 송별회
> rude 혱 무례한, 예의 없는

B 다음 빈칸에 **for**와 **of** 중 알맞은 것을 쓰시오.

1 It is polite _____ you to hold the door for me.

2 It is important _____ us to choose the right person as a leader.

3 It was careless _____ Kate to leave the lights on.

4 It is necessary _____ everyone to express their thoughts.

> polite 혱 정중한, 예의 바른
> right 혱 적절한, 옳은
> careless 혱 부주의한
> express 됭 표현하다
> thought 몡 생각

C 다음 두 문장의 의미가 같도록 빈칸에 알맞은 말을 쓰시오.

1 It seems that this snack is made from rice.
→ This snack seems _____ _____ _____ from rice.

2 It seems that Karen found the solution to her problem.
→ Karen seems _____ _____ _____ the solution to her problem.

3 It seems that the scientists are surprised at the outcome of the experiment.
→ The scientists seem _____ _____ _____ at the outcome of the experiment.

> solution 몡 해결책
> outcome 몡 결과
> experiment 몡 실험

D 우리말과 같도록 괄호 안의 말을 활용하여 빈칸에 쓰시오.

1 에어컨은 가능한 한 빨리 수리될 필요가 있다. (repair)
= The air conditioner needs _____ _____ _____ as soon as possible.

2 그가 한 시간 동안 수업에 집중하는 것은 불가능하다. (impossible, concentrate)
= It is _____ _____ _____ _____ _____ on the class for an hour.

3 나의 팔은 내가 농구를 하는 동안 부러졌던 것 같다. (seem, break)
= My arm _____ _____ _____ _____ while I was playing basketball.

> repair 됭 수리하다
> concentrate 됭 집중하다

UNIT 05 | to부정사 구문, 독립부정사

1 to부정사를 이용한 구문

❶ 「too + 형용사/부사 + to부정사」: …하기에 너무 ~한/하게 (= so + 형용사/부사 + that + 주어 + can't + 동사원형)

Tim is **too** tired **to do** his assignment.
→ Tim is **so** tired **that** he **can't do** his assignment.

The lecture was **too** difficult *for us* **to understand**.
→ *The lecture* was **so** difficult **that** *we* **couldn't understand** *it*.
　　　　↳ 문장의 주어가 to부정사의 목적어인 경우 that절에 반드시 목적어를 쓴다.

❷ 「형용사/부사 + enough + to부정사」: …할 만큼 충분히 ~한/하게 (= so + 형용사/부사 + that + 주어 + can + 동사원형)

This elevator is big **enough to hold** 30 people.
→ This elevator is **so** big **that** it **can hold** 30 people.

These books are easy **enough** *for kids* **to read**.
→ *These books* are **so** easy **that** *kids* **can read** *them*.

❸ 「It takes + 목적어 + 시간 + to부정사」: …가 ~하는 데 (시간)이 걸리다

It takes me 20 minutes **to take** a shower.
It took the architects over a year **to design** the skyscraper.

2 독립부정사

독립적인 의미를 갖는 to부정사 표현으로, 문장 전체를 수식한다.

to begin with 우선, 먼저	so to speak 말하자면
to be sure 확실히	strange to say 이상한 얘기지만
to be frank (with you) 솔직히 말하면	to make matters worse 설상가상으로
to tell (you) the truth 사실대로 말하면	to make a long story short 간단히 말하면

To begin with, I will tell you the class rules.
To make matters worse, I sprained my ankle.

다음 빈칸에 들어갈 알맞은 것을 고르시오.

1 Kevin is tall _____ to reach the ceiling.
　① so　　　　　　　② too　　　　　　　③ enough

2 This sweater is _____ small for her to wear.
　① so　　　　　　　② too　　　　　　　③ enough

3 _____ frank with you, I don't like your new hairstyle.
　① Be　　　　　　　② Are　　　　　　　③ To be

Practice

Answers p.7

A 괄호 안에서 알맞은 것을 고르시오.

1 The soup was (too / enough) spicy for me to eat.

2 It takes (Emily / for Emily) 15 minutes to get to school on foot.

3 This room is (large enough / enough large) to throw a banquet.

4 (Tell / To tell) the truth, I don't think your idea will work.

5 (To be / Being) sure, some TV programs are not appropriate for kids.

on foot 걸어서, 도보로
throw 통 (모임 등을) 개최하다
banquet 명 연회
work 통 효과가 있다
appropriate 형 적절한

B 다음 두 문장의 의미가 같도록 문장을 완성하시오.

1 This knife is so sharp that it can cut anything.
→ This knife is _____.

2 The environmental issue is so serious that we can't ignore it.
→ The environmental issue is _____.

3 Some fish are poisonous enough to make us sick.
→ Some fish are _____.

4 The light was too dim for me to read the book.
→ The light was _____.

5 I am so exhausted that I can't walk anymore.
→ I am _____.

6 Lindsay studied hard enough to get a perfect score.
→ Lindsay studied _____.

environmental 형 환경의
serious 형 심각한, 중대한
ignore 통 무시하다, 모르는 체하다
poisonous 형 유독한
dim 형 희미한, 약한
exhausted 형 탈진한

C 우리말과 같도록 괄호 안의 말을 활용하여 빈칸에 쓰시오.

1 이상한 얘기지만, 나는 사실은 습한 날씨를 선호한다. (strange)
= _____ _____ _____, I actually prefer humid weather.

2 그 야구 선수는 메이저 리그에서 뛸 만큼 충분히 유능하다. (capable, play)
= The baseball player is _____ _____ _____ _____ in the major leagues.

3 나의 남동생은 혼자 여행하기에 너무 어리다. (young, travel)
= My younger brother is _____ _____ _____ _____ alone.

4 간단히 말하면, David는 지시를 따르는 것을 거부했다. (make, story)
= _____ _____ _____ _____ _____ _____, David refused to follow directions.

actually 부 사실은
prefer 통 선호하다
humid 형 습한
capable 형 유능한
play 통 (특정 경기에서) 뛰다
direction 명 지시

Writing Exercise

A 밑줄 친 부분이 어법상 맞으면 O를 쓰고, 틀리면 바르게 고쳐 쓰시오.

1 Carol let her cat <u>to stay</u> on her bed. → _____

2 I'm watching American dramas <u>to improving</u> my English. → _____

3 It is exciting for me <u>to act</u> in a play. → _____

4 Henry seems <u>to be shock</u> at his grades. → _____

5 I saw the truck <u>enter</u> the no-parking zone. → _____

6 All the dishes need <u>to wash</u> after a meal. → _____

B 우리말과 같도록 to부정사와 괄호 안의 말을 활용하여 문장을 완성하시오.

1 Julian은 그의 개에게 짖는 것을 멈추라고 명령했다. (order, stop)

= Julian _____ barking.

2 정부는 내년에 세금을 인상할 예정이다. (be, increase, taxes)

= The government _____ next year.

3 바다는 지금 당장 수영하기에 너무 춥다. (cold, swim in)

= The sea _____ right now.

4 나의 여동생은 칼로 사과의 껍질을 어떻게 벗기는지 모른다. (peel, an apple)

= My sister doesn't know _____ with a knife.

5 코끼리는 물을 마시기 위해 그들의 코를 사용한다. (use, their trunks, drink)

= The elephants _____ .

6 Megan의 계획은 내일 도서관에 책을 반납하는 것이다. (return, books)

= Megan's plan _____ to the library tomorrow.

C 우리말과 같도록 괄호 안의 말을 알맞게 배열하시오.

1 Ella는 최고의 피아니스트들 중 한 명이 될 만큼 충분히 재능이 있다. (enough, be, talented, to, is)

= Ella _____ one of the best pianists.

2 이 약은 네가 잘 자는 것을 돕는다. (well, you, sleep, to, helps)

= This medicine _____ .

3 사실대로 말하면, 나는 그녀의 연설 도중에 지루함을 느꼈다. (truth, the, to, tell)

= _____ , I felt bored in the middle of her speech.

4 나는 미래를 상상하는 것이 흥미롭다는 것을 알게 되었다. (it, interesting, to, found, imagine)

= I _____ the future.

5 런던에서 로마까지 비행기로 가는 데 두 시간이 걸린다. (to, hours, takes, fly, two)

= It _____ from London to Rome.

6 Evan은 내가 그 퀴즈의 정답을 확인하게 했다. (the, check, me, to, got, answers)

= Evan _____ of the quiz.

D 다음 그림을 보고 괄호 안의 말을 활용하여 빈칸에 쓰시오.

1

2

3

1 They asked me _____ _____ their pictures in front of the fountain. (take)

2 Some pigs know _____ _____ _____ mushrooms. (where, find)

3 I heard _____ _____ _____ _____ at night. (the fire alarm, ring)

Chapter Test

[1-3] 다음 빈칸에 들어갈 알맞은 것을 고르시오.

1

It is always helpful _____ ahead.

① plan
② planned
③ to plan
④ to planning
⑤ be planning

2

The crying baby wants a toy _____.

① play
② played with
③ to playing
④ to play with
⑤ to playing with

3

Ms. Tompson had the mechanic _____ her car.

① fix
② fixed
③ to fix
④ to fixing
⑤ to be fixed

4 다음 빈칸에 공통으로 들어갈 알맞은 것은?

- It is generous _____ you to help your friends in need.
- It was foolish _____ him to lose his wallet again.

① to
② for
③ of
④ with
⑤ from

5 다음 빈칸에 들어갈 말로 <u>어색한</u> 것은?

Mom _____ me to finish my homework before dinner.

① wanted
② told
③ advised
④ made
⑤ encouraged

서술형

[6-8] 다음 두 문장의 의미가 같도록 빈칸에 알맞은 말을 쓰시오.

6

It seems that Kelly cried last night.
→ Kelly _____ _____ _____ _____ last night.

7

The weather is so hot that we can't play outside.
→ The weather is _____ _____ _____ _____ _____ _____ outside.

8

The students discussed when they should hold the school festival.
→ The students discussed _____ _____ the school festival.

서술형

[9-11] 괄호 안의 동사를 활용하여 문장을 완성하시오.

9

> I forgot to bring my pencil case, so Peter let me _____ his pen. (use)

10

> The broken window needs _____ as soon as possible. (repair)

11

> It took the scientists a year _____ the research. (complete)

12 다음 중 밑줄 친 부분을 바르게 고친 것은?

① The teacher ordered the students to being silent. (→ being)

② I was happy to give many presents by friends. (→ to be given)

③ The children need some paper to write. (→ to writing)

④ Dad got us to bringing the newspaper. (→ bring)

⑤ Daniel heard someone to cry out loud. (→ to crying)

13 다음 중 어법상 바른 것은?

① It is impossible of Karen to tell a lie.

② The soup is too hot for me to eat quickly.

③ George found it hard understand the Korean language.

④ The conference room was enough big to hold 50 people.

⑤ The doctor helped her to dealing with her stress.

고난도

14 다음 중 짝지어진 두 문장의 의미가 다른 것은?

① It is cheaper to buy the same item online.
   → To buy the same item online is cheaper.

② You must stay away from the wild animals.
   → You are to stay away from the wild animals.

③ Jeffrey went to a flower shop to buy some flower seeds.
   → Jeffrey went to a flower shop in order to buy some flower seeds.

④ The sun is so bright that we can't see it with our bare eyes.
   → The sun is bright enough for us to see with our bare eyes.

⑤ It seems that the printer stopped working.
   → The printer seems to have stopped working.

[15-16] 다음 빈칸에 들어갈 말이 순서대로 짝지어진 것을 고르시오.

15

> • Eric seems _____ a good boy when he was little.
> • I was very proud _____ a scholarship from school.

① to be – to give
② to be – to be given
③ being – to give
④ to have been – to give
⑤ to have been – to be given

16

> • The doctor advised my grandmother _____ less salt for her health.
> • Rebecca had her hair _____ last week.

① eat – cut
② to eat – to cut
③ to eat – cut
④ eating – to cut
⑤ eating – cut

[17-19] 우리말과 같도록 부정사와 괄호 안의 말을 활용하여 문장을 완성하시오.

17
> 그 신입생은 벌써 대화할 친구들을 사귀었다.
> (friends, talk with)

= The new student has already made _____

_____ .

18
> 나는 나의 여동생이 마실 차를 샀다. (sister, drink)

= I bought tea _____

_____ .

19
> 안내인은 방문객들에게 전시품을 만지지 않을 것을 요청했다. (touch, the exhibits)

= The guide asked the visitors _____

_____ .

[20-21] 다음 중 어법상 <u>어색한</u> 것을 고르시오.

20 ① Laura hopes to travel to Italy someday.
② The teacher taught us how to play volleyball.
③ To be frank, I'm not good at science.
④ Mom doesn't let us to watch TV late at night.
⑤ She saw something moving in the darkness.

21 ① To make matters worse, it began to rain hard.
② She didn't know where to visiting in Seoul.
③ He was brave enough to try skydiving.
④ Nothing was to be found in the cabinet.
⑤ Her grandfather lived to be 90 years old.

[22-23] 주어진 문장의 밑줄 친 **to**부정사와 용법이 같은 것을 고르시오.

22
> It would be exciting <u>to meet</u> my favorite actor.

① If you are <u>to succeed</u>, you should be diligent.
② She must be upset <u>to hear</u> the bad news.
③ He has a suit <u>to wear</u> for his speech.
④ Andrew's hobby is <u>to swim</u> in the sea.
⑤ The athletes practiced hard <u>to get</u> a medal.

23
> Ms. Evans doesn't have a lot of time <u>to exercise</u>.

① <u>To reach</u> the top of the mountain is tough.
② The little kid grew up <u>to be</u> a pilot.
③ Sandra refused <u>to join</u> the chess club.
④ <u>To see</u> him solve math problems, you would admit that he is smart.
⑤ Christopher finally found a bench <u>to sit</u> on.

24 우리말과 같도록 주어진 <조건>에 맞게 영작하시오.

> 네가 그를 또 믿다니 어리석었다.

> <조건> 1. 가주어 it을 사용하시오.
>   2. silly, trust, again을 포함하시오.
>   3. 9단어로 쓰시오.

= _____ .

Chapter

05

동명사

동명사는 「동사원형 + -ing」의 형태로 문장 안에서 명사 역할을 한다.

1 주어/목적어/보어

동명사는 문장 안에서 주어, 목적어, 보어로 쓰인다.

Taking pictures of wild animals can be dangerous. <주어>
You should *stop* **complaining** so much. <동사의 목적어>
Tommy is afraid *of* **getting** a shot. <전치사의 목적어>
Linda's hobby is **knitting** sweaters and hats. <보어>

2 동명사의 의미상 주어

동명사가 나타내는 행위의 주체가 문장의 주어와 다를 때 동명사 앞에 소유격이나 목적격을 써서 의미상 주어를 나타낸다.

Do you mind **my[me]** *turning* on the heater?
We hate **his[him]** *making* fun of other kids.

3 동명사의 시제

❶ 단순 동명사: 「동사원형 + -ing」의 형태로, 동명사의 시제가 주절의 시제와 같을 때 쓴다.

She enjoys **drinking** hot tea when it rains.

❷ 완료 동명사: 「having + p.p.」의 형태로, 동명사의 시제가 주절의 시제보다 앞설 때 쓴다.

I apologize for **having caused** the trouble.

4 동명사의 수동태

❶ 단순형: 「being + p.p.」의 형태로, 동명사가 수동의 의미이고 시제가 주절의 시제와 같을 때 쓴다.

Cindy doesn't like **being left** alone.

❷ 완료형: 「having been + p.p.」의 형태로, 동명사가 수동의 의미이고 시제가 주절의 시제보다 앞설 때 쓴다.

She is glad about **having been accepted** into the soccer team.

Smart Check 다음 빈칸에 들어갈 알맞은 것을 고르시오.

1 Mr. Smith is thinking about _____ his job.
　① quit　　　　　　　　② to quit　　　　　　　③ quitting

2 My parents are proud of _____ winning the speech contest.
　① I　　　　　　　　　② my　　　　　　　　　③ for me

3 He doesn't admit _____ the rules in yesterday's game.
　① broke　　　　　　　② been broken　　　　　③ having broken

Practice

Answers p.8

A 괄호 안에서 알맞은 것을 고르시오.

1 (Explore / Exploring) a new city is fascinating.

2 David has always liked (I / my) singing.

3 I'm sorry for not (to call / calling) you sooner.

4 She was glad about (given / being given) helpful advice.

explore ⑧ 탐험하다, 답사하다
fascinating ⑱ 대단히 흥미로운, 매력적인
helpful ⑱ 도움이 되는
advice ⑲ 조언

B 괄호 안의 말을 알맞은 형태로 바꿔 문장을 완성하시오.

1 I don't mind _____ joining our conversation. (he)

2 People can't keep _____ without electricity. (live)

3 Lena's father doesn't like _____ watching too much TV. (she)

4 Aaron was worried about _____ the deadline. (miss)

conversation ⑲ 대화
electricity ⑲ 전기
deadline ⑲ 기한, 마감 시간

C 다음 두 문장의 의미가 같도록 빈칸에 알맞은 말을 쓰시오.

1 Susan was upset that I spilled water on her laptop.
 → Susan was upset about _____ _____ water on her laptop.

2 He remembered that he had watched the movie before.
 → He remembered _____ _____ the movie before.

3 They were proud that they were chosen to represent the school.
 → They were proud of _____ _____ to represent the school.

spill ⑧ 흘리다, 쏟다
proud ⑱ 자랑스러운
represent ⑧ 대표하다, 대신하다

D 우리말과 같도록 괄호 안의 말을 활용하여 빈칸에 쓰시오.

1 그의 신뢰를 얻는 것은 많은 시간이 걸린다. (gain his trust, take)
 = _____ _____ _____ _____ a lot of time.

2 나는 그녀가 나의 비밀을 지켜주는 것을 안다. (keep)
 = I'm aware of _____ _____ my secret.

3 Daniel은 마지막 경기에서 패배 당한 것에 대해 슬펐다. (defeat)
 = Daniel was sad about _____ _____ in the final game.

gain ⑧ 얻다, 획득하다
trust ⑲ 신뢰, 믿음
be aware of ~을 알다
defeat ⑧ 패배시키다, 물리치다

UNIT 02 | 동명사와 to부정사를 목적어로 쓰는 동사

1 **동명사를 목적어로 쓰는 동사**

> enjoy   finish   avoid   keep   mind   give up   stop   quit   deny   admit   consider   put off   ···

Why did you *give up* **becoming** a nurse?

2 **to부정사를 목적어로 쓰는 동사**

> want   hope   wish   would like   decide   plan   need   expect   promise   agree   refuse   afford   ···

The suspect *refused* **to answer** the question.

3 **동명사와 to부정사를 모두 목적어로 쓰는 동사**

❶ 의미 차이가 없는 경우: like, love, hate, prefer, begin, start, continue 등

Kate *loves* **talking[to talk]** about herself.

❷ 의미 차이가 있는 경우

forget + 동명사 forget + to부정사	(과거에) ~한 것을 잊다 (미래에) ~할 것을 잊다	Ken *forgot* **meeting** her last month. She *forgot* **to buy** milk this week.
remember + 동명사 remember + to부정사	(과거에) ~한 것을 기억하다 (미래에) ~할 것을 기억하다	Do you *remember* **reading** the novel? Please *remember* **to call** me tonight.
regret + 동명사 regret + to부정사	~한 것을 후회하다 ~하게 되어 유감이다	I *regret* **yelling** at my sister. I *regret* **to inform** you of the news.
try + 동명사 try + to부정사	(시험 삼아) ~해보다 ~하려고 노력하다	*Try* **drinking** eight glasses of water a day. Liam *tried* **to exercise** more regularly.

4 **동명사 관용 표현**

> go + V-ing ~하러 가다
> be busy + V-ing ~하느라 바쁘다
> be worth + V-ing ~할 가치가 있다
> cannot help + V-ing ~하지 않을 수 없다
> look forward to + V-ing ~하는 것을 기대하다
>
> There is no + V-ing ~할 수 없다
> be good at + V-ing ~하는 것을 잘하다
> be used to + V-ing ~하는 데 익숙하다
> spend + 시간/돈 + V-ing ~하는 데 시간/돈을 쓰다
> keep[prevent] ··· from + V-ing ~가 ~하지 못하게 하다
>
> on[upon] + V-ing ~하자마자
> feel like + V-ing ~하고 싶다
> It is no use + V-ing ~해도 소용없다

The musical **is worth seeing** many times.

 Smart Check   다음 빈칸에 들어갈 알맞은 것을 고르시오.

1 She is considering _____ a new phone.

　　① get　　　　　　② getting　　　　　③ to get

Practice

Answers p.8

A 괄호 안에서 알맞은 것을 고르시오.

1 The clock on my desk stopped (working / to work).

2 I still remember (visiting / to visit) Hawaii when I was a child.

3 Why did your family decide (moving / to move) to New York?

4 On (see / seeing) her mother, the baby grinned happily.

work 图 작동하다
grin 图 활짝 웃다

B 괄호 안의 동사를 알맞은 형태로 바꿔 문장을 완성하시오.

1 My sister denied _____ my glasses. (hide)

2 Ethan felt like _____ something sweet. (eat)

3 The farmer hopes _____ the apples for a good price. (sell)

4 The scientists will continue _____ on the project. (work)

hide 图 숨기다
price 명 가격
project 명 연구 과제

C 다음 빈칸에 알맞은 말을 <보기>에서 한 번씩만 골라 알맞은 형태로 바꿔 쓰시오.

<보기>	build	learn	charge	respect

1 Diana gave up _____ a new instrument.

2 We cannot help _____ his courageous actions.

3 When does the city plan _____ a new bridge?

4 Joe forgot _____ his phone, so it's running out of power.

respect 图 존경하다
courageous 형 용감한
run out of ~이 다 떨어지다

D 우리말과 같도록 괄호 안의 말을 활용하여 빈칸에 쓰시오.

1 너는 너의 시간을 낭비하는 것을 피해야 한다. (avoid, waste)
= You should _____ _____ your time.

2 나는 카펫 위의 얼룩을 제거하기 위해 비누를 사용해봤다. (try, use)
= I _____ _____ soap to remove the stain on the carpet.

3 낙타는 더운 날씨에서 사는 데 익숙하다. (live)
= A camel _____ _____ _____ _____ in hot weather.

4 은행원들은 고객들을 대하느라 바쁘다. (deal)
= The bank tellers _____ _____ _____ with customers.

waste 图 낭비하다
stain 명 얼룩
deal with 대하다, 다루다

Writing Exercise

A   <보기>와 같이 동명사나 to부정사를 이용하여 다음 두 문장을 한 문장으로 연결하시오.

> <보기>   It is dangerous to drink old milk. You'd better avoid it.
> → You'd better avoid _drinking old milk_ .

1   I'm reading books. It is a great way to relax.

    → _____ is a great way to relax.

2   My mother was to pick me up after class. But she forgot it.

    → My mother forgot _____ after class.

3   Ollie delivers pizzas. It's his part-time job.

    → Ollie's part-time job is _____ .

4   I asked Jake to join the volunteer program with me. He agreed to it.

    → Jake agreed _____ with me.

5   I went to Hanoi with my parents last year. I remember it.

    → I remember _____ last year.

B   우리말과 같도록 괄호 안의 말을 활용하여 문장을 완성하시오.

1   Ashley는 너무 많은 도넛을 먹은 것을 후회했다. (regret, eat)

    = Ashley _____ too many doughnuts.

2   우리는 불공평하게 대우받았던 것에 대해 여전히 화가 난다. (treat, unfairly)

    = We're still angry about _____ .

3   Davis씨는 해외에서 일하는 것을 고려하고 있다. (consider, work)

    = Mr. Davis _____ abroad.

4   그들은 그런 큰 실수를 했었다는 것을 부인한다. (deny, make)

    = They _____ such a big mistake.

5   내가 로비에서 기다려도 되니? (mind, I, wait)

    = Do you _____ at the lobby?

6   그 학자의 연설은 경청할 가치가 있었다. (worth, listen to)

    = The scholar's speech _____ .

C 우리말과 같도록 괄호 안의 말을 알맞게 배열하시오.

1 아빠는 옛 시절에 대한 이야기를 하기 시작했다. (about, times, talking, the, began, old)

= Dad _____ .

2 겨울에 눈사람을 만드는 것은 즐겁다. (winter, snowman, building, a, in)

= _____ is enjoyable.

3 Rebecca는 검은색 옷을 입은 남자를 봤던 것을 기억했다. (the, remembered, man, seeing)

= Rebecca _____ in black clothes.

4 정원사는 혼자서 큰 바위를 옮기려고 노력했다. (move, to, the, rock, tried, large)

= The gardener _____ on his own.

5 그 끔찍한 소식을 들은 후에 나는 울지 않을 수 없었다. (help, could, crying, not)

= I _____ after hearing the terrible news.

6 그 배우는 그의 가족에 대해 질문받는 것을 싫어한다. (asked, being, family, hates, his, about)

= The actor _____ .

D 다음 그림을 보고 <보기>의 말과 괄호 안의 동사를 활용하여 문장을 완성하시오.

1  **2**  **3**

<보기>	on	be busy	look forward to

1 Jordan _____ for the exam last weekend. (prepare)

2 We _____ to Paris next month. (go)

3 _____ the room, Eva turned on the air conditioner. (enter)

Chapter Test

[1-3] 다음 빈칸에 들어갈 알맞은 것을 고르시오.

1

> The members considered _____ off the chess club meeting.

① put
② putting
③ to put
④ being put
⑤ to be put

2

> He decided _____ a hotel with a view of the ocean.

① book
② will book
③ to book
④ booking
⑤ to booking

3

> I cannot help _____ when I see small animals.

① smile
② smiled
③ to smile
④ smiling
⑤ having been smiled

4 다음 빈칸에 들어갈 말로 <u>어색한</u> 것은?

> We _____ going to the large shopping mall.

① hate
② enjoy
③ plan
④ avoid
⑤ love

서술형

[5-6] 괄호 안의 동사를 활용하여 문장을 완성하시오.

5

> I finished _____ in my journal and then went to bed. (write)

6

> Philip forgot _____ his lunchbox, so he had to buy something to eat. (bring)

[7-8] 다음 중 어법상 <u>어색한</u> 것을 고르시오.

7
① Taking care of babies is not easy.
② I don't like he telling silly jokes to me.
③ Marie feels sorry for having made trouble.
④ Jackson hates being pointed at.
⑤ Do you mind opening the window?

8
① We all tried eating the spicy noodles.
② The injured man needed to go to the hospital right away.
③ The latest novel is worth to read twice.
④ Mr. Wright stopped drinking coffee.
⑤ The customer continued to complain about the product.

서술형

[9-11] 다음 문장에서 어법상 <u>어색한</u> 부분을 찾아 쓰고 바르게 고쳐 쓰시오.

9
> Judy has confidence in give speeches in front of big audience.

_____ → _____

10
> Ms. Tompson's kids love taking to the amusement park.

_____ → _____

11
> Sam regrets to buy the expensive sneakers yesterday.

_____ → _____

고난도

12 주어진 문장의 밑줄 친 부분과 쓰임이 <u>다른</u> 것은?

> My sister enjoys <u>making</u> fun of me.

① He kept <u>shaking</u> his legs during the test.
② They quit <u>using</u> plastic bags for the environment.
③ Terry's goal is <u>becoming</u> a baseball player.
④ We don't mind her <u>coming</u> with us on a camping trip.
⑤ Anne avoids <u>going</u> into the sea.

13 다음 중 밑줄 친 부분을 바르게 고치지 <u>못한</u> 것은?

① We gave up <u>persuade</u> him to go skiing with us.
　　　　→ to persuade
② My dad admitted <u>having been eaten</u> my salad.
　　　　→ having eaten
③ Sara promised <u>studying</u> hard for the exam.
　　　　→ to study
④ I started <u>to feeling</u> nervous on the stage.
　　　　→ feeling
⑤ Alan hopes <u>visiting</u> Busan in the summer.
　　　　→ to visit

서술형

[14-16] 우리말과 같도록 괄호 안의 말을 활용하여 문장을 완성하시오.

14
> Albert는 나에게서 지우개를 빌려간 것을 기억하지 못한다. (remember, borrow)

= Albert _____ an eraser from me.

15
> 그 아이는 어젯밤 컵을 깼던 것을 부인한다. (deny, break)

= The kid _____ the cup last night.

16
> Jessie는 새 컴퓨터를 구입하는 것을 생각하고 있다. (think of, purchase)

= Jessie _____ a new computer.

17 다음 우리말을 알맞게 영작한 것은?

이 영화를 함께 본 것을 잊지 마.

① Don't forget watch this movie together.
② Don't forget to watch this movie together.
③ Don't forget to watching this movie together.
④ Don't forget watching this movie together.
⑤ Don't forget having been watched this movie together.

[18-19] 다음 빈칸에 들어갈 말이 순서대로 짝지어진 것을 고르시오.

18
• I felt like _____ some hot tea.
• Upon _____ our aunt, we hugged her.

① drink – see
② to drink – to see
③ to drink – seeing
④ drinking – seeing
⑤ drinking – to seeing

19
• Paul is still upset about _____ for what he hadn't done.
• Her illness kept her from _____ to school.

① blaming – going
② blaming – being gone
③ being blamed – being gone
④ having been blamed – going
⑤ having been blamed – being gone

20 다음 빈칸에 들어갈 수 있는 것을 <u>모두</u> 고르시오.

Peter prefers _____ home on Sunday.

① stay
② stayed
③ staying
④ to stay
⑤ to staying

[21-22] 동명사를 이용하여 다음 두 문장을 한 문장으로 연결하시오.

21
He is late again. His teacher is quite disappointed about it.
→ His teacher is quite disappointed about _____ again.

22
I was disturbed by the noise from upstairs. But I didn't mind it.
→ I didn't mind _____ by the noise from upstairs.

23 우리말과 같도록 괄호 안의 말을 알맞게 배열하시오.

과거를 후회해도 소용없다. (past, it, use, the, is, regretting, no)

= _____.

24 다음 중 어법상 바른 것은?

① Everyone agreed waiting for Tim a little longer.
② Jeff is busy watch the soccer match.
③ I spent a lot of money buying the tickets.
④ The child refused going to the dentist.
⑤ Mr. Parker is proud of to have been a firefighter.

Chapter

06

분사

분사는 동사가 V-ing형이나 p.p.형으로 쓰여
문장 안에서 형용사 역할을 하는 것이다.

UNIT 01 | 현재분사와 과거분사

1 분사의 쓰임

분사는 V-ing(현재분사)나 p.p.(과거분사)의 형태로, 형용사처럼 명사를 수식하거나 문장 안에서 보어로 쓰인다.

❶ 명사 수식: 분사가 단독으로 쓰이면 명사 앞에 오고, 구를 이루어 쓰이면 명사 뒤에 온다.

Are you able to fix the **broken** *computer*?
We saw a *girl* **playing the flute**.

❷ 보어: 주격 보어나 목적격 보어로 쓰인다.

The man sat **reading** a magazine. <주격 보어>
Nate had his room **painted** last week. <목적격 보어>

2 현재분사와 과거분사

❶ 현재분사(V-ing): 능동(~하는)·진행(~하고 있는)
The firefighters went into the **burning** house.
The boy **jogging** along the river is my classmate.

❷ 과거분사(p.p.): 수동(~된, ~당한)·완료(~된)

I couldn't find my **stolen** wallet.
Let's sweep the leaves **fallen** on the street.

3 감정을 나타내는 분사

분사가 수식하거나 설명하는 대상이 감정을 일으키는 원인일 때는 현재분사를 쓰고, 감정을 느낄 때는 과거분사를 쓴다.

surprising 놀라운 - surprised 놀란	interesting 흥미로운 - interested 흥미로워하는
amazing 놀라운 - amazed 놀란	boring 지루한 - bored 지루해하는
exciting 신나는 - excited 신이 난	pleasing 기쁜 - pleased 기뻐하는
shocking 충격적인 - shocked 충격받은	disappointing 실망스러운 - disappointed 실망스러워하는
exhausting 지치게 하는 - exhausted 지친	confusing 혼란스러운 - confused 혼란스러워하는

Ben had a **disappointing** dinner. He was **disappointed**.

Smart Check 다음 빈칸에 들어갈 알맞은 것을 고르시오.

1 Mr. Hart always keeps his shoes _____.
　① polish　　　　　② polishing　　　　　③ polished

2 No one could answer the _____ math question.
　① confuse　　　　　② confusing　　　　　③ confused

Practice

A 괄호 안에서 알맞은 것을 고르시오.

1 I saw a bird (flying / flown) into my bedroom window.

2 Stephanie couldn't read the sign (writing / written) in Spanish.

3 He heard me (practicing / practiced) a song in the auditorium.

4 Staying in school all day makes students (exhausting / exhausted).

auditorium 몡 강당
all day 하루 종일

B 괄호 안의 동사를 알맞은 형태로 바꿔 빈칸에 쓰시오.

1 The children tried to catch the _____ snow. (fall)

2 Anna looked _____ because she was lost. (confuse)

3 The boy _____ round glasses is my brother. (wear)

4 The cat found a mouse _____ in the trap. (catch)

lost 혱 길을 잃은
trap 몡 덫, 함정

C 우리말과 같도록 <보기>의 말을 한 번씩만 골라 알맞은 형태로 바꿔 쓰시오.

<보기>	amaze	interest	please

1 너는 세계사에 흥미가 있니?
= Are you _____ in world history?

2 그 산은 정상에서 보이는 놀라운 경치로 유명하다.
= The mountain is famous for the _____ view from the top.

3 Smith씨는 학생들로부터 온 편지에 기뻐했다.
= Mr. Smith was _____ with the letters from students.

be famous for ~으로 유명하다

D 우리말과 같도록 괄호 안의 말을 활용하여 빈칸에 쓰시오.

1 Jacob은 나무 밑에 숨겨진 보물을 찾아냈다. (the treasure, hide)
= Jacob found _____ _____ _____ under the tree.

2 그 금이 간 거울은 어제 교체되었다. (crack, mirror)
= The _____ _____ was replaced yesterday.

3 이 지역에는 홍수에 의해 피해를 입은 많은 집들이 있다. (many houses, damage)
= There are _____ _____ _____ by the flood in this area.

crack 통 금이 가다
replace 통 교체하다
damage 통 피해를 입히다

UNIT 02 | 분사구문

1 분사구문

❶ 분사구문은 분사를 이용하여 「접속사 + 주어 + 동사」 형태의 부사절을 부사구로 바꾼 것이다.

❷ 분사구문은 부사절과 주절의 주어가 같을 때 부사절의 접속사와 주어를 생략하고 부사절의 동사를 V-ing형으로 바꿔서 만든다.

As I trust Jane, I can tell her my secrets.
→ **Trusting** Jane, I can tell her my secrets.

While Eric climbed the mountain, he sprained his ankle.
→ **Climbing** the mountain, Eric sprained his ankle.

> **TIP** 분사구문의 부정형은 분사 앞에 **not**을 붙여 만든다.
> **Not feeling** well, I took the medicine.

2 분사구문의 다양한 의미

시간	when ~할 때 while ~하는 동안 after ~한 후에 as soon as ~하자마자	**Hearing** the thunder, the puppies were surprised. (← When the puppies heard the thunder)
이유	because/as/since ~하기 때문에	**Making** the same mistake again, I was angry at myself. (← As I made the same mistake again)
동시동작	while/as ~하면서	**Having** dinner, they watch TV together. (← While they have dinner)
조건	if 만약 ~한다면	**Taking** the subway Line 2, you can get to city hall. (← If you take the subway Line 2)
양보	although/though 비록 ~이지만	**Although singing** well, he is afraid of singing in public. (← Although he sings well) **TIP** 양보를 나타내는 분사구문은 주로 접속사를 생략하지 않는다.

Smart Check 다음 밑줄 친 부사절을 분사구문으로 바꿀 때 빈칸에 알맞은 말을 쓰시오.

1 As he turned around, he saw his friend.
→ _____ around, he saw his friend.

2 Because Emily wasn't sleepy, she stayed up late.
→ _____ _____ sleepy, Emily stayed up late.

3 Though I live in France, I can't speak French.
→ _____ _____ in France, I can't speak French.

Practice

Answers p.9

A 괄호 안에서 알맞은 것을 고르시오.

1 (Running / Ran) up the hill, I sweated a lot.

2 (Knowing not / Not knowing) what to do, she asked her teacher.

3 (To follow / Following) your dream, you'll become successful.

4 (Graduating / Graduated) from university, he became a lawyer.

hill 똉 언덕
sweat 똉 땀을 흘리다
successful 똉 성공적인
graduate 똉 졸업하다

B 다음 밑줄 친 부사절을 분사구문으로 바꿀 때 빈칸에 알맞은 말을 쓰시오.

1 Because I felt dizzy, I came home early.
→ _____ dizzy, I came home early.

2 When she reached the hospital, she found it closed.
→ _____ the hospital, she found it closed.

3 If you go straight two blocks, you can see a train station.
→ _____ straight two blocks, you can see a train station.

4 While people listened to the songs, they danced.
→ _____ to the songs, people danced.

dizzy 똉 어지러운
reach 똉 도착하다, 도달하다

C 다음 밑줄 친 부분을 접속사 when, since, if를 이용하여 부사절로 바꿔 쓰시오.

1 Not having money, he couldn't take a taxi.
→ _____ money, he couldn't take a taxi.

2 Looking up, I saw a rainbow appear in the sky.
→ _____, I saw a rainbow appear in the sky.

3 Turning right, you'll find the city library.
→ _____, you'll find the city library.

appear 똉 나타나다

D 우리말과 같도록 괄호 안의 말을 활용하여 빈칸에 쓰시오.

1 나는 그 무서운 영화를 보는 동안, 두려움에 떨었다. (watch the scary movie)
= _____ _____ _____ _____, I trembled with fear.

2 그녀는 빙판 위에서 넘어졌기 때문에, 무릎에 멍이 들었다. (fall down on the ice)
= _____ _____ _____ _____ _____, she got a
bruise on her knee.

3 비록 그는 부자이지만, 많은 돈을 쓰지 않는다. (be rich)
= _____ _____ _____, he doesn't spend a lot of money.

tremble 똉 (몸을) 떨다
bruise 똉 멍, 타박상

UNIT 03 | 주의해야 할 분사구문

1 완료형 분사구문

「having + p.p.」의 형태로, 부사절의 시제가 주절의 시제보다 앞설 때 쓴다.

Having watched the movie, I know the ending. (← As I *watched* the movie, I *know* the ending.)

---

2 수동형 분사구문

「being[having been] + p.p.」의 형태로, being이나 having been은 생략할 수 있다.

(**Being**) **Given** a present, Nina felt touched.
(← When Nina *was given* a present, she *felt* touched.)
(**Having been**) **Injured** last week, he can't join today's game.
(← As he *was injured* last week, he *can't join* today's game.)

---

3 독립분사구문

❶ 부사절의 주어와 주절의 주어가 다를 때 부사절의 주어를 생략하지 않으며, 이를 독립분사구문이라고 한다.

It being rainy, *we* need an umbrella. (← As <u>it</u> *is* rainy, <u>we</u> need an umbrella.)

❷ 분사구문의 주어가 막연한 일반인인 경우 주어를 생략하고 관용적으로 쓰기도 한다.

Generally speaking 일반적으로 말하면	Strictly speaking 엄밀히 말하면	Frankly speaking 솔직히 말하면
Judging from ~으로 판단하건대	Speaking of ~에 대해 말하자면	Considering ~을 고려하면

Strictly speaking, the rumor isn't true.

---

4 접속사를 생략하지 않는 분사구문

분사구문의 의미를 분명하게 하기 위해 접속사를 생략하지 않기도 한다.

While running in the race, he felt thirsty. (← *While* he ran in the race, he felt thirsty.)

---

5 with + (대)명사 + 분사

'~가 -한 채로/하면서'라는 의미로, 동시 동작을 나타낸다. (대)명사와 분사의 관계가 능동이면 현재분사, 수동이면 과거분사를 쓴다.

The band finished a song **with the crowd cheering**.
Samuel listened to me carefully **with his arms crossed**.

Smart Check 다음 빈칸에 들어갈 알맞은 것을 고르시오.

1 _____ with fur, this sofa is really soft.
① Covering   ② Having covered   ③ Being covered

2 He is sleeping with the TV _____ on.
① turn   ② turned   ③ turning

Practice

Answers p.10

A 괄호 안에서 알맞은 것을 고르시오.

1 (Watching / Watched) by a lot of people, the video got popular.

2 (Today being Sunday / Being today Sunday), I got up late.

3 (Taken / Having taken) the medicine, I feel better now.

4 The boy preferred to stay in his room with the door (closing / closed).

take medicine 약을 먹다
prefer 동 선호하다

B 괄호 안의 동사를 알맞은 형태로 바꿔 빈칸에 쓰시오.

1 Generally _____, kids learn languages faster than adults. (speak)

2 He played the guitar with his legs _____. (cross)

3 Before _____ the sweater, I turned it inside out. (wash)

4 _____ by a fire, the house needs to be rebuilt. (destroy)

inside out (안팎을) 뒤집어
rebuild 동 다시 세우다
destroy 동 파괴하다, 무너뜨리다

C 다음 두 문장의 의미가 같도록 분사구문을 이용하여 문장을 완성하시오. (단, 접속사를 생략하시오.)

1 As I had enough sleep last night, I'm in good condition.
→ _____, I'm in good condition.

2 Because a violin is made of wood, it is easy to break.
→ _____, a violin is easy to break.

3 After they had completed the work, they felt proud of themselves.
→ _____, they felt proud of themselves.

4 When the snow started to fall, I arrived home.
→ _____, I arrived home.

in good condition 몸 상태가 좋은
break 동 깨지다, 부서지다
complete 동 완료하다, 마치다
proud 형 자랑스러운

D 우리말과 같도록 괄호 안의 말을 활용하여 빈칸에 쓰시오.

1 그녀는 이전에 이곳에서 살았었기 때문에, 거리들에 익숙하다. (live, here)
= _____ _____ _____ before, she is familiar with the streets.

2 가격을 고려하면, 그 식당은 실망스러웠다. (consider, the price)
= _____ _____ _____, the restaurant was disappointing.

3 David는 그의 개가 따라오는 채로 공원에서 조깅을 했다. (dog, follow)
= David jogged in the park _____ _____ _____ _____.

familiar 형 익숙한
price 명 가격
follow 동 따라오다

Writing Exercise

A 다음 문장에서 틀린 부분을 바르게 고쳐 완전한 문장을 쓰시오.

1 Strictly speak, this is not the best solution.

→ _____ .

2 Being walked along the lake, I listened to my favorite song.

→ _____ .

3 He focused on the game with his arms folding.

→ _____ .

4 Please avoid beverages contain a large amount of caffeine.

→ _____ .

5 I bought a basket filling with lemon cookies.

→ _____ .

6 The teacher's storytelling made the lecture more interested.

→ _____ .

B 우리말과 같도록 괄호 안의 말을 활용하여 분사구문을 완성하시오. (단, 접속사를 생략하시오.)

1 그녀는 큰 소리로 울면서, 그녀의 침대에 누웠다. (cry, loudly)

= _____ , she lied on her bed.

2 그는 프랑스어를 배우지 않았었기 때문에, 프랑스어로 쓰인 책을 읽을 수 없다. (learn, French)

= _____ , he can't read the book written in French.

3 나는 나의 오랜 친구를 보자마자, 그를 안기 위해 달려갔다. (see, my old friend)

= _____ , I ran to hug him.

4 그는 캐나다에서 태어났기 때문에, 그것의 관광지에 대해 잘 알고 있다. (be born, Canada)

= _____ , he knows well about its tourist sites.

5 우리는 산을 오르면서, 경치를 즐겼다. (climb up, the mountain)

= _____ , we enjoyed the view.

6 호텔들이 비쌌기 때문에, Lucas는 호스텔에 머무는 것을 선택했다. (the hotels, expensive)

= _____ , Lucas chose to stay at a hostel.

C 우리말과 같도록 괄호 안의 말을 알맞게 배열하시오.

1 나는 촛불을 끄면서, 소원을 빌었다. (the, out, blowing, candles)

= _____, I made a wish.

2 소포를 들고 있는 그 소년은 우체국으로 향했다. (boy, a, carrying, the, parcel)

= _____ headed to the post office.

3 우리는 배관공에 의해 부엌의 싱크대가 수리되게 했다. (repaired, kitchen, the, had, sink)

= We _____ by the plumber.

4 나는 이전에 몰디브에 방문했기 때문에, 그곳이 멋지다는 것을 안다. (before, having, Maldives, visited)

= _____, I know the place is wonderful.

5 하늘에 있는 잿빛의 구름으로 판단하건대, 비가 올 것이다. (the, in, gray, judging, the, clouds, sky, from)

= _____, it is going to rain.

6 Grace는 게시판에 꽂힌 모든 메모들을 제거했다. (pinned, to, memos, bulletin board, the)

= Grace removed all the _____.

D 다음 그림을 보고 괄호 안의 말을 활용하여 빈칸에 쓰시오.

1

2

3

1 I found a red dress _____ _____ _____ _____. (keep, the closet)

2 _____ _____ _____ _____, we watched the sunset. (sit on, the bench)

3 He left the room _____ _____ _____ _____ _____. (with, his computer, turn on)

Chapter 06

분사

Hackers Grammar Smart Level 3

Chapter Test

[1-3] 다음 빈칸에 들어갈 알맞은 것을 고르시오.

1

> The man _____ beside the door is my dad.

① stand ② stands
③ standing ④ stood
⑤ to stand

2

> _____ her students, Ms. Rogers waved her hands at them.

① Sees ② Saw
③ Seen ④ Seeing
⑤ Being seen

3

> I felt _____ when I heard that Jenny was going abroad.

① shock ② shocking
③ shocked ④ to shock
⑤ to shocked

4 다음 중 어법상 바른 것은?

① Jeff was surprising at the car accident.
② I had my shirts washing last weekend.
③ We found the door locked from the outside.
④ That girl worn a wide hat is Jessica.
⑤ The documentary about lions is interested.

[5-6] 다음 빈칸에 들어갈 말이 순서대로 짝지어진 것을 고르시오.

5

> • The exhibits in this museum look _____.
> • Frank was _____ at the result of the baseball game.

① amaze – disappoint
② amazed – disappointed
③ amazed – disappointing
④ amazing – disappointed
⑤ amazing – disappointing

6

> • _____ the plants, I saw a beautiful butterfly.
> • Mr. Jenkins had the wall _____ white.

① Watering – painting
② Watering – painted
③ Watered – painting
④ Watered – painted
⑤ Having watered – painting

서술형

[7-8] 다음 문장에서 어법상 어색한 부분을 찾아 쓰고 바르게 고쳐 쓰시오.

7

> I listened to the music with my eyes closing.

_____ → _____

8

> Although having been had a lot of food for breakfast, she still feels hungry.

_____ → _____

[9-10] 다음 중 어법상 <u>어색한</u> 것을 고르시오.

9
① Do you see the people waiting in line?
② The girl run across the field is my niece.
③ I gently touched the kitten sleeping on the couch.
④ The writer got his novel published in 2020.
⑤ The rescuers discovered a house damaged by the hurricane.

10
① Sweeping the floor, I found an earring.
② Not having a driver's license, my older brother can't drive.
③ Having wiped, the window is now clean.
④ Left alone, the child started to cry.
⑤ It being rainy, we decided to stay home.

<u>서술형</u>
[11-12] 괄호 안의 동사를 알맞은 형태로 바꿔 빈칸에 쓰시오.

11
_____ _____ _____ by Picasso, the painting is priceless. (create)

12
_____ his daughter's name, the man searched for his lost child. (call)

<u>서술형</u>
[13-15] 다음 문장의 밑줄 친 부분을 분사구문으로 바꿔 쓰시오.

13
<u>When Lisa won the award</u>, she cried with joy.
→ _____, Lisa cried with joy.

14
<u>Because Mark grew up here</u>, he knows many residents in this town.
→ _____, Mark knows many residents this town.

15
<u>If you turn left</u>, you will be on the main street.
→ _____, you will be on the main street.

16 다음 밑줄 친 부분을 부사절로 바꾼 것 중 <u>어색한</u> 것은?
① <u>Digging into the ground</u>, he found some old pots. (→ While he dug into the ground)
② <u>Having enough money</u>, I can buy those sneakers. (→ As I had enough money)
③ <u>Arriving at school</u>, I ran into my best friend. (→ As soon as I arrived at school)
④ <u>Being a genius</u>, she can solve any problem. (→ Since she is a genius)
⑤ <u>Leaving Korea</u>, they promised to come back. (→ When they left Korea)

[17-20] 우리말과 같도록 괄호 안의 말을 활용하여 빈칸에 쓰시오.

17 비록 그는 어리지만, 매우 현명하다. (be, young)

= _____ _____ _____ _____,
he is very wise.

= _____ _____ _____, he is very
wise.

18 만약 네가 열심히 공부한다면, 좋은 성적을 받을
것이다. (study, hard)

= _____ _____ _____ _____,
you will get good grades.

= _____ _____, you will get good
grades.

19 그녀는 산을 올랐기 때문에, 지금 목마르다. (climb,
the mountain)

= _____ _____ _____ _____
_____, she is thirsty now.

= _____ _____ _____ _____,
she is thirsty now.

20 그 개는 씻겨지는 동안, 계속 짖었다. (wash)

= _____ _____ _____ _____
_____, it kept barking.

= _____ _____, the dog kept barking.

21 주어진 문장의 밑줄 친 부분과 쓰임이 <u>다른</u> 것은?

> Mom is looking after the <u>crying</u> baby.

① Tiffany sat <u>waiting</u> for her friends.
② My dream is <u>traveling</u> around the world.
③ There are children <u>playing</u> in the playground.
④ The rules of the board game were <u>confusing</u>.
⑤ We saw Jack <u>studying</u> in the library.

22 다음 글의 밑줄 친 ⓐ~ⓔ 중 어법상 어색한 것을 찾아
기호를 쓰고 바르게 고쳐 쓰시오.

> ⓐStarting the third grade, I felt upset to be
> separated from my friends. ⓑSat beside
> a new classmate, Matt, I was too shy to
> start a conversation. Frankly ⓒspeaking, I
> didn't know Matt last year. However, after
> ⓓspending some time with him, I realized
> that he was a nice guy. I was ⓔpleasing to
> get to know him better.

(1) _____ → _____
(2) _____ → _____

23 다음 중 어법상 바른 것의 개수는?

> ⓐ Do not touch the broken cup.
> ⓑ Having not a pen, Jim had to borrow one.
> ⓒ Jamie found his stealing wallet.
> ⓓ Felt hot, she took off her scarf.
> ⓔ Having sprained her arm, Maria can't hold
>   her bag.

① 1개   ② 2개   ③ 3개
④ 4개   ⑤ 5개

Chapter

07

관계사

관계사는 두 문장을 연결하는 접속사 역할을 하며,
관계사가 이끄는 절은 앞 문장의 명사를 꾸민다.
관계사에는 관계대명사와 관계부사가 있다.

UNIT 01 | 관계대명사

관계대명사는 접속사와 대명사 역할을 하며, 관계대명사가 이끄는 절은 선행사(앞 문장의 명사)를 수식한다.

I listened to the song. It was popular in the 1990s.

→ I listened to *the song* **which** was popular in the 1990s.

선행사   관계대명사절

선행사 ＼ 관계대명사의 격	주격	목적격	소유격
사람	who	who(m)	whose
사물, 동물	which	which	
사람, 사물, 동물	that	that	-
선행사 포함	what	what	-

TIP 선행사가 「사람 + 사물/동물」, -thing으로 끝나는 대명사이거나 선행사에 최상급, 서수, **the only, the same, the very, all, every, no** 등이 포함될 때 주로 관계대명사 **that**을 사용한다.

Linda was *the first person* **that** arrived at the meeting.

1 주격 관계대명사 : who, which, that

I have *a friend* **who[that]** speaks both Korean and English.

He ate *the apples* **which[that]** were in the basket.

2 목적격 관계대명사 : who(m), which, that

The girl **who(m)[that]** I met at the festival was friendly.

Jack returned *the shoes* **which[that]** he bought yesterday.

3 소유격 관계대명사 : whose

Did you see *the man* **whose** beard was really long?

Kate wants to live in *a house* **whose** windows are big.
（= the windows of which）

4 관계대명사 what

선행사를 포함하고 있으며, '~한 것'이라는 의미이다. the thing(s) which[that]으로 바꿔 쓸 수 있다.

What she told me wasn't true.
（= The thing which[that]）

Can you understand **what** the teacher explained?
（= the thing which[that]）

 Smart Check   다음 빈칸에 들어갈 알맞은 것을 고르시오.

    1 The lamp _____ is by my bed isn't working.

      ① who   ② which   ③ whose

Practice

Answers p.11

A 괄호 안에서 알맞은 것을 고르시오.

1 Here is your key (who / which) you lost yesterday.

2 This is the coldest winter (whom / that) I have ever experienced.

3 Let's rest under the tree (which / whose) leaves are very large.

4 There are some people (whom / whose) I don't know in the group.

5 Have you decided (that / what) you are going to do this weekend?

experience ⑧ 겪다, 경험하다
rest ⑧ 쉬다
decide ⑧ 결정하다

B 다음 빈칸에 알맞은 말을 <보기>에서 한 번씩만 골라 쓰시오.

<보기>	which	whom	that

1 There are some kids and dogs _____ are playing in the pool.

2 The tour guide _____ I recommended is very kind.

3 We'll go to the restaurant _____ uses organic ingredients.

recommend ⑧ 추천하다
organic ⑲ 유기농의
ingredient ⑲ 재료

C 관계대명사를 이용하여 다음 두 문장을 한 문장으로 연결하시오.

1 Can you pick up the pen? It is under your desk.
→ Can you pick up the pen _____?

2 Nick will join the soccer team. Its star player is injured.
→ Nick will join the soccer team _____.

3 The students were Chinese. We saw them at the entrance.
→ The students _____ were Chinese.

pick up ~을 집어 올리다
star player 인기 선수
injured ⑲ 부상을 입은
entrance ⑲ 입구

D 우리말과 같도록 관계대명사와 괄호 안의 말을 활용하여 빈칸에 쓰시오.

1 Frank는 Maria가 제안한 것에 대해 신중하게 생각했다. (suggest)
= Frank carefully thought about _____ _____ _____.

2 나는 주인공이 형사인 책들을 좋아한다. (the books, main character)
= I like _____ _____ _____ _____ is a detective.

3 수리공은 기계를 정비하는 사람이다. (a person, maintain)
= A mechanic is _____ _____ _____ machines.

suggest ⑧ 제안하다
main character ⑲ 주인공
detective ⑲ 형사, 탐정
maintain ⑧ 정비하다
mechanic ⑲ 수리공

UNIT 02 | 관계부사

관계부사는 접속사와 부사 역할을 하며, 관계부사가 이끄는 절은 선행사를 수식한다. 관계부사는 장소, 시간, 이유, 방법을 나타내며, 「전치사 + 관계대명사」로 바꿔 쓸 수 있다.

	선행사	관계부사	「전치사 + 관계대명사」
장소	the place, the house, the city 등	where	at/on/in/to + which
시간	the time, the day, the year 등	when	at/on/in/during + which
이유	the reason	why	for + which
방법	the way	how	in + which

1 where

This is *the place* **where**[**at which**] we play after school.
London is *the city* **where**[**in which**] Jackson was born.

2 when

Do you know *the time* **when**[**at which**] the concert starts?
April 5 is *the day* **when**[**on which**] people plant trees.

3 why

Tell me *the reason* **why**[**for which**] you arrived late.
Coffee is *the reason* **why**[**for which**] George can't fall asleep.

4 how

the way와 how는 둘 중 하나만 쓸 수 있다.

I want to learn **how** you solved this puzzle.
= I want to learn *the way* (**in which**) you solved this puzzle.

> **TIP** 선행사가 **the place, the time, the reason**과 같은 일반적인 명사인 경우 선행사나 관계부사 둘 중 하나를 생략할 수 있다.
> That bakery is *(the place)* **where** I buy bread every morning.
> = That bakery is *the place* (**where**) I buy bread every morning.

Smart Check 다음 빈칸에 들어갈 알맞은 것을 고르시오.

1 Jane forgot the place _____ she left her wallet.
  ① where　　　　　　② when　　　　　　③ why

2 2010 is the year _____ my family moved to Seoul.
  ① where　　　　　　② when　　　　　　③ how

3 Is there any reason _____ Adam is so upset?
  ① when　　　　　　② why　　　　　　③ how

Practice

Answers p.11

A 괄호 안에서 알맞은 것을 고르시오.

1 5 A.M. is the time (where / when) the first bus starts running.

2 Good service is the reason (when / why) our customers are satisfied.

3 I don't like (the way how / how) Thomas talks to me.

4 She knows a place (where / how) we can see a nice sunset.

run ⑧ 운행하다
satisfy ⑧ 만족시키다
sunset ⑨ 일몰

B 다음 빈칸에 알맞은 말을 <보기>에서 한 번씩만 골라 쓰시오.

<보기>	when	why	how

1 Brian taught me _____ I can use the Bluetooth speaker.

2 I heard the reason _____ Jenny refused to join the club.

3 Do you remember the date _____ you ordered the item?

refuse ⑧ 거절하다, 거부하다
order ⑧ 주문하다

C 다음 두 문장의 의미가 같도록 관계부사를 이용하여 문장을 완성하시오.

1 Ms. Wilson showed me the way the copy machine works.
→ Ms. Wilson showed me _____.

2 The shop at which I always buy clothes is closed today.
→ The shop _____ is closed today.

3 December is the month in which the winter begins.
→ December is the month _____.

4 Kate told me the reason for which she decided to do volunteer work.
→ Kate told me the reason _____.

work ⑧ 작동하다
volunteer work ⑨ 자원 봉사

D 우리말과 같도록 관계부사와 괄호 안의 말을 활용하여 빈칸에 쓰시오.

1 이곳은 졸업식이 열릴 강당이다. (the hall)
= This is _____ _____ _____ the graduation will be held.

2 나는 멕시코 사람들이 새해 첫날을 축하하는 방법을 배웠다. (Mexicans, celebrate)
= I learned _____ _____ _____ New Year's Day.

3 강의가 끝나는 시간을 나에게 말해줄 수 있니? (the time)
= Can you tell me _____ _____ _____ the lecture ends?

graduation ⑨ 졸업식, 졸업
celebrate ⑧ 축하하다, 기념하다
lecture ⑨ 강의, 강연

UNIT 03 | 주의해야 할 관계사의 쓰임

1 관계대명사의 생략

❶ 목적격 관계대명사 who(m), which, that은 생략할 수 있다.

Ken is the friend (**who(m)**[**that**]) I trust the most.
I keep thinking about the movie (**which**[**that**]) I saw yesterday.

❷ 「주격 관계대명사 + be동사」는 생략할 수 있다.

The woman (**who**[**that**] **is**) waving at us is my aunt.
He gave me a box (**which**[**that**] **was**) filled with cookies.

---

2 전치사 + 관계대명사

관계대명사가 전치사의 목적어인 경우, 전치사는 관계대명사절의 맨 뒤나 관계대명사 바로 앞에 온다.

Who is the boy (**who(m)**[**that**]) you were speaking **to**?
→ Who is the boy **to whom** you were speaking?
  └→ 관계대명사 바로 앞에 전치사가 올 때는 목적격 관계대명사를 생략할 수 없고, 관계대명사 who나 that을 쓸 수 없다.

She is looking for a bench (**which**[**that**]) she can sit **on**.
→ She is looking for a bench **on which** she can sit.

---

3 관계사의 계속적 용법

선행사에 부가적인 설명을 덧붙일 때 사용하며, 관계사 앞에 콤마(,)를 쓴다. 계속적 용법으로 쓰인 관계사는 생략할 수 없다.

❶ 관계대명사의 계속적 용법: who와 which만 쓸 수 있고, 「접속사 + 대명사」로 바꿔 쓸 수 있다.

This is Mr. Jones, **who**(= **and he**) taught me English.
My sister bought a new watch, **which**(= **but it**) broke the next day.

> **TIP** 관계대명사 which는 계속적 용법으로 쓸 때 앞에 나온 구나 절을 선행사로 취할 수 있다.
> *The boy fell down the stairs*, **which**(= **and it**) made him cry.

❷ 관계부사의 계속적 용법: where와 when만 쓸 수 있고, 「접속사 + 부사」로 바꿔 쓸 수 있다.

Cam went to the market, **where**(= **and there**) he met his friend.
It snowed last weekend, **when**(= **and then**) we built a snowman.

Smart Check 다음 빈칸에 들어갈 알맞은 것을 고르시오.

1 I know the girl about _____ you are talking.
① who   ② whom   ③ that

2 Everyone likes Daniel, _____ is friendly and humorous.
① who   ② which   ③ that

Practice

Answers p.11

A 괄호 안에서 알맞은 것을 고르시오.

1 That is the bank at (which / that) my father works.

2 We like going to the ice rink, (which / where) we can enjoy ice skating.

3 Amy drank a bottle of juice, (which / what) she bought in the morning.

4 Owen watched a movie (directed / was directed) by Steven Spielberg.

direct 통 감독하다, 연출하다

B 밑줄 친 부분을 생략할 수 있으면 O를 쓰고, 생략할 수 없으면 X를 쓰시오.

1 Joshua is my friend <u>who</u> is scared of insects. → _____

2 I'm eating some chocolate <u>that</u> I brought from Belgium. → _____

3 The mushroom <u>which</u> he touched was poisonous. → _____

4 They found old coins <u>which were</u> buried in the ground. → _____

be scared of ~을 두려워하다
insect 명 곤충
poisonous 형 독성이 있는
bury 통 묻다

C 다음 두 문장의 의미가 같도록 빈칸에 알맞은 관계사를 쓰시오.

1 Nancy went to the theater, and there she ran into Tommy.
→ Nancy went to the theater, _____ she ran into Tommy.

2 I participated in a drawing contest, and it was a good experience.
→ I participated in a drawing contest, _____ was a good experience.

3 He broke the record last year, and then he became the world champion.
→ He broke the record last year, _____ he became the world champion.

run into 통 ~와 우연히 만나다
participate 통 참가하다
experience 명 경험
break the record 기록을 깨다

D 우리말과 같도록 괄호 안의 말을 활용하여 빈칸에 쓰시오.

1 영어는 내가 흥미가 있는 과목이다. (interest)
= English is the subject in _____ _____ _____ _____.

2 Johnson씨는 한국에 살고 있는 미군이다. (live in)
= Mr. Johnson is an American soldier _____ _____ Korea.

3 항공편이 지연됐는데, 그것은 많은 사람들을 공항에서 기다리게 했다. (make)
= The flight was delayed, _____ _____ many people wait at the airport.

interest 통 흥미를 갖게 하다
subject 명 과목
delay 통 지연시키다

UNIT 04 | 복합관계사

1 복합관계대명사

「관계대명사 + -ever」의 형태로 명사절이나 부사절을 이끈다.

복합관계대명사	명사절	부사절
who(m)ever	anyone who(m) ~하는 누구든지	no matter who(m) 누가[누구를] ~하더라도
whichever	anything that ~하는 어느 것이든지	no matter which 어느 것이[을] ~하더라도
whatever	anything that ~하는 무엇이든지	no matter what 무엇이[을] ~하더라도

Whoever turns in the homework first will be rewarded.
= *Anyone who*

You can bring **who(m)ever** you like to the concert.
          = *anyone who(m)*

Whatever my friends say, I won't change my mind.
= *No matter what*

TIP whichever와 whatever는 뒤에 오는 명사를 수식하는 복합관계형용사로도 쓰인다.
Order **whichever** *dish* you want to eat.
Whatever *topic* we discuss, it's going to be interesting.

2 복합관계부사

「관계부사 + -ever」의 형태로 장소·시간·방법이나 양보의 부사절을 이끈다.

복합관계부사	장소·시간·방법의 부사절	양보의 부사절
wherever	at any place where ~하는 곳은 어디든지	no matter where 어디서 ~하더라도
whenever	at any time when ~할 때는 언제나	no matter when 언제 ~하더라도
however	in whatever way that ~하는 어떤 방법으로든지	no matter how 아무리 ~하더라도

You may put your bag **wherever** you like.
                    = *at any place where*

Whenever he called Jane, she didn't answer.
= *No matter when*

However noisy it was, the dog slept well.
= *No matter how*

 다음 빈칸에 들어갈 알맞은 것을 고르시오.

1 The store will give a free gift to _____ comes on the opening day.
① whoever   ② whichever   ③ whatever

2 _____ hard James pushed, he couldn't open the door.
① Wherever   ② Whenever   ③ However

Practice

Answers p.11

A 괄호 안에서 알맞은 것을 고르시오.

1 (Whoever / Whichever) signs up on our website will get a coupon.

2 Please pick (whichever / whenever) you want to read from the bookshelf.

3 (Wherever / However) I looked, there was beautiful scenery.

4 (Wherever / Whatever) you request will be handled immediately.

sign up 图 가입하다
scenery 图 경치
handle 图 처리하다, 다루다
immediately 图 즉시

B 다음 빈칸에 알맞은 말을 <보기>에서 한 번씩만 골라 쓰시오.

<보기>	whomever	whenever	however

1 _____ hard I tried, I couldn't persuade my mother.

2 He told the good news to _____ he met.

3 You can ask for more drinks _____ you want.

persuade 图 설득하다
drink 图 음료

C 다음 두 문장의 의미가 같도록 빈칸에 알맞은 말을 쓰시오.

1 No matter where you are from, we can be friends.

→ _____ you are from, we can be friends.

2 No matter what he attempts, he is sure that he will succeed.

→ _____ he attempts, he is sure that he will succeed.

3 Anyone who visits this museum will be given a souvenir.

→ _____ visits this museum will be given a souvenir.

4 No matter which room you choose, you will be satisfied.

→ _____ room you choose, you will be satisfied.

attempt 图 시도하다
succeed 图 성공하다
souvenir 图 기념품

D 우리말과 같도록 복합관계사와 괄호 안의 말을 활용하여 빈칸에 쓰시오.

1 아무리 덥더라도, Tim은 절대 반바지를 입지 않는다. (hot)

= _____ _____ _____ _____, Tim never wears shorts.

2 내가 무엇을 요리하더라도, 그것은 항상 맛있다. (cook)

= _____ _____ _____, it always tastes good.

3 네가 어느 길로 가더라도 너는 교통 혼잡에 갇힐 것이다. (way, go)

= You will be stuck in traffic _____ _____ _____ _____.

shorts 图 반바지
be stuck in traffic 교통 혼잡에 갇히다

Writing Exercise

A 빈칸에 알맞은 말을 <보기>에서 골라 관계대명사를 이용하여 쓰시오. (단, **that**은 쓰지 마시오.)

> <보기>   worked in the mines
> roof was covered with snow
> likes to sleep in the sun

1 The man _____ in the past was injured.

2 Jonathan has a cat _____.

3 I remember seeing the house _____.

> <보기>   Henry hates the most
> was written by Hemingway
> was driving too fast

4 The police chased the driver _____.

5 _____ is waking up early on Saturday.

6 *A Farewell to Arms* is a novel _____.

B 다음 두 문장의 의미가 같도록 문장을 완성하시오.

1 There must be a reason for which Alice behaved strangely.
   → There must be a reason _____.

2 No matter what you buy, we provide a five-year guarantee.
   → _____, we provide a five-year guarantee.

3 Please tell me about the city in which you grew up.
   → Please tell me about the city _____.

4 The birds built a nest, and it is still in good shape.
   → The birds built a nest, _____.

5 I intend to buy a tablet PC no matter how much it costs.
   → I intend to buy a tablet PC _____.

6 This picture was taken near the lake, and there I used to ride a bicycle.
   → This picture was taken near the lake, _____.

C 우리말과 같도록 괄호 안의 말을 알맞게 배열하시오.

1 이 식료품점에서 파는 과일은 비싸다. (store, this, sold, grocery, fruits, in)

= _____ _____ are expensive.

2 에드먼드 힐러리는 에베레스트산을 등반했던 첫 번째 사람이다. (climbed, the, man, first, that)

= Edmund Hillary is _____ Mount Everest.

3 우리는 Luke가 필요한 무슨 조언이든지 그에게 해주고 싶다. (needs, whatever, he, advice)

= We'd like to give Luke _____.

4 설문 결과는 우리가 예상했던 것과 달랐다. (we, expected, from, what, different)

= The survey result was _____.

5 이것은 로빈 후드 이야기에 대한 책이다. (tale, which, a, about, book, the, is)

= This is _____ of Robin Hood.

6 Eric은 그가 사랑에 빠진 소녀에게 편지를 썼다. (fell, whom, with, he, in, love)

= Eric wrote a letter to the girl _____.

D 다음 글의 빈칸에 알맞은 관계사를 쓰시오. (단, that은 쓰지 마시오.)

Dear Angela,

During my vacation, I went to Sydney **1** _____ Justin lives. Justin is my old friend **2** _____ I met in elementary school. I had a great time with him in Sydney. First, I visited the Opera House **3** _____ is one of the most famous places in Australia. The shell-like shape of the building was amazing. On the next day, we went to Sydney Tower Eye. It is 309 meters high and is the city's tallest building. It offered a 4D cinema experience, **4** _____ provided descriptions of the city's major tourist attractions. I'll never forget the days **5** _____ I visited there.

I hope you had a nice vacation, too! I really miss you. See you soon.
From Julie

Chapter 07

관계사

Hackers Grammar Smart Level 3

Chapter Test

[1-3] 다음 빈칸에 들어갈 알맞은 것을 고르시오.

1

> The girl _____ won first prize in the speech contest is Betty.

① which   ② who   ③ whose
④ whom   ⑤ what

2

> Busan is the city _____ lots of people go for a vacation.

① where   ② how   ③ when
④ which   ⑤ why

3

> All the flowers in the garden bloomed, _____ made me happy.

① who   ② when   ③ which
④ that   ⑤ and which

4 다음 중 밑줄 친 부분을 생략할 수 <u>없는</u> 것은?

① This is the movie <u>which</u> I read a review of.
② Jogging is an activity <u>that</u> many people enjoy.
③ He is the baseball player <u>who</u> received an MVP award.
④ Jessica is the friend <u>whom</u> I met online last month.
⑤ Volunteers are people <u>who are</u> willing to help others.

[5-6] 다음 중 어법상 <u>어색한</u> 것을 고르시오.

5

① What Joy said made me feel nervous.
② The country to which Chris went was Italy.
③ Whichever menu you choose, you will like it.
④ I bought some toys with that my baby sister could play.
⑤ Do you know the name of the man whose hair is red?

6

① Tell me the reason why you broke your promise.
② The children were thrilled whenever they visited the amusement park.
③ Is this the place where your mom works?
④ Tina won't forget the summer when she stayed at the peaceful island.
⑤ Jeff showed us the way how he painted the wall.

서술형
[7-8] 다음 두 문장의 의미가 같도록 빈칸에 알맞은 말을 쓰시오.

7

> Anyone who wants to enter the building needs an ID card.
> → _____ wants to enter the building needs an ID card.

8

> Did you find the thing that you were looking for?
> → Did you find _____ you were looking for?

서술형

[9-10] 우리말과 같도록 괄호 안의 말을 활용하여 빈칸에 쓰시오.

9

> 내가 아무리 열심히 노력했더라도, 나는 이전보다 더 낮은 점수를 받았다. (hard, try)

= _____ _____ _____ _____,

I got a lower grade than before.

10

> 자정은 Mark가 자러 가는 시간이다. (go to bed)

= Midnight is the time _____ _____

_____ _____ _____.

서술형

11 우리말과 같도록 주어진 <조건>에 맞게 영작하시오.

> 네가 이 문제를 푼 방법은 창의적이었다.

> <조건>   1. how를 쓰지 마시오.
> 　　　　 2. solve, problem, creative를 활용하시오.
> 　　　　 3. 8단어로 쓰시오.

= _____ .

12 다음 중 어법상 바른 것은?

① Edison, that made the light bulb, was a great inventor.

② We don't know the time which Sam left.

③ Whatever hungry you are, try to eat slowly.

④ The bag lying on the floor belongs to Ben.

⑤ I have been to PyeongChang, which the 2018 Winter Olympics was held.

[13-14] 다음 빈칸에 공통으로 들어갈 알맞은 것을 고르시오.

13

> • The new laptop _____ I bought is very light.
> • Spring is the season in _____ plants start to grow again.

① what　　② that　　③ which

④ when　　⑤ why

14

> • _____ Anne dreamed of last night was shocking.
> • We told the police _____ we saw at the scene of the accident.

① what　　② that　　③ which

④ who　　⑤ why

서술형

[15-16] 다음 문장에서 어법상 어색한 부분을 찾아 쓰고 바르게 고쳐 쓰시오.

15

> There is Steve, that lives next door to me.

_____ → _____

16

> The scientist was praised for which he discovered.

_____ → _____

17 다음 우리말을 알맞게 영작한 것은?

> 나는 어디서 공부하더라도, 잘 집중할 수 있다.

① Where I study, I can concentrate well.
② The place where I study, I can concentrate well.
③ No matter which I study, I can concentrate well.
④ Whenever I study, I can concentrate well.
⑤ Wherever I study, I can concentrate well.

서술형
[18-20] 알맞은 관계사를 이용하여 다음 두 문장을 한 문장으로 연결하시오.

18
> My family is staying at the hotel. Its view is wonderful.
> → My family is staying at the hotel _____
> _____.

19
> Jason helped me move the chairs. It saved much time.
> → Jason helped me move the chairs, _____
> _____.

20
> I want to know the reason. Tom looks excited for that reason.
> → I want to know the reason _____
> _____.

고난도
21 다음 빈칸에 들어갈 관계대명사가 나머지 넷과 다른 것은?

① I bought _____ you recommended yesterday.
② They couldn't believe _____ they heard.
③ His parents always give him _____ he wants.
④ _____ we saw on TV made us sad.
⑤ The smartphone _____ color is gold is the most expensive.

고난도
22 다음 중 밑줄 친 부분이 어법상 어색한 것은?

① Sam was the only person that was late.
② We laugh at anything that Jake tells us.
③ It rained heavily, that caused some damage.
④ Look for a restaurant that serves seafood.
⑤ The girl and the dog that were running around together is now going home.

[23-24] 다음 빈칸에 들어갈 말이 순서대로 짝지어진 것은?

23
> • I went to an exhibit, _____ I ran into Liam.
> • The band released the new album, _____ made their fans excited.

① where – that　　② where – which
③ which – that　　④ that – which
⑤ that – what

24
> • John was the student of _____ the teacher felt proud.
> • Tomorrow is the day _____ we finally start our journey.

① which – when　　② which – where
③ who – when　　④ whom – when
⑤ whom – where

Chapter

08

접속사

접속사는 단어와 단어, 구와 구, 절과 절을 연결하는 말이다.

UNIT 01 | 부사절을 이끄는 접속사

1 **시간을 나타내는 접속사** : when(~할 때), as(~하고 있을 때, ~하면서), while(~하는 동안), until[till](~할 때까지), since(~한 이후로), as soon as(~하자마자)

Susie will go to Gyeongbokgung **when** she visits Korea.
> 시간을 나타내는 부사절에서는 미래시제 대신 현재시제를 쓴다.

As I was cleaning the bedroom, I found my lost necklace.
Tim set the table **while** his mom was preparing dinner.
I'm not going to give up **until[till]** I achieve my goal.
The classroom has been noisy **since** the teacher left.
As soon as David opened the window, a bird flew in.

2 **이유를 나타내는 접속사** : because, since, as(~하기 때문에)

She is upset **because** her favorite watch is broken.
Since the traffic was bad, some were late for the class.
As the team lost in the semifinals, it can't play in the finals.

3 **결과를 나타내는 접속사** : so ~ that …(너무 ~해서 …한)

The shirt was **so** small **that** Ben had to return it.

4 **조건을 나타내는 접속사** : if(만약 ~한다면), unless(= if ~ not)(만약 ~하지 않는다면)

If you apologize to Cameron, he will forgive you.
> 조건을 나타내는 부사절에서는 미래시제 대신 현재시제를 쓴다.
I can't finish the work on time **unless** I get help.
(= I can't finish the work on time **if** I do**n't** get help.)

5 **양보를 나타내는 접속사** : although[though/even though](비록 ~이지만), even if(비록 ~일지라도)

Although[Though/Even though] we live in the same building, we hardly see each other.
Jack will keep trying **even if** he fails to win the medal.

Smart Check 다음 빈칸에 들어갈 알맞은 것을 고르시오.

1 I'll let you know as soon as I _____ the news.
① hear   ② heard   ③ will hear

2 _____ you don't know the word's meaning, look it up in a dictionary.
① While   ② If   ③ Unless

Practice

Answers p.13

A 괄호 안에서 알맞은 것을 고르시오.

1 Her teddy bear fell from the bed (while / until) she was sleeping.

2 (Since / Though) we came early, we can sit anywhere we want.

3 (If / Unless) you have any food in your bag, please take it out.

4 The sun is so bright (that / if) people can't look at it directly.

fall from ~로부터 떨어지다
anywhere 🖳 어디든, 아무데나
take out 꺼내다
directly 🖳 똑바로

B 다음 빈칸에 가장 알맞은 말을 <보기>에서 한 번씩만 골라 쓰시오.

<보기>	because	so	although

1 Emily couldn't play with anyone _____ she was ill.

2 _____ I didn't eat breakfast, I wasn't hungry.

3 Larry walks _____ fast that his friends can't follow him.

<보기>	as	until	unless

4 Eric's teacher will get angry _____ he brings his textbook.

5 _____ I opened the door, a cat came into the house.

6 The mother duck sits on the eggs _____ they hatch.

ill 🖳 아픈
follow 🖳 따라가다
hatch 🖳 부화하다

C 우리말과 같도록 괄호 안의 말을 활용하여 빈칸에 쓰시오.

1 그가 열 살 때 그 연못은 물로 가득 차 있었다. (be)
= The pond was full of water _____ _____ _____ ten.

2 나의 언니는 너무 키가 커서 선반 맨 위에 손이 닿는다. (tall)
= My sister is _____ _____ _____ she can reach the top shelf.

3 Melissa는 마지막 기차를 탔기 때문에 운이 좋다고 느꼈다. (catch)
= Melissa felt lucky _____ _____ _____ the last train.

4 만약 당신이 불만이 있다면, 저희 고객 서비스 센터에 전화할 수 있습니다. (have)
= _____ _____ _____ a complaint, you can call our customer service center.

pond 🖳 연못
be full of ~으로 가득 차 있다
reach 🖳 (손이) 닿다
catch 🖳 (시간 맞춰) 타다
complaint 🖳 불만

UNIT 02 | 상관접속사, 간접의문문

1 상관접속사

❶ both A and B(A와 B 둘 다)

I have been to **both** *Germany* **and** *France*.

❷ not only A but (also) B(= B as well as A)(A뿐만 아니라 B도)

This website is **not only** *useful* **but** (**also**) *free*.
(= This website is *free* **as well as** *useful*.)

❸ either A or B(A나 B 둘 중 하나)

You can **either** *call* **or** *send* me an e-mail.

❹ neither A nor B(A도 B도 아닌)

Samantha is good at **neither** *singing* **nor** *dancing*.

TIP both A and B 뒤에는 항상 복수동사를 쓰고, 나머지 상관접속사 뒤에 오는 동사는 **B**에 수일치시킨다.
Both *Janice* **and** *Paul* (~~was~~, **were**) at the restaurant.
Either *my sister* **or** *I* (~~has~~, **have**) to do the laundry.

2 간접의문문

다른 문장의 일부로 쓰여 질문의 내용을 간접적으로 묻는 의문문을 간접의문문이라 한다.

❶ 의문사가 있는 경우: 「의문사 + 주어 + 동사」

Can you tell me? + Where is the train station?

→ Can you tell me **where the train station is**?

I wonder. + Who invented the light bulb?

→ I wonder **who invented** the light bulb.
└→ 의문사가 간접의문문의 주어이므로 「의문사(주어) + 동사」의 어순이 된다.

Do you think? + When can you finish the report?

→ **When** do you *think* **you can finish** the report?
└→ 간접의문문을 포함하는 문장의 동사가 생각이나 추측을 나타내는 think, believe, guess, suppose 등인 경우 간접의문문의 의문사를 문장 맨 앞에 쓴다.

❷ 의문사가 없는 경우: 「if[whether](~인지 아닌지) + 주어 + 동사」

I'm not sure. + Will Amy come to my birthday party?

→ I'm not sure **if[whether] Amy will come** to my birthday party.

Smart Check 다음 빈칸에 들어갈 알맞은 것을 고르시오.

1 Frogs can live both in water _____ on land.
　① or　　　　　　　② but　　　　　　　③ and

2 Please tell me _____ so early.
　① why you left　　② you left why　　③ why did you leave

Practice

Answers p.13

A 괄호 안에서 알맞은 것을 고르시오.

1 Both Alice (and / or) Jason put up the campaign posters.

2 The sculptor used not only wood (also / but also) marble.

3 Neither the bank nor the hospital (is / are) open today.

4 He wants to know if (does Christine like / Christine likes) red roses.

put up 내붙이다, 게시하다
sculptor 뎽 조각가
marble 뎽 대리석

B <보기>의 말을 활용하여 다음 두 문장을 한 문장으로 연결하시오.

<보기>	both	either	neither

1 You can get to the mall by bus. Or you can get there by subway.
→ You can get to the mall by _____ bus _____ subway.

2 Summer isn't my favorite season. Winter isn't my favorite season, either.
→ _____ summer _____ winter is my favorite season.

3 The community center offers violin lessons. It offers piano lessons, too.
→ The community center offers _____ violin lessons _____ piano lessons.

season 뎽 계절
community center 뎽 지역 문화 센터
offer 뎽 제공하다

C 다음 두 문장을 한 문장으로 연결하시오.

1 Can you tell me? + When will Ms. Jones give a presentation?
→ Can you tell me _____?

2 I'm not sure. + Who left this empty box here?
→ I'm not sure _____.

3 Sarah doesn't know. + Is Berlin the capital of Germany?
→ Sarah doesn't know _____.

presentation 뎽 발표
leave 뎽 두다, 떠나다
empty 뎽 비어 있는
capital 뎽 수도

D 우리말과 같도록 괄호 안의 말을 활용하여 빈칸에 쓰시오.

1 천장뿐만 아니라 벽도 새로 칠해졌다. (the ceiling, be)
= The walls _____ _____ _____ _____ _____ _____ newly painted.

2 나는 6월이나 7월에 휴가를 갈 것이다. (June, July)
= I will go on a vacation in _____ _____ _____ _____.

3 너는 네가 어디에서 너의 여권을 잃어버렸다고 추측하니? (guess)
= _____ _____ _____ _____ you lost your passport?

ceiling 뎽 천장
newly 뎽 새로
guess 뎽 추측하다

Writing Exercise

A 다음 빈칸에 가장 알맞은 말을 <보기>에서 골라 쓰시오.

<보기>	until I find my lost wallet	because she was taking a shower
	since it rained heavily	that she needs to wear a belt
	if you have a coupon	though the sun was shining

1 Kate couldn't answer the phone _____ .

2 _____ , you can get 10 percent discount.

3 Her jeans are so big _____ .

4 I'll have to keep searching _____ .

5 _____ , the streets were flooded.

6 It wasn't warm _____ .

B 우리말과 같도록 괄호 안의 말을 알맞게 배열하시오.

1 Peter도 Noah도 거리에 쓰레기를 버리지 않았다. (threw, nor, neither, Noah, Peter, away)

= _____ the trash on the street.

2 내가 너에게 말하고 있을 동안 나를 봐라. (you, talking, while, am, to, I)

= Look at me _____ .

3 너는 밥이나 면 둘 중 하나를 선택할 수 있다. (or, rice, noodles, either)

= You can choose _____ .

4 Linda는 서점에서 소설과 잡지 둘 다 샀다. (a, bought, a, novel, magazine, and, both)

= Linda _____ at the bookstore.

5 만약 그녀 자신이 그것을 직접 하지 않는다면, 그녀는 만족하지 않을 것이다. (she, herself, unless, does, it)

= _____ , she will not be satisfied.

6 Ron뿐만 아니라 Fred도 선생님이 말했던 것을 기억한다. (Ron, also, not, Fred, but, remembers, only)

= _____ what the teacher said.

C 다음 두 문장을 한 문장으로 연결하시오.

1 They wonder. + How were the pyramids built?

→ _____ .

2 Do you know? + Who found out the answer to the question?

→ _____ ?

3 Do you think? + When should we change the batteries?

→ _____ ?

4 I'm not sure. + Why does Nathan disagree with your idea?

→ _____ .

5 He doesn't know. + How much is this picture worth?

→ _____ .

6 Can you tell me? + Where did you see Sally last night?

→ _____ ?

D 다음 그림을 보고 <보기>의 접속사와 괄호 안의 말을 활용하여 문장을 완성하시오. (단, 과거시제로 쓰시오.)

1

2

3

| <보기> | while | because | although |

1 I stayed in bed _____ . (have a fever)

2 _____ , I broke my favorite cup. (wash the dishes)

3 _____ , I kept running. (be exhausted)

Chapter Test

[1-3] 다음 빈칸에 들어갈 가장 알맞은 것을 고르시오.

1

> You will be able to see the sunrise _____ you wake up early.

① if   ② while   ③ though
④ unless   ⑤ until

2

> Jason is not sure _____ he can complete his book report today.

① what   ② who   ③ unless
④ since   ⑤ whether

3

> _____ Mary nor I like drinking soda.

① Either   ② Neither   ③ Not only
④ Both   ⑤ And

4 다음 중 밑줄 친 as의 의미가 나머지 넷과 다른 것은?

① As the road was slippery, Ms. Wilson had to drive slowly.
② As I was jogging in the park, I listened to music.
③ As Emma lives near my house, I often visit her.
④ As the athlete wanted to win, he did his best.
⑤ As you enjoy reading detective novels, you will love this new book.

서술형

[5-7] 다음 문장에서 어법상 어색한 부분을 찾아 쓰고 바르게 고쳐 쓰시오.

5

> Both Linda and David participates in the soccer practice every morning.

_____ → _____

6

> We will go to that restaurant when it will open next month.

_____ → _____

7

> The egg was very hard that I couldn't break it easily.

_____ → _____

8 다음 두 문장을 한 문장으로 연결한 것 중 어색한 것을 모두 고르시오.

① Can you tell me? + Where is the public toilet?
  → Can you tell me where is the public toilet?
② I'm not sure. + When does the market close?
  → I'm not sure when the market closes.
③ Do you think? + Who is the suspect?
  → Who do you think is the suspect?
④ Lisa doesn't know. + Will Kevin join the band?
  → Lisa doesn't know that Kevin will join the band.
⑤ We wonder. + Why is Jeffery angry at us?
  → We wonder why Jeffrey is angry at us.

서술형

[9-10] 우리말과 같도록 괄호 안의 말을 활용하여 빈칸에 쓰시오.

9

> 너는 택시나 버스 둘 중 하나로 미술관에 갈 수 있다. (taxi, bus)

= You can get to the art museum by _____ _____ _____ _____.

10

> 나의 친구와 나 둘 다 그 문제에 책임이 있다. (friend, be)

= _____ _____ _____ _____ _____ _____ responsible for the issue.

서술형

11 우리말과 같도록 주어진 <조건>에 맞게 영작하시오.

> 나는 그 편지를 받자마자 답장할 것이다.

> <조건> 1. 접속사를 문장 맨 앞에 쓰시오.
>   2. get, letter, reply를 활용하시오.
>   3. 10단어로 쓰시오.

= _____.

12 다음 중 어법상 바른 것은?

① Let's wait inside until everyone will arrive.

② Unless you don't help her, she will be upset.

③ Both Mike and I am able to understand Chinese.

④ Do you think where we should buy a present for Jane?

⑤ Either my sister or I have to look after the cat.

서술형

[13-14] 다음 두 문장의 의미가 같도록 빈칸에 알맞은 말을 쓰시오.

13

> Not only the original novel but also the movie was fantastic.
> → _____ _____ _____ _____ _____ _____ _____ _____ was fantastic.

14

> Unless it rains on Sunday, we will go hiking.
> → _____ _____ _____ _____ _____ _____, we will go hiking.

[15-16] 다음 빈칸에 들어갈 말이 순서대로 짝지어진 것은?

15

> • We can get sunburn _____ we apply sunscreen.
> • I'm not hungry _____ I have just eaten lunch.

① unless – until   ② unless – although

③ even if – because   ④ even if – although

⑤ until – because

16

> • _____ we don't leave now, we will miss the event.
> • Evan doesn't practice hard _____ he wants to be a better dancer.

① If – because   ② If – even though

③ Unless – because   ④ Unless – even though

⑤ Since – because

[17-18] 다음 중 어법상 <u>어색한</u> 것을 고르시오.

17 ① When Jerry sings, his voice becomes lower.
② Though he isn't tall, he is good at basketball.
③ We don't have to go to school today because it is a national holiday.
④ I will look for the café while you will wait here.
⑤ As soon as Josh got to the beach, he went swimming.

18 ① Both my wallet and cell phone were stolen.
② We wonder if Daniel will accept our invitation.
③ Neither the pants nor the shirt were sold out.
④ I don't remember what the password is.
⑤ Not only the students but also the teacher was excited about the field trip.

[19-20] 다음 빈칸에 공통으로 들어갈 알맞은 것을 고르시오.

19
> • My uncle has worked at a bank _____ he was 28 years old.
> • _____ I don't have flour, I can't bake the cake now.

① as   ② if   ③ since
④ though   ⑤ unless

20
> • _____ you buy roses for your mom, she will be so happy.
> • I wonder _____ Ms. Parker will be my homeroom teacher this year.

① if   ② unless   ③ as
④ whether   ⑤ even if

21 알맞은 접속사를 이용하여 다음 두 문장을 한 문장으로 연결하시오.

> Luke didn't see the rainbow yesterday.
> I didn't see the rainbow yesterday, either.
> → _____ saw the rainbow yesterday.

22 다음 우리말을 알맞게 영작한 것은?

> 너는 누가 늦게 올 거라고 추측하니?

① Do you guess will who come late?
② Do you guess who came late?
③ Do you guess who will come late?
④ Who do you guess came late?
⑤ Who do you guess will come late?

23 다음은 세 명의 학생에 대한 정보를 나타낸 표이다. 상관접속사를 이용하여 빈칸에 알맞은 말을 쓰시오.

	Age	Favorite Subject	Dream Job
Sarah	16	English	Teacher
Charles	15	Math	Teacher
Emily	16	Art	Painter

(1) _____ _____ Sarah _____ _____ Emily is 16 years old.

(2) _____ Math _____ Art is Sarah's favorite subject.

(3) _____ Sarah _____ Charles want to be a teacher.

Chapter

09

가정법

가정법은 사실과 반대되거나 실현 가능성이
거의 없는 일을 가정하여 말하는 것이다.

UNIT 01 | 가정법 과거/과거완료, 혼합 가정법

1 가정법 과거

'만약 ~한다면 …할 텐데'의 의미로 현재의 사실과 반대되거나 실현 가능성이 거의 없는 일을 가정할 때 쓴다.

| If | + | 주어 | + | 동사의 과거형
(be동사는 were) | ~, | 주어 | + | would, could,
might | + | 동사원형 | … |

If Nate **were** here, he **could give** us helpful advice.
(← As Nate isn't here, he can't give us helpful advice.)

If I **lived** close to school, I **wouldn't have** to wake up early.
(← As I don't live close to school, I have to wake up early.)

> **TIP** 가정법은 실현 가능성이 거의 없는 일을 가정할 때 쓰고, 조건문은 현재나 미래에 일어날 수 있는 상황을 나타낼 때 쓴다. 조건문의 부사절에서는 미래를 나타내더라도 현재시제를 쓴다.
> If it **rained**, the field trip **would be** canceled. <가정법: 비가 올 가능성이 거의 없음>
> If it **rains**, the field trip **will be** canceled. <조건문: 비가 올 가능성이 있음>

2 가정법 과거완료

'만약 ~했더라면 …했을 텐데'의 의미로 과거의 사실과 반대되는 일을 가정할 때 쓴다.

| If | + | 주어 | + | had p.p. | ~, | 주어 | + | would, could,
might | + | have p.p. | … |

If Kerry **hadn't slipped** on the stairs, her legs **wouldn't have been** broken.
(← As Kerry slipped on the stairs, her legs were broken.)

3 혼합 가정법

'만약 ~했더라면 …할 텐데'의 의미로 과거의 사실과 반대되는 일이 현재까지 영향을 미치는 상황을 가정할 때 쓴다.

| If | + | 주어 | + | had p.p. | ~, | 주어 | + | would, could,
might | + | 동사원형 | … |

If you **had brought** your coat, you **wouldn't feel** cold now.
(← As you didn't bring your coat, you feel cold now.)

Smart Check 다음 빈칸에 들어갈 알맞은 것을 고르시오.

1 If Jane _____ shy, she could easily make friends.
① isn't　　　　　　② aren't　　　　　　③ weren't

2 If I had practiced harder, I _____ better on stage.
① will perform　　　② would performed　　　③ would have performed

3 If my brother had done his homework, he _____ with me now.
① can play　　　　　② could play　　　　　③ could have played

Practice

Answers p.14

A 괄호 안에서 알맞은 것을 고르시오.

1 If I (know / knew) how to ski, we could ski together.

2 If I hadn't forgotten to water the flower, it (could live / could have lived).

3 If the kids (are / were) taller, they could ride the roller coaster.

4 If you had exercised regularly, you (would be / would have been) healthier now.

B 괄호 안의 말을 활용하여 가정법 과거완료 문장을 완성하시오.

1 If it _____ so much, we could have gone hiking. (not, snow)

2 If he had come to the festival, he _____ himself. (will, enjoy)

3 If the question _____ easier, Brian could have answered it. (be)

4 If I had been more careful, I _____ my phone. (will, not, drop)

C 다음 문장을 가정법 문장으로 바꿔 쓰시오.

1 As the air conditioner doesn't work, the room is hot.
→ If _____, the room wouldn't be hot.

2 As you helped me yesterday, I'm not tired today.
→ If you hadn't helped me yesterday, I _____.

3 As the soup was spicy, Eric had a stomachache.
→ If _____, Eric wouldn't have had a stomachache.

D 우리말과 같도록 괄호 안의 말을 활용하여 빈칸에 쓰시오.

1 만약 강이 오염되지 않았다면, 많은 물고기들이 그곳에 살 텐데. (be, will, live)
= If the river _____ polluted, many fish _____ _____ in it.

2 만약 네가 너의 돈을 모두 쓰지 않았더라면, 노트북을 지금 살 수 있을 텐데. (spend, can, buy)
= If you _____ _____ all your money, you _____ _____ the laptop now.

3 만약 그녀가 주의를 기울였더라면, 빵을 태우지 않았을 텐데. (pay, will, burn)
= If she _____ _____ attention, she _____ _____ _____ the bread.

---

forget 동 잊다
regularly 부 규칙적으로

enjoy oneself 즐거운 시간을 보내다
drop 동 떨어뜨리다

have a stomachache 배탈이 나다

pollute 동 오염시키다
pay attention 주의를 기울이다
burn 동 태우다

1 I wish 가정법

❶ 「I wish + 가정법 과거」는 '~하면 좋을 텐데'라는 의미로 현재 이룰 수 없거나 실현 가능성이 거의 없는 일을 소망할 때 쓴다.

| I wish | + | 주어 | + | 동사의 과거형 (be동사는 were) |

I wish I **understood** Chinese. (← I'm sorry that I don't understand Chinese.)

❷ 「I wish + 가정법 과거완료」는 '~했더라면 좋았을 텐데'라는 의미로 과거에 이루지 못한 일에 대한 아쉬움을 나타낼 때 쓴다.

| I wish | + | 주어 | + | had p.p. |

I wish I **had woken** up earlier in the morning. (← I'm sorry that I didn't wake up earlier in the morning.)

2 as if 가정법

❶ 「as if + 가정법 과거」는 '마치 ~인 것처럼'이라는 의미로 주절의 시제와 같은 시점의 사실과 반대되는 일을 가정한다.

| 주어 | + | 동사 | + | as if | + | 주어 | + | 동사의 과거형 (be동사는 were) |

He *acts* **as if** he **owned** a sports car. (← In fact, he *doesn't own* a sports car.)
He *acted* **as if** he **owned** a sports car. (← In fact, he *didn't own* a sports car.)

❷ 「as if + 가정법 과거완료」는 '마치 ~이었던 것처럼'이라는 의미로 주절의 시제보다 앞선 시점의 사실과 반대되는 일을 가정한다.

| 주어 | + | 동사 | + | as if | + | 주어 | + | had p.p. |

Anna *talks* **as if** she **hadn't heard** the rumor. (← In fact, Anna *heard* the rumor.)
Anna *talked* **as if** she **hadn't heard** the rumor. (← In fact, Anna *had heard* the rumor.)

3 It's time 가정법

'~해야 할 때이다'의 의미로 했어야 하는 일을 하지 않은 것에 대한 유감을 나타낸다.

| It's time | + | 주어 | + | 동사의 과거형 |

It's time I **fed** my goldfish.
It's already midnight. **It's time** you **went** to bed.

Smart Check 다음 빈칸에 들어갈 알맞은 것을 고르시오.

1 I wish James _____ to my advice yesterday.
① listens ② listened ③ had listened

2 Linda looks as if she _____ ill, but she isn't.
① are ② were ③ had been

3 It's time we _____ our bedroom. It's messy.
① cleaned ② are cleaning ③ had cleaned

Practice

Answers p.14

A 괄호 안에서 알맞은 것을 고르시오.

1 I wish I (saw / had seen) William before he left school.

2 The player acted as if he (were / had been) injured, but he hadn't.

3 It's time we (started / will start) packing for the camping.

4 I wish I (had / had had) a raincoat right now.

injure 图 부상을 입히다
pack 图 (짐을) 싸다

B 괄호 안의 동사를 활용하여 가정법 문장을 완성하시오.

1 Mr. Jade talks as if he _____ an actor, but he isn't. (be)

2 I wish she _____ her photos on the blog, but she doesn't want to do it. (share)

3 Sam describes the accident as if he _____ it. In fact, he didn't see anything. (see)

4 The dance performance ended too soon. I wish it _____ longer. (be)

describe 图 묘사하다
performance 명 공연

C 다음 문장을 가정법 문장으로 바꿔 쓰시오.

1 I'm sorry that you feel so depressed.
→ I wish you _____ so depressed.

2 In fact, my friends knew my secret.
→ My friends act as if they _____ my secret.

3 I'm sorry that Jacob didn't do his best in the game.
→ I wish Jacob _____ his best in the game.

depressed 형 우울한

D 우리말과 같도록 괄호 안의 말을 활용하여 문장을 완성하시오.

1 네가 너의 조부모님을 방문해야 할 때이다. (visit, grandparents)
= It's time _____.

2 Kelly는 마치 많은 돈을 저축했던 것처럼 말했다. (save, a lot of money)
= Kelly talked as if _____.

3 네가 유리 꽃병을 조심해서 다루면 좋을 텐데. (be, careful)
= I wish _____ with the glass vase.

grandparents 명 조부모
save 图 저축하다
careful 형 조심하는

UNIT 03 | Without[But for] 가정법, if를 생략한 가정법

1 Without[But for] 가정법

'~가 없(었)다면'의 의미로, 가정법 과거와 과거완료에 모두 쓸 수 있다. 이때 「Without[But for] + 명사(구)」는 가정법의 if절을 대신한다.

Without[But for] air and water, everything on the earth **couldn't live**.
→ *If it were not for* air and water, everything on the earth couldn't live.

Without[But for] your support, I **would have given** up.
→ *If it had not been for* your support, I would have given up.

2 if를 생략한 가정법

가정법에서 if절의 동사가 were나 「had + p.p.」인 경우 if를 생략할 수 있으며, 이때 주어와 동사의 위치가 바뀐다.

Were I outgoing, I would make new friends more easily.
(← If I were outgoing, I would make new friends more easily.)

Had it been sunny yesterday, we could have gone to the beach.
(← If it had been sunny yesterday, we could have gone to the beach.)

Had I known the truth, I would have told my friend.
(← If I had known the truth, I would have told my friend.)

> **TIP** 「If it were not for ~」와 「If it had not been for ~」에서도 if를 생략하여 「Were it not for ~」와 「Had it not been for ~」로 쓸 수 있다.
> **Were it not for** the heater, the room would be very cold.
> **Had it not been for** the traffic jam, Amy could have arrived on time.

Smart Check 다음 빈칸에 들어갈 알맞은 것을 고르시오.

1 _____ his glasses, he couldn't read small text.

① But   ② If   ③ Without

2 _____ you, I would listen to the doctor's advice.

① I were   ② Were I   ③ Had I

3 _____ helped her, she could have found her wallet.

① Someone had   ② Had someone   ③ If had someone

4 _____ for Jake's suggestion, I wouldn't have watched the movie.

① Had it not been   ② It had not been   ③ If it had not

Practice

Answers p.14

A 괄호 안에서 알맞은 것을 고르시오.

1 (Was / Were) it Saturday, I wouldn't go to school.

2 (If / Had) it not been for Mr. Wilson's car, we would have been late.

3 (Without / But) the teacher's detailed explanation, I couldn't understand the lecture.

detailed ⑬ 상세한
explanation ⑬ 설명

B 다음 두 문장의 의미가 같도록 빈칸에 알맞은 말을 쓰시오.

1 If I were you, I would book the hotel right away.

→ _____ _____ _____, I would book the hotel right away.

2 If I had owned a hamster, I would have named it Fluffy.

→ _____ _____ _____ _____ _____, I would have named it Fluffy.

3 If it were not for electricity, all the machines couldn't run.

→ _____ _____ _____ _____ _____, all the machines couldn't run.

book ⑧ 예약하다
own ⑧ 소유하다
electricity ⑬ 전기
run ⑧ 작동하다

C 다음 두 문장의 의미가 같도록 괄호 안의 말로 시작하는 가정법 문장을 완성하시오.

1 If it had not been for the map, I would have been lost. (without)

→ _____, I would have been lost.

2 If it were not for the Wi-Fi, we couldn't use the Internet on the bus. (but)

→ _____, we couldn't use the Internet on the bus.

3 If Tim had brought his wallet, I wouldn't have lent him money. (had)

→ _____, I wouldn't have lent him money.

lost ⑬ 길을 잃은
lend ⑧ 빌려주다

D 우리말과 같도록 괄호 안의 말을 알맞게 배열하시오.

1 만약 내가 로마에 있다면, 나의 삼촌을 만날 수 있을 텐데. (in, were, Rome, I)

= _____, I could meet my uncle.

2 기부금이 없었더라면, 우리는 가난한 사람들을 돕지 못했을 텐데. (for, not, it, donation, been, had, the)

= _____, we couldn't have helped the poor.

3 냉장고가 없다면, 음식은 더 오래가지 못할 텐데. (fridge, for, not, it, the, were)

= _____, the food wouldn't last longer.

donation ⑬ 기부금
last long 오래가다

Writing Exercise

A   <보기>와 같이 빈칸에 알맞은 말을 써서 가정법 문장을 완성하시오.

> <보기>   I wish George _had kept_ his promise.
> (I'm sorry that George didn't keep his promise.)

1   I wish I _____ English better than Jacob.
(I'm sorry that I don't speak English better than Jacob.)

2   The dog seems as if it _____.
(In fact, the dog didn't run around for hours.)

3   I wish the plumber _____ the sink.
(I'm sorry that the plumber didn't fix the sink.)

4   Frank's bicycle looked as if it _____ before.
(In fact, Frank's bicycle had been ridden before.)

B   다음 두 문장의 의미가 같도록 문장을 완성하시오.

1   As the lake isn't frozen, we can't go ice skating.
→ If _____, we could go ice skating.

2   If he were in Peru, he could visit Machu Picchu.
→ Were _____, he could visit Machu Picchu.

3   I'm sorry that you didn't clean the room before your friends came.
→ I wish _____ before your friends came.

4   Without the Internet, searching for information would be difficult.
→ If _____, searching for information would be difficult.

5   If Helen hadn't been so nervous, she wouldn't have made such mistakes.
→ Had _____, she wouldn't have made such mistakes.

C 우리말과 같도록 괄호 안의 말을 알맞게 배열하시오.

1 전화기가 없다면, 우리는 다른 사람들과 쉽게 의사소통하지 못할 텐데. (not, were, telephone, it, for, the)

= _____, we couldn't communicate easily with others.

2 만약 네가 너의 부모님께 진실을 말했더라면, 그들은 화가 나지 않았을 텐데. (been, would, upset, not, they, have)

= If you had told your parents the truth, _____.

3 Amy가 그녀의 노트북을 수리받아야 할 때이다. (her, time, Amy, repaired, it's, got, laptop)

= _____.

4 너의 노력이 없었다면, 우리는 성공할 수 없었을 텐데. (been, your, it, not, effort, for, had)

= _____, we couldn't have succeeded.

5 만약 네가 현대 미술에 관심이 있다면, 그 전시회에 갈 텐데. (modern, you, in, were, art, interested)

= _____, you would go to that exhibition.

D <보기>의 말을 활용하여 대화를 완성하시오.

<보기>	have another pen	will buy a private plane	be good at math

1 A ⟨ I need to fill out the application. Can I borrow a pen?

I only have one. I wish I _____ to give you. ⟩ B

2 A ⟨ Lena acts as if she _____.

Well, I know she struggles with math. ⟩ B

3 A ⟨ What would you do if you were a billionaire?

Were I a billionaire, I _____. ⟩ B

Chapter Test

[1-3] 다음 빈칸에 들어갈 알맞은 것을 고르시오.

1

> If my dog _____ a human, it would be 40 years old.

① be   ② were
③ is   ④ being
⑤ has been

2

> If I _____ the coupon that day, I wouldn't get a free gift now.

① lose   ② lost
③ have lost   ④ had lost
⑤ would have lost

3

> _____ you asked Jamie, he would have gladly helped you.

① Were   ② Have
③ Has   ④ Are
⑤ Had

[서술형]
4 다음 세 문장의 의미가 같도록 빈칸에 알맞은 말을 쓰시오.

> But for the alarm clock, she would have been late for the class.
> → _____ the alarm clock, she would have been late for the class.
> → _____ _____ _____
> _____ _____ _____ the
> alarm clock, she would have been late for the class.

[5-6] 다음 중 어법상 어색한 것을 고르시오.

5

① If you lend me a pen, I'll draw you a picture.
② It's time you made a study plan for the exam.
③ Eva talks as if she had been sick yesterday.
④ If Matt's leg weren't broken, he would participate in the marathon.
⑤ I wish she has joined our party last Sunday.

6

① If he hadn't forgotten to bring an umbrella, he wouldn't have gotten wet.
② Without the sunscreen, I would have gotten a sunburn.
③ If he had checked the city map, he wouldn't have been lost now.
④ Had Lisa come home, she could have seen her aunt.
⑤ But for the calendar, we couldn't know the date.

7 다음 우리말을 알맞게 영작한 것은?

> 만약 Tina가 지난주에 서울에 머물렀더라면, 그 축제를 즐겼을 텐데.

① If Tina stays in Seoul last week, she will enjoy the festival.
② If Tina stayed in Seoul last week, she would enjoy the festival.
③ If Tina stayed in Seoul last week, she would have enjoyed the festival.
④ If Tina had stayed in Seoul last week, she would have enjoyed the festival.
⑤ If Tina had stayed in Seoul last week, she would enjoy the festival.

8 다음 대화의 빈칸에 들어갈 말이 순서대로 짝지어진 것은?

> A: We waited outside for a long time until we finally bought the tickets.
> B: I know. If we _____ the ticket online, we _____ in line so long.

① book – didn't wait
② booked – wouldn't wait
③ booked – wouldn't have waited
④ had booked – wouldn't wait
⑤ had booked – wouldn't have waited

서술형

9 다음 문장의 밑줄 친 부분을 if를 생략하여 다시 쓰시오.

> If it had not been for my family, my life would have been less meaningful.
> → _____, my life would have been less meaningful.

10 다음 중 밑줄 친 부분이 어법상 바른 것은?

① I wish I saved more money before.
② If Paul is here, he would have fun with us.
③ But for Patricia's help, I couldn't have caught up with the class.
④ It's time you go outside for some exercise.
⑤ Were I sleepy, I would have gone to bed early.

서술형

11 다음 두 문장의 의미가 같도록 문장을 완성하시오.

> But for your efforts, we would have failed then.
> → If _____, we would have failed then.

[12-13] 다음 빈칸에 들어갈 말이 순서대로 짝지어진 것을 고르시오.

12
> • My sister talks as if she _____ my shirt. In fact, she did.
> • If the first chapter of the book had been interesting, I _____ it to the end last night.

① wore – would read
② didn't wear – would read
③ didn't wear – would have read
④ hadn't worn – would read
⑤ hadn't worn – would have read

13
> • _____ the MVP, the team would have lost the game.
> • I wish I _____ Italian well. I want to study art in Italy.

① Without – could speak
② Without – could have spoken
③ With – could speak
④ But – could have spoken
⑤ But for – can have spoken

서술형

[14-15] 다음 문장에서 어법상 어색한 부분을 찾아 쓰고 바르게 고쳐 쓰시오.

14
> If I ate breakfast, I wouldn't be hungry now.
> _____ → _____

15
> Without for water, people wouldn't survive.
> _____ → _____

16 다음 중 짝지어진 두 문장의 의미가 <u>다른</u> 것은?

① I wish I were a university student.

→ I'm sorry that I'm not a university student.

② If the road hadn't been closed for repair, we would have arrived sooner.

→ As the road was closed for repair, we didn't arrive sooner.

③ But for the news, we wouldn't have known about the upcoming storm.

→ If it were not for the news, we wouldn't have known about the upcoming storm.

④ If you weren't with me, I would be lonely.

→ As you are with me, I'm not lonely.

⑤ If Ben hadn't been there last night, he wouldn't have seen the accident.

→ As Ben was there last night, he saw the accident.

[17-18] 우리말과 같도록 괄호 안의 말을 활용하여 빈칸에 쓰시오.

17

지난달에 비가 왔더라면, 식물들이 죽지 않았을 텐데. (rain)

= _____ _____ _____ _____ last month, the plants wouldn't have died.

18

사람들이 기후 변화에 대해 걱정할 때이다. (people, worry)

= _____ _____ _____ _____ about climate change.

[19-21] 다음 문장을 가정법 문장으로 바꿔 쓰시오.

19

As Ashley didn't study hard, she couldn't pass the exam.

→ If Ashley _____,

_____.

20

I'm sorry that today is not sunny.

→ I wish _____.

21

As you didn't take the medicine, you feel worse now.

→ If you _____,

_____.

22 다음 중 밑줄 친 부분을 바르게 고치지 <u>못한</u> 것은?

① I wish you <u>came</u> to the concert yesterday.

(→ have come)

② <u>Were it not for</u> your warning, I would have slipped on the ice. (→ Had it not been for)

③ It's time you <u>submit</u> your assignment.

(→ submitted)

④ <u>With</u> gravity, we couldn't stand on the ground.

(→ Without)

⑤ Larry talks as if he <u>saw</u> a UFO when he was a child. (→ had seen)

Chapter

10

비교구문

둘 이상의 대상의 성질·상태·수량 등을 서로 견주어 비교하는 것을
비교구문이라고 한다. 형용사나 부사를 그대로 사용하거나
형태를 바꿔 원급, 비교급, 최상급 비교를 표현할 수 있다.

UNIT 01 | 원급/비교급/최상급 비교

1

「as + 형용사/부사의 원급 + as」: …만큼 ~한/하게

비교하는 두 대상의 정도가 비슷하거나 같음을 나타낸다.

Fred is **as strong as** his brother.
Sarah can type **as fast as** I can(= me).
→ as나 than 뒤의 「주어 + 동사」는 목적격으로 바꿔 쓸 수 있다.

Your backpack is **not as[so] heavy as** mine.
We do **not** play this game **as[so] well as** Luke (does).

2

「형용사/부사의 비교급 + than」: …보다 더 ~한/하게

❶ 비교하는 두 대상 간 정도의 차이를 나타내며, 비교급 앞에 much, even, far, a lot 등을 써서 '훨씬'이라는 의미로 비교급을 강조할 수 있다.

Russia is *much* **bigger than** South Korea.
This smartphone is **more popular than** that one.

❷ 「less + 형용사/부사의 원급 + than」은 '…보다 덜 ~한/하게'라는 의미이다.

The fabric bag is **less expensive than** the leather bag.

TIP than 대신 to를 쓰는 비교급: **superior**(우수한), **inferior**(열등한), **prior**(이전의), **senior**(상위의, 연장자의) 등
This company's product is **superior to** its competitor's.

3

「the + 형용사/부사의 최상급」: 가장 ~한/하게

❶ 셋 이상의 비교 대상 중 하나의 정도가 가장 높음을 나타내며, 보통 in이나 of를 사용하여 비교 범위를 나타낸다.

Lucy is **the most positive** girl *in the class*. <in + 장소/집단>
I am **the shortest** *of all my friends*. <of + 비교 대상>

❷ 부사의 최상급 앞에는 the를 생략하기도 한다.

Marcus sings (**the**) **best** in the band.

Smart Check 다음 빈칸에 들어갈 알맞은 것을 고르시오.

1 A candle isn't as bright _____ a light bulb.
① as   ② so   ③ than

2 My dress is far _____ than hers.
① colorful   ② more colorful   ③ most colorful

3 This is _____ movie in the theater now.
① scary   ② scarier   ③ the scariest

Practice

Answers p.16

A 괄호 안에서 알맞은 것을 고르시오.

1 This brown curtain is not as (wide / wider) as that white one.

2 Children's bones are (flexible / more flexible) than adults'.

3 The Missouri River is the (longer / longest) river in North America.

4 People say that the new model is inferior (than / to) the previous one.

wide 형 폭이 넓은
bone 명 뼈
flexible 형 유연한
previous 형 이전의

B 괄호 안의 말을 활용하여 다음 문장을 한 문장으로 바꿔 쓰시오.

1 The chair is $20. The desk is $100. The sofa is $200. (cheap)
→ The chair is _____ of the three.

2 Seoul's population is 9,839,000. Hanoi's population is 8,054,000. (big)
→ Seoul's population is _____ Hanoi's.

3 Tyler arrived home at 11 P.M. Eva also arrived home at 11 P.M. (late)
→ Tyler arrived home _____ Eva.

4 The apple weighs 195 g. The coconut weighs 680 g. (light)
→ The apple is _____ the coconut.

population 명 인구
weigh 동 무게가 ~이다

C 우리말과 같도록 괄호 안의 말을 활용하여 빈칸에 쓰시오.

1 역사 소설은 공상 과학 소설보다 덜 흥미롭다. (interesting)
= A historical novel is _____ _____ _____ a sci-fi novel.

2 Karen은 그녀의 팀에서 가장 나이가 어린 선수이다. (young, player)
= Karen is _____ _____ _____ on her team.

3 이 컵은 싱크대에 있는 것만큼 더럽지 않다. (dirty)
= This cup is not _____ _____ _____ the one in the sink.

historical 형 역사의
novel 명 소설
sci-fi 형 공상 과학 소설의

D 우리말과 같도록 괄호 안의 말을 알맞게 배열하시오.

1 John은 그의 엄마만큼 깔끔하게 그의 옷을 갰다. (mom, as, did, neatly, his, as)
= John folded his clothes _____.

2 그 소음은 천둥보다 훨씬 더 소리가 컸다. (even, thunder, than, louder)
= The noise was _____.

3 Laura의 집은 이 마을에서 가장 호화로운 집이다. (house, the, luxurious, most)
= Laura's house is _____ in this town.

neatly 부 깔끔하게
fold 동 개다, 접다
thunder 명 천둥
luxurious 형 호화로운

UNIT 02 | 비교구문을 이용한 표현

1 원급을 이용한 표현

❶ 「배수사 + as + 원급 + as」: …보다 -배 더 ~한/하게 (= 「배수사 + 비교급 + than」)

The tree is **three times as tall as** me. (= The tree is **three times taller than** me.)

❷ 「as + 원급 + as + possible」: 가능한 한 ~한/하게 (= 「as + 원급 + as + 주어 + can[could]」)

Please reply to me **as soon as possible**. (= Please reply to me **as soon as you can**.)

2 비교급을 이용한 표현

❶ 「the + 비교급, the + 비교급」: ~하면 할수록 더 …하다

The more time he spent on his essay, **the better** its quality got.

❷ 「비교급 + and + 비교급」: 점점 더 ~한/하게

Emily's headache is getting **worse and worse**.
Making new friends became **more and more difficult** as I grew up.
↳ 비교급이 「more + 원급」의 형태인 경우 「more and more + 원급」으로 쓴다.

3 최상급을 이용한 표현

❶ 「one of the + 최상급 + 복수명사」: 가장 ~한 것들 중 하나

Kim is **one of the most common last names** in Korea.

❷ 「the + 최상급 + 명사 + (that) + 주어 + have/has + (ever) + p.p.」: …한 것 중에서 가장 ~한

This is **the funniest video (that) I have (ever) watched**.

4 원급과 비교급을 이용한 최상급 표현

the + 최상급	= No (other) + 단수명사 ~ as[so] + 원급 + as	(다른) 어떤 …도 -만큼 ~하지 않은
	= No (other) + 단수명사 ~ 비교급 + than	(다른) 어떤 …도 -보다 더 ~하지 않은
	= 비교급 + than any other + 단수명사	다른 어떤 …보다 더 ~한
	= 비교급 + than all the other + 복수명사	다른 모든 …보다 더 ~한

Neptune is **the coldest planet** in the solar system.
= **No (other) planet** in the solar system is **as[so] cold as** Neptune.
= **No (other) planet** in the solar system is **colder than** Neptune.
= Neptune is **colder than any other planet** in the solar system.
= Neptune is **colder than all the other planets** in the solar system.

Smart Check 다음 빈칸에 들어갈 알맞은 것을 고르시오.

1 _____ the music got, the more my ears hurt.

① The loud   ② The louder   ③ The loudest

Practice

Answers p.16

A 괄호 안에서 알맞은 것을 고르시오.

1 My scores were (twice as high / high as twice) as Mark's.

2 The more heavily it rained, the (bad / worse) the traffic jam became.

3 Sandra is one of the best (cellist / cellists) in the orchestra.

4 As the wind blew, the weather got (cold and cold / colder and colder).

traffic jam 명 교통 체증
cellist 명 첼로 연주자
blow 동 불다

B 다음 문장들의 의미가 같도록 문장을 완성하시오.

1 I'm going to keep studying as hard as possible.
→ I'm going to keep studying _____.

2 A basketball is 14 times as heavy as a golf ball.
→ A basketball is 14 times _____ a golf ball.

3 David answered the questions as honestly as possible.
→ David answered the questions _____.

4 The salmon steak is the most popular dish on the menu.
→ No other dish on the menu is _____ as the salmon steak.
→ The salmon steak is _____ dish on the menu.

5 This lake is four times as deep as the one in my town.
→ This lake is four times _____ the one in my town.

6 August is the hottest month of the year.
→ No other month of the year is _____ than August.
→ August is _____ months of the year.

answer 동 대답하다
honestly 부 정직하게, 솔직하게
salmon 명 연어
dish 명 요리

C 우리말과 같도록 괄호 안의 말을 활용하여 빈칸에 쓰시오.

1 Amy는 가능한 한 현실적으로 사자를 그렸다. (realistically)
= Amy drew the lion _____ _____ _____ _____ _____.

2 바다가 깊으면 깊을수록 그것은 더 어둡다. (deep, dark)
= _____ _____ the ocean is, _____ _____ it is.

3 그는 내가 만난 소년 중에서 가장 게으른 소년이다. (lazy, meet)
= He is the _____ _____ _____ _____ _____.

realistically 부 현실적으로
ocean 명 바다
lazy 형 게으른

Writing Exercise

A   다음 두 문장의 의미가 같도록 문장을 완성하시오.

1 The Sun is 330,000 times as heavy as the Earth.
→ The Sun is _____ the Earth.

2 If you invite more people to the party, it will be more exciting.
→ _____ you invite to the party, _____ it will be.

3 Friendship is the most important thing in my life.
→ No _____ as friendship.

4 Mr. Jones will let you know the test result as soon as possible.
→ Mr. Jones will let you know the test result _____.

B   우리말과 같도록 괄호 안의 말을 활용하여 문장을 완성하시오.

1 오늘은 내가 경험한 것 중에서 가장 더운 날이었다. (hot, day)
= Today was _____ I have ever experienced.

2 이 자동차 브랜드는 저것보다 더 우수하다. (superior)
= This automobile brand is _____ that one.

3 가능한 한 많이 읽는 것에 반드시 주력해라. (much, can)
= Be sure to concentrate on reading _____.

4 산은 가을에 점점 더 다채로워진다. (colorful)
= The mountains get _____ in fall.

5 12월은 우리 가족에게 가장 바쁜 달이다. (busy, month)
= December is _____ for my family.

6 사람들은 충분한 휴식을 취한 후에 훨씬 더 효율적으로 일한다. (much, effectively)
= People work _____ after they get enough rest.

C 우리말과 같도록 괄호 안의 말을 알맞게 배열하시오.

1 가능한 한 주의 깊게 설명서를 읽어라. (carefully, can, as, instructions, as, the, you)
= Read _____ .

2 비행기 표는 지난주보다 덜 비싸다. (last, than, less, week, expensive)
= The plane ticket is _____ .

3 버즈 칼리파는 세계에서 가장 높은 건물들 중 하나이다. (the, buildings, of, tallest, one)
= Burj Khalifa is _____ in the world.

4 Paul은 뉴스가 다큐멘터리보다 더 흥미롭다고 생각한다. (documentaries, more, than, interesting)
= Paul thinks the news is _____ .

5 이 머핀은 내가 만든 것만큼 맛있지 않다. (as, one, delicious, as, the, not)
= This muffin is _____ that I made.

6 Helena는 그 배구팀에서 가장 열심히 훈련한다. (in, team, hardest, volleyball, the)
= Helena trains _____ .

D 다음은 세 종류의 스마트폰을 비교하는 표이다. 괄호 안의 말을 활용하여 문장을 완성하시오.

스마트폰	A	B	C
출시 연도	2016	2019	2020
가격	$899	$1,100	$750
판매량	3,000,000	1,500,000	2,000,000

1 Smartphone A is _____ smartphone of the three. (old)

2 Smartphone B is _____ as smartphone A and C. (cheap)

3 Smartphone C sold _____ than smartphone B. (well)

Chapter Test

[1-3] 다음 빈칸에 들어갈 알맞은 것을 고르시오.

1

Jack can speak French as _____ as Tina.

① fluent
② more fluent
③ fluently
④ more fluently
⑤ the most fluently

2

Learning the piano was _____ than I thought.

① difficult
② as difficult
③ most difficult
④ more difficult
⑤ difficulter

3

My grandmother is _____ than me.

① four old
② four times older
③ four as old
④ four times so old
⑤ four times the oldest

4 다음 중 어법상 바른 것은?

① Angela jumps highest in our class.
② Mathew exercises so often as I do.
③ This is most crowded street in Seoul.
④ She felt more and more good after taking a break.
⑤ The Pacific Ocean is deepest than the Arctic Ocean.

서술형

[5-6] 괄호 안의 말을 활용하여 다음 문장을 한 문장으로 바꿔 쓰시오.

5

• The brown bag costs 20 dollars.
• The yellow bag costs 60 dollars.

→ The yellow bag is _____
_____ the brown bag.
(three, expensive)

6

• The dog is 5 kg.
• The cat is 4 kg.
• The rabbit is 2 kg.

→ The rabbit is _____ of
the three animals. (light)

7 다음 중 밑줄 친 부분을 바르게 고치지 못한 것은?

① The hard the test got, the more puzzled the students became. (→ harder)
② Today was the goodest day in my life. (→ best)
③ Try to solve the problems as patiently as you possible. (→ can)
④ This is one of the most popular movie in the country. (→ movies)
⑤ I love my dad as most as my mom. (→ more)

8 주어진 문장과 의미가 다른 것은?

He is the most talented actor.

① No actor is as talented as him.
② He is as talented as any other actor.
③ He is more talented than any other actor.
④ No other actor is more talented than him.
⑤ He is more talented than all the other actors.

서술형

[9-11] 우리말과 같도록 괄호 안의 말을 활용하여 문장을 완성하시오.

9

온라인 쇼핑은 점점 더 편리해지고 있다.
(convenient)

= Online shopping is becoming _____

_____ .

10

너는 그 대회에 대해 생각하면 할수록 더 불안함을 느낄 것이다. (nervous, feel)

= The more you think about the contest, _____

_____ .

11

그 퀴즈는 내가 예상했던 것보다 훨씬 더 쉬웠다.
(a lot, easy)

= The quiz was _____

I expected.

12 다음은 세 명의 학생을 비교하는 표이다. 다음 표를 바르게 설명한 것은?

이름	Brian	Aaron	Joshua
나이	15	17	13
키	165 cm	170 cm	160 cm

① Brian is younger than Joshua.

② Aaron is as short as Brian.

③ Joshua is older than Aaron.

④ Joshua is as tall as Brian.

⑤ Aaron is the oldest of the three.

13 다음 빈칸에 들어갈 말로 어색한 것은?

To me, cooking is _____ more boring
than doing the dishes.

① even　　　　② much

③ far　　　　④ very

⑤ a lot

서술형

[14-16] 다음 문장에서 어법상 어색한 부분을 찾아 쓰고 바르게 고쳐 쓰시오.

14

The blue whale is one of the heaviest animal
in the world.

_____ → _____

15

Judy is as stronger as an athlete.

_____ → _____

16

This is softest chair in our house.

_____ → _____

[17-19] 다음 두 문장의 의미가 같도록 빈칸에 알맞은 말을 쓰시오.

17

A melon is three times bigger than an apple.
→ A melon is _____ _____
_____ _____ _____ an
apple.

18

The giraffe is the tallest animal on the earth.
→ No other _____ on the earth
_____ _____ _____
_____ the giraffe.

19

As the traveler became more exhausted, he walked more slowly.
→ _____ _____ _____ the
traveler became, _____ _____
_____ he walked.

20 다음 중 짝지어진 두 문장의 의미가 다른 것을 모두 고르시오.

① Helen's voice is not as loud as yours.
　→ Helen's voice is not so loud as yours.
② I will call you back as soon as possible.
　→ I will call you back as soon as I can.
③ No other subject is more difficult than math.
　→ Math is one of the most difficult subjects.
④ Sneakers are more comfortable than sandals.
　→ Sandals are less comfortable than sneakers.
⑤ The rose is the prettiest flower in the garden.
　→ All the other flower in the garden is as
　　pretty as the rose.

[21-22] 다음 중 어법상 어색한 것을 고르시오.

21 ① The flight to Bangkok was longer than I
　thought.
② The story got more and more exciting.
③ Tom does not dance so better as Emily.
④ Scott is the smartest of all his friends.
⑤ Tiffany is even more active than her brother.

22 ① The more the singer practiced, the best he
　performed.
② The new machine is superior to the old one.
③ This was the most thrilling roller coaster I
　have ever ridden.
④ Your shirt is as colorful as mine.
⑤ Picasso was one of the most creative artists
　in history.

23 다음 빈칸에 들어갈 말이 순서대로 짝지어진 것은?

• She writes in English _____ well as a
native speaker does.
• Simon is far more witty _____ any other
student in his class.

① as – as ② as – than
③ so – as ④ so – than
⑤ as – so

24 다음 빈칸에 공통으로 들어갈 알맞은 것은?

• Fruits and vegetables are _____
healthier than junk food.
• Lena studies three times as _____ as
me.

① even ② a lot
③ very ④ much
⑤ many

Chapter

11

일치와 화법

문장 안에서 주어와 동사의 수를 맞추거나,
주절과 종속절의 시제를 맞추는 것을 일치라고 한다.
화법은 말이나 생각을 전달하는 방식으로,
직접 화법과 간접 화법이 있다.

UNIT 01 | 수의 일치

1 단수 취급하는 경우

다음과 같은 주어 뒤에는 항상 단수동사를 쓴다.

each, every가 포함된 주어	*Each pen* **costs** five dollars. *Every student* in my class **has** to give a presentation.
-thing, -one, -body	*No one* **thinks** that it is a good plan. *Somebody* **has** taken my shoes.
학과명, 국가명, 질병명	*Physics* **is** difficult for many students. *The United States* **consists** of 50 states.
시간, 거리, 무게, 금액 등의 단위	*45 minutes* **is** enough time to eat lunch. *Five hundred dollars* **was** given to the winner.
동명사구나 명사절	*Mastering foreign languages* **takes** a lot of time. *What I told my friends* **was** a lie.

2 복수 취급하는 경우

다음과 같은 주어 뒤에는 항상 복수동사를 쓴다.

(both) A and B	*(Both) Judy and I* **are** interested in classical music. **TIP** 「A and B」가 하나의 개념을 나타낼 때는 단수 취급한다. *Curry and rice* **is** what I had for dinner.
the + 형용사(~한 사람들)	*The deaf* **use** their hands to communicate.
a number of + 복수명사 (많은 ~)	*A number of people* **are** enjoying the concert. **TIP** 「the number of + 복수명사」(~의 수)는 단수 취급한다. *The number of elementary school students* **is** decreasing.

Smart Check 다음 빈칸에 들어갈 알맞은 것을 고르시오.

1 Ethan and Eric _____ twin brothers.
　① be　　　　　　　　② is　　　　　　　　③ are

2 Each person _____ a different appearance and personality.
　① has　　　　　　　② have　　　　　　　③ is having

3 The injured _____ to be taken to the hospital immediately.
　① needs　　　　　　② need　　　　　　　③ is needing

Practice

Answers p.17

A 괄호 안에서 알맞은 것을 고르시오.

1 Every participant (is / are) going to get a free gift.

2 Both my laptop and tablet PC (was / were) broken.

3 Thirty dollars (is / are) enough for me to buy the shirt I wanted.

4 Measles (was / were) dangerous before the vaccine was developed.

participant 명 참가자
measles 명 홍역
vaccine 명 백신
develop 동 개발하다

B 괄호 안의 동사를 알맞은 형태로 바꿔 빈칸에 쓰시오. (단, 현재시제로 쓰시오.)

1 The disabled _____ government assistance. (get)

2 Both Mary and Daniel _____ sweet desserts. (like)

3 A number of students _____ the school's new policy. (support)

4 The number of tourists visiting Jejudo _____ every year. (increase)

disabled 형 장애를 가진
government 명 정부
assistance 명 보조, 도움
policy 명 정책
increase 동 증가하다

C 다음 빈칸에 알맞은 말을 <보기>에서 한 번씩만 골라 알맞은 형태로 바꿔 쓰시오. (단, 현재시제로 쓰시오.)

<보기>	be	have	train	create

1 Everyone on the soccer team _____ very hard.

2 Each shirt in the closet _____ unique in design.

3 Trial and error _____ better results.

4 The young _____ the chance to experience different jobs.

train 동 훈련하다
create 동 만들어내다
unique 형 독특한
trial and error 시행착오
experience 동 경험하다

D 우리말과 같도록 괄호 안의 말을 활용하여 빈칸에 쓰시오.

1 숙제에 두 시간이 소요되었다. (spend)

= _____ _____ _____ _____ on homework.

2 많은 군인들은 평화를 위해 싸운다. (number, soldier, fight)

= _____ _____ _____ _____ _____ for peace.

3 Jacob이 주문한 것은 내 것보다 더 맛있었다. (what, order, be)

= _____ _____ _____ _____ _____ tastier than mine.

soldier 명 군인
peace 명 평화
order 동 주문하다
tasty 형 맛있는

Chapter 11

일치와 화법

Hackers Grammar Smart Level 3

UNIT 02 | 시제의 일치

1 시제의 일치

❶ 주절이 현재시제인 경우 종속절에는 의미에 따라 모든 시제를 쓸 수 있다.

I *believe* that Jane **isn't telling** the truth.
I *believe* that Jane **didn't tell** the truth.
I *believe* that Jane **won't tell** the truth.

❷ 주절이 과거시제인 경우 종속절에는 의미에 따라 과거시제나 과거완료시제를 쓴다.

We *heard* that Peter **moved** to Seoul.
We *heard* that Peter **had moved** to Seoul.
We *heard* that Peter <u>would move</u> to Seoul.
  └→ 주절이 과거시제인 경우 종속절의 조동사도 과거형(would, could, might 등)을 쓴다.

2 시제 일치의 예외

❶ 다음과 같은 경우에는 주절의 시제와 상관없이 종속절에 항상 현재시제를 쓴다.

현재의 습관이나 반복되는 일을 나타낼 때	Linda *said* that she **plays** tennis every weekend.
일반적·과학적 사실을 나타낼 때	They *didn't know* that Big Ben **is** in London. Mr. Hall *taught* us that some turtles **live** up to 100 years.
속담·격언을 말할 때	My parents *said* that haste **makes** waste. The coach *told* me that the early bird **catches** the worm.

❷ 역사적 사실을 나타낼 때는 주절의 시제와 상관없이 종속절에 항상 과거시제를 쓴다.

She *knows* that 2018 Winter Olympics **was held** in Pyeongchang.
The students *learned* that Neil Armstrong **landed** on the moon in 1969.

Smart Check 다음 빈칸에 들어갈 알맞은 것을 고르시오.

1 We thought that Jake _____ the window.
① breaks   ② had broken   ③ may break

2 The boy promised that he _____ more careful.
① is   ② will be   ③ would be

3 I found out that Ottawa _____ the capital of Canada.
① is   ② was   ③ had been

Practice

Answers p.17

A 괄호 안에서 알맞은 것을 고르시오.

1 I wondered why she (won't / wouldn't) answer her phone.

2 I heard that the last bus for Seoul (have / had) left ten minutes ago.

3 David knew that light (travels / traveled) faster than sound.

4 The tour guide told us that the biggest city festival (is / was) held in May every year.

wonder 통 궁금하다
answer 통 (전화를) 받다
last 형 맨 마지막의
travel 통 이동하다

B 괄호 안의 동사를 알맞은 형태로 바꿔 빈칸에 쓰시오.

1 The teacher said that Hangeul _____ invented in 1443. (be)

2 The kids learned that metal _____ in hot weather. (expand)

3 My brother didn't know that the Eiffel Tower _____ in Paris. (be)

4 I knew that Kelly always _____ the violin at 2 P.M. (practice)

invent 통 발명하다
metal 명 금속
expand 통 팽창하다

C 다음 문장을 과거시제로 바꿀 때 빈칸에 알맞은 말을 쓰시오.

1 I think that you will like the director's new film.
→ I thought that you _____ _____ the director's new film.

2 Mark says that he visits the national library once a month.
→ Mark said that he _____ the national library once a month.

3 The woman complains that she heard noises from upstairs.
→ The woman complained that she _____ _____ noises from upstairs.

national library 명 국립 도서관
once 부 한 번
upstairs 명 위층

D 우리말과 같도록 괄호 안의 말을 활용하여 빈칸에 쓰시오.

1 Mia는 더 조심할 것을 약속했다. (will, be)
= Mia promised that _____ _____ _____ more careful.

2 나의 아버지는 나에게 아는 것이 힘이라고 말씀하셨다. (knowledge, be)
= My father told me that _____ _____ power.

3 그는 알래스카가 1959년에 미국의 49번째 주가 되었다고 말했다. (Alaska, become)
= He said that _____ _____ the 49th state of the U.S. in 1959.

careful 형 조심하는
knowledge 명 아는 것, 지식
state 명 (미국 등의) 주

UNIT 03 | 화법

다른 사람이 말한 내용을 큰따옴표(" ")를 사용하여 그대로 전달하는 것을 직접 화법이라고 하고, 큰따옴표 없이 전달하는 사람의 입장에서 말하는 것을 간접 화법이라고 한다.

1 평서문의 직접 화법 → 간접 화법 전환

Jim said to me, "I want to watch this movie with you."
→ Jim told me (that) he wanted to watch that movie with me.
　　　ⓐ　　ⓑ　ⓒ　ⓓ　　　　　ⓔ　　　　　ⓒ

> ⓐ 전달동사가 say인 경우 그대로 쓰고, say to인 경우 tell로 바꾼다.
> ⓑ 콤마(,)와 큰따옴표(" ")를 없애고 접속사 that으로 두 절을 연결한다. 이때 that은 생략할 수 있다.
> ⓒ that절의 인칭대명사를 전달하는 사람의 입장에 맞게 바꾼다.
> ⓓ 전달동사가 현재시제인 경우 that절의 시제를 바꾸지 않고, 과거시제인 경우 과거시제나 과거완료시제로 바꾼다.
> ⓔ 지시대명사나 부사(구)를 전달하는 사람의 입장에 맞게 바꾼다.
>
> | this/these → that/those | ago → before | today → that day |
> |---|---|---|
> | here → there | next ~ → the following ~ | yesterday → the previous day[the day before] |
> | now → then | last ~ → the previous ~ | tomorrow → the next[the following] day |

2 의문문의 직접 화법 → 간접 화법 전환

❶ 의문사가 있는 의문문: 「ask (+ 목적어) + 의문사 + 주어 + 동사」

I said to him, "What are you doing now?"
→ I **asked** him **what he was doing** then.

My mom said, "Who broke the cup?"
→ My mom **asked who had broken** the cup.
　　　　　　　↳ 의문사가 주어인 경우 「의문사 + 동사」의 어순을 그대로 쓴다.

❷ 의문사가 없는 의문문: 「ask (+ 목적어) + if[whether] + 주어 + 동사」

She said to me, "Will you join the chess club?"
→ She asked me **if[whether] I would join** the chess club.

3 명령문의 직접 화법 → 간접 화법 전환: 「tell[ask, order, advise 등] + 목적어 + to부정사」

He said to me, "Exercise at least three times a week."
→ He **told** me **to exercise** at least three times a week.

The police said to the man, "Don't drive fast here."
→ The police **ordered** the man **not to drive** fast there.
　　　　　　　↳ 부정명령문을 간접 화법으로 바꿀 때는 to부정사 앞에 not을 쓴다.

Smart Check 다음 문장을 간접 화법으로 바꿀 때 빈칸에 들어갈 알맞은 것을 고르시오.

1 The forecast said, "It will rain tomorrow." → The forecast said that it _____ the following day.
　① will rain　　　　　② would rain　　　　　③ is raining

Practice

Answers p.17

A 괄호 안에서 알맞은 것을 고르시오.

1 He (said / told) her that he didn't know how to use the scanner.

2 The guests said (that / if) they had been satisfied with the meal.

3 My mom told me (to forget not / not to forget) to take the umbrella.

4 Anthony asked me what sport (I liked / did I like) the most.

satisfy 图 만족시키다

B 다음 직접 화법을 간접 화법으로 바꾼 문장에서 밑줄 친 부분을 바르게 고쳐 쓰시오.

1 I said to my dad, "Is it cold outside?"
→ I <u>asked to my dad</u> if it was cold outside.   → _____

2 Hannah said, "Where can I buy a light bulb?"
→ Hannah asked <u>where could she</u> buy a light bulb. → _____

3 The teacher said to me, "Participate in the debate."
→ The teacher told me <u>participate</u> in the debate.   → _____

light bulb 图 전구
debate 图 토론

C 다음 문장을 간접 화법으로 바꿔 쓰시오.

1 Ryan said to me, "I had a car accident last week."
→ Ryan _____ a car accident the previous week.

2 I said to the police officer, "Is there a bus stop nearby?"
→ I _____ a bus stop nearby.

3 My baseball coach said to me, "Practice hitting the ball."
→ My baseball coach _____ hitting the ball.

car accident 자동차 사고
previous 图 이전의
nearby 图 인근에
hit 图 치다

D 우리말과 같도록 괄호 안의 말을 활용하여 빈칸에 쓰시오.

1 Natalie는 나에게 내가 언제 나의 안경을 바꿨는지 물었다. (change)
= Natalie asked me _____ _____ _____ _____ my glasses.

2 보안 요원은 나에게 빨간색 버튼을 만지지 말라고 말했다. (touch)
= The security guard told me _____ _____ _____ the red button.

3 그는 누가 도서관에서 큰 소리로 이야기하고 있는지 물었다. (talk)
= He asked _____ _____ _____ loudly in the library.

security guard 图 보안 요원
loudly 图 큰 소리로

Writing Exercise

A 우리말과 같도록 괄호 안의 말을 활용하여 문장을 완성하시오.

1 초록색과 파란색 둘 다 너에게 잘 어울린다. (both, look)

= _____ good on you.

2 50달러는 잃기엔 많은 돈이다. (be)

= _____ a lot of money to lose.

3 각각의 물품은 철저한 점검 후에 배송된다. (each, item, ship)

= _____ after a thorough inspection.

4 봄이 오면서, 많은 꽃들이 핀다. (number, bloom)

= As spring comes, _____ .

5 Robert가 말한 것은 매우 놀라웠다. (what, say, be)

= _____ very surprising.

6 요즘에 젊은 사람들은 온라인으로 쇼핑하는 것을 즐긴다. (young, enjoy)

= Nowadays, _____ shopping online.

B 다음 문장의 밑줄 친 부분을 과거시제로 바꿔 완전한 문장을 쓰시오.

1 Kelly says that she may arrive late.

→ Kelly _____ .

2 My teacher tells me that a bad workman blames his tools.

→ My teacher _____ .

3 Dean says that the *Titanic* sank on April 15, 1912.

→ Dean _____ .

4 I don't know that the package was delivered to me.

→ I _____ .

5 Most people know that a koala spends most of its time sleeping.

→ Most people _____ .

6 The hikers think that it will be hard to reach the top of the mountain.

→ The hikers _____ .

C 다음 문장을 간접 화법으로 바꿔 쓰시오.

1 Brian said to me, "I prefer classical music to rock music."
→ Brian _____ .

2 Julie said to him, "How long can I borrow this magazine?"
→ Julie _____ .

3 I told my brother, "Turn off your phone before the movie starts."
→ I _____ before the movie started.

4 She said to me, "I will look after your dog tomorrow."
→ She _____ .

5 Sarah said to me, "Can you get a towel for me?"
→ Sarah _____ .

6 The teacher said to Anna, "Translate these English sentences into Korean."
→ The teacher _____ .

D 다음 그림을 보고 괄호 안의 말을 활용하여 빈칸에 쓰시오. (단, 현재시제로 쓰시오.)

1

2

3

1 _____ _____ _____ _____ _____ to get tickets for the show.
(number, fan, want)

2 _____ _____ _____ the distance between my house and Nancy's house.
(kilometer, be)

3 _____ _____ _____ a different number during the race. (each, runner, wear)

[1-4] 다음 빈칸에 들어갈 알맞은 것을 고르시오.

1

| Annie knew that I _____ the tennis team. |

① join　　　　② joins
③ joined　　　④ have joined
⑤ will join

2

| I learned that the Taj Mahal _____ in 1648. |

① is built　　　　② was built
③ has been built　④ had been built
⑤ had built

3

| Did you know that the highest mountain in Korea _____ Mount Halla? |

① is　　　　② was
③ will be　④ would be
⑤ had been

4

| The doctor asked me _____ I had any other symptoms. |

① that　　　② what
③ which　　④ unless
⑤ whether

[5-7] 다음 문장을 간접 화법으로 바꿔 쓰시오.

5

| My sister said to me, "When will you call me back?"
→ My sister asked me _____
_____. |

6

| The technician said to us, "Don't use the air conditioner until tomorrow."
→ The technician told us _____
_____. |

7

| He said, "I enjoyed the fireworks yesterday."
→ He said that _____
_____. |

8 다음 중 어법상 바른 것은?

① I heard that Pompeii had been discovered in 1748.
② Six kilometers are too long for me to walk.
③ The young is called the hope of the future.
④ We were taught that Venus was the hottest planet in the solar system.
⑤ A number of trucks are parked on the street.

서술형

[9-11] 다음 문장에서 어법상 <u>어색한</u> 부분을 찾아 쓰고 바르게 고쳐 쓰시오.

9

Economics are the subject that I'm good at.

_____ → _____

10

We learned that our body temperature decreased as we get older.

_____ → _____

11

Steve asked if had I visited the museum.

_____ → _____

고난도

12 다음 중 직접 화법을 간접 화법으로 <u>잘못</u> 바꾼 것은?

① I said to Emma, "Do you know this song?"
  → I asked Emma if she knew that song.

② Ken said, "I met Jimmy three days ago."
  → Ken said he had met Jimmy three days before.

③ Betty said to me, "I want to stay here."
  → Betty told me that she wanted to stay there.

④ Mr. Brown said to us, "Don't go into the water without warm-up exercises."
  → Mr. Brown advised us not go into the water without warm-up exercises.

⑤ Dad said to me, "Where did you put your sweater?"
  → Dad asked me where I had put my sweater.

13 다음 대화의 빈칸에 들어갈 알맞은 것은?

> A: What did the police officer ask you?
> B: She asked me _____.

① if did I see any stranger
② if had I seen any stranger
③ if I saw any stranger
④ that I see any stranger
⑤ that I saw any stranger

14 다음 빈칸에 들어갈 말이 순서대로 짝지어진 것은?

> • The researcher said that the biggest earthquake ever _____ in 1960.
> • We thought that Jeff _____ get a better score.

① occurs – will   ② occurred – will
③ occurred – would   ④ had occurred – will
⑤ had occurred – would

서술형 고난도

15 우리말과 같도록 주어진 <조건>에 맞게 영작하시오.

> 많은 학생들은 그 요리 수업을 듣는다.

> <조건>
> 1. number, student, take, cooking class를 활용하시오.
> 2. 8단어로 쓰시오.

= _____.

[16-17] 다음 중 어법상 <u>어색한</u> 것을 고르시오.

16 ① We didn't know that Lisa could speak three languages.
② Mom told me that banks are closed on weekends.
③ I thought that the school trip will be canceled.
④ Lauren asked why Josh was angry at her.
⑤ The teacher was certain that his students had done their best.

17 ① Both the man and his son are feeding the dog.
② The poor was provided with food and shelter.
③ Anything is possible if you believe in yourself.
④ Two days wasn't enough to read the whole book.
⑤ A number of boats are floating on the river.

18 다음 문장을 과거시제로 바꿀 때 밑줄 친 부분이 어법상 어색한 것은?

> People know that the earth is round.
> → People <u>knew</u> that the <u>earth</u> was <u>round</u>.
>   ①   ②   ③   ④   ⑤

서술형
19 괄호 안의 동사를 활용하여 빈칸에 쓰시오. (단, 현재시제로 쓰시오.)

> I think that every person _____ unique and precious. (be)

서술형
[20-22] 우리말과 같도록 괄호 안의 말을 활용하여 문장을 완성하시오.

20
> 나는 번개가 1초에 100번 정도 친다는 것을 배웠다. (strike)

= I learned that lightning _____ about 100 times in a second.

21
> 교통사고 건수는 계속해서 증가하고 있다. (increase)

= The number of traffic accidents _____ continuously.

22
> Mark는 내가 그에게 펜 한 개를 빌려줄 수 있는지 물었다. (can, lend)

= Mark asked _____ him a pen.

고난도
23 다음 중 어법상 바른 것끼리 묶인 것은?

> ⓐ Two dollars are enough to buy a snack.
> ⓑ Mom said that practice makes perfect.
> ⓒ Tim told that he didn't want to go to the dentist.
> ⓓ What the scientists found was amazing.
> ⓔ The museum guide said that *The Starry Night* had been painted by Vincent van Gogh in 1889.

① ⓐ, ⓑ   ② ⓐ, ⓒ   ③ ⓑ, ⓒ
④ ⓑ, ⓓ   ⑤ ⓓ, ⓔ

Chapter

12

특수구문

강조 등의 특정 목적을 위해 일반적인 문장 구조를
따르지 않는 것을 특수구문이라고 한다.

UNIT 01 | 강조, 도치

1 강조

❶ do를 이용한 동사 강조: '정말 …하다'의 의미로 동사원형 앞에 do/does/did를 쓴다.

I **do** *wish* to become a doctor.
Laura **did** *go* to the library yesterday.

❷ 「It is[was] ~ that …」 구문을 이용한 강조: '…한 것은 바로 ~이다'의 의미로 동사를 제외한 문장 성분(주어, 목적어, 부사(구/절) 등)을 It is[was]와 that 사이에 쓴다.

<u>Peter</u> <u>met</u> <u>Liam</u> <u>on the street</u> <u>yesterday</u>.
→ **It was** *Peter* **that[who]** met Liam on the street yesterday. <주어 강조>
→ **It was** *Liam* **that[who(m)]** Peter met on the street yesterday. <목적어 강조>
→ **It was** *on the street* **that[where]** Peter met Liam yesterday. <부사구(장소) 강조>
→ **It was** *yesterday* **that[when]** Peter met Liam on the street. <부사(시간) 강조>
  └→ 강조하는 대상에 따라 that 대신 who(m), which, where, when을 쓸 수 있다.

2 도치

부사(구)의 의미를 강조하기 위해 부사(구)를 문장 맨 앞으로 보낼 때 주어와 동사의 순서가 바뀐다.

❶ 장소나 방향의 부사(구)를 강조하기 위한 도치: 「장소나 방향의 부사(구) + 동사 + 주어」

On the desk **is my computer**. (← My computer is on the desk.)
Into the pool **dived Thomas**. (← Thomas dived into the pool.)

> **TIP** 주어가 대명사일 경우 주로 주어와 동사가 도치되지 않는다.
> *Here* **she comes**.

❷ 부정어를 강조하기 위한 도치

ⓐ be동사나 조동사가 있는 문장: 「부정어(never, hardly, rarely, little 등) + be동사/조동사 + 주어」
Hardly **can he** believe the rumor.

ⓑ 일반동사가 있는 문장: 「부정어(never, hardly, rarely, little 등) + do/does/did + 주어 + 동사원형」
Rarely **does Laura complain** about small things.

❸ 「so/neither + 동사 + 주어」(~도 그렇다/아니다)

A: I am good at playing the piano.　　B: *So* **am I**.
A: I don't like spicy food.　　B: *Neither* **does Samuel**.

Smart Check 다음 빈칸에 들어갈 알맞은 것을 고르시오.

1 Kevin _____ tired now.
　① do looks　　　　　② does look　　　　　③ do look

2 Rarely _____ expensive things.
　① she buys　　　　　② she does buy　　　　　③ does she buy

Practice

Answers p.19

A 괄호 안에서 알맞은 것을 고르시오.

1 I (do / did) like reading comic books when I was young.

2 Among the tall trees (a cabin stood / stood a cabin).

3 It is at the entrance (that / when) I'm going to meet Julie.

4 Little (I dreamed / did I dream) that I would get a scholarship.

cabin 몡 오두막집
entrance 몡 입구
scholarship 몡 장학금

B 다음 문장을 밑줄 친 부분을 강조하는 문장으로 바꿔 쓰시오.

1 Nick <u>won</u> the lottery last month.

→ _____ .

2 She drinks <u>a glass of milk</u> every morning.

→ _____ .

3 They felt the ground shaking <u>an hour ago</u>.

→ _____ .

lottery 몡 복권
ground 몡 땅바닥, 지면
shake 동 흔들리다

C 다음 두 문장의 의미가 같도록 문장을 완성하시오.

1 The white horse jumped over the fence.
→ Over the fence _____ .

2 Lightning hardly strikes the same place twice.
→ Hardly _____ .

3 I have never been to the movie theater alone.
→ Never _____ .

lightning 몡 번개
strike 동 (세게) 치다
alone 부 혼자

D 우리말과 같도록 괄호 안의 말을 알맞게 배열하시오.

1 그 의자 뒤에 작은 고양이 한 마리가 숨었다. (hid, cat, chair, a, the, small)
= Behind _____ .

2 Sally가 새로운 노트북을 산 때는 바로 지난주였다. (last, that, was, it, week)
= _____ Sally bought a new laptop.

3 나는 약간의 물을 마시고 싶어. – 나도 그래. (do, so, I)
= I want to have some water. – _____ .

hide 동 숨다

Chapter 12

UNIT 02 | 병렬, 부정, 동격, 생략

1 병렬

등위접속사(and, but, or 등)나 상관접속사(both A and B, either A or B, not only A but also B 등)로 연결되는 말은 문법적으로 형태가 같아야 한다.

Tina is **polite**, **friendly**, *and* **smart**.
You can *either* **take a subway** *or* **walk five blocks**.

2 부정

❶ 전체 부정: no/none/neither/never가 문장에 쓰여 '아무것도/아무도/둘 다/결코 ~ 않다'라는 의미를 나타낸다.

None of the seats is empty.
Neither of her parents was at home.

❷ 부분 부정: 「not + always/all/every/both」의 형태로 쓰여 '항상/모두/둘 다 ~인 것은 아니다'라는 의미를 나타낸다.

Eating salty food is **not always** bad.
Not every flower smells nice.

3 동격

명사나 대명사 뒤에 콤마(,), of, that을 써서 부연 설명을 덧붙일 수 있다.

❶ 「명사 + 콤마(,) + 명사」

Andrew, **my best friend**, always helps me.

❷ 「명사 + of + 명사(상당어구)」

We had **a hope** *of* **seeing a rainbow** after the rain.

❸ 「명사(news, fact, rumor, idea, thought, promise 등) + that절」

The news *that* **the building was on fire** surprised everyone.

4 생략

❶ 문장 내에서 반복되는 어구는 생략할 수 있다.

Sophia got up late and (**Sophia**) missed the bus.
You don't have to go there if you don't want to (**go there**).

❷ 부사절의 주어가 주절과 같고 부사절의 동사가 be동사인 경우, 부사절에서 「주어 + be동사」를 생략할 수 있다.

The boy broke his leg while (**he was**) playing soccer.

Smart Check 다음 빈칸에 들어갈 알맞은 것을 고르시오.

1 Bill and Harry don't like shopping. _____ of them likes shopping.
　① Both　　　　　　　　② All　　　　　　　　③ Neither

Practice

Answers p.19

A 괄호 안에서 알맞은 것을 고르시오.

1 You can either call me or (send / to send) a text message.

2 The kids went to the amusement park and (have / had) a great time.

3 The author's latest novel was long but (interesting / interestingly).

4 We practiced not only catching but also (to hit / hitting) balls.

author 몡 작가
latest 혱 최신의
catch 동 잡다

B 다음 두 문장의 의미가 같도록 <보기>에서 알맞은 말을 골라 빈칸에 쓰시오.

<보기>   no   none   not

1 Some of my cousins came to the family trip, but others didn't.

→ _____ all of my cousins came to the family trip.

2 All of the citizens agreed with the new policy.

→ _____ of the citizens disagreed with the new policy.

3 Everyone knows that Beijing is the capital of China.

→ There is _____ one who doesn't know that Beijing is the capital of China.

citizen 몡 시민
policy 몡 정책
disagree 동 동의하지 않다
capital 몡 수도

C 다음 문장의 밑줄 친 부분과 동격인 부분에 밑줄을 치시오.

1 Mike had the goal of winning the award.

2 Ice hockey, a winter sport, is popular in Canada.

3 The fact that the climate is changing makes me scared.

4 I like the idea of throwing a party at the restaurant.

climate 몡 기후
throw a party 파티를 열다

D 다음 문장에서 생략할 수 있는 부분에 밑줄을 치시오.

1 When I am at home, I wear comfortable clothes.

2 You can bring friends here if you want to bring friends here.

3 Henry found a coin while he was sweeping the floor.

4 Eva made some cookies and Eva gave them to me.

comfortable 혱 편한
sweep 동 쓸다

Writing Exercise

A   다음 문장을 괄호 안의 지시대로 바꿔 쓰시오.

1   Jenny saw a deer in the forest. (a deer 강조)

→ _____ .

2   The teacher rarely finishes his class early. (rarely를 문장 맨 앞으로)

→ _____ .

3   Some of my friends didn't laugh at my joke. (not all of를 활용한 문장으로)

→ _____ .

4   My mother came into the room. (into the room을 문장 맨 앞으로)

→ _____ .

5   The football team has a big match on Saturday. (on Saturday 강조)

→ _____ .

B   밑줄 친 부분이 어법상 맞으면 O를 쓰고, 틀리면 바르게 고쳐 완전한 문장을 쓰시오.

1   Steven is a hardworking student, and so <u>do</u> I.

→ _____ .

2   Lisa couldn't talk on the phone <u>while riding</u> a bicycle.

→ _____ .

3   Hardly <u>I have played</u> tennis since I was a child.

→ _____ .

4   In the deep ocean <u>the octopus lives</u>.

→ _____ .

5   Ron is good at both dancing and <u>sing</u>.

→ _____ .

6   Emily didn't spread the rumors, and <u>so</u> did I.

→ _____ .

C 우리말과 같도록 괄호 안의 말을 알맞게 배열하시오.

1 아이들은 캠프파이어 앞에 모였다. (the, gathered, of, kids, the, campfire, front)
= In _____.

2 새로운 사람들을 만나는 것이 항상 즐거운 것은 아니다. (not, it, meet, always, fun, is, to)
= _____ new people.

3 이 항아리들이 만들어진 때는 바로 18세기였다. (century, was, it, when, the, 18th, in)
= _____ these pots were made.

4 나는 그렇게 아름다운 풍경을 이전에 본 적이 없다. (such, I, sight, seen, have, a, beautiful)
= Never _____ before.

5 그 선수는 부상을 당하는 것에 대한 두려움이 있었다. (being, a, of, injured, fear, had)
= The player _____.

6 나는 실패를 경험해볼 가치가 있다는 생각에 반대한다. (worth, it, experiencing, that, idea, is, the, failure)
= I'm against _____.

D 다음 그림을 보고 <보기 1>과 <보기 2>의 말을 한 번씩만 골라 문장을 완성하시오.

1  **2**  **3**

| <보기 1> | not every | neither of | none of |

| <보기 2> | the shoes | rose | the girls |

1 _____ is playing online games.

2 _____ in the vase is red.

3 _____ on the website is available.

Chapter Test

[1-3] 다음 빈칸에 들어갈 알맞은 것을 고르시오.

1

> You _____ look great in the black suit last night.

① are   ② were
③ do   ④ does
⑤ did

2

> Never _____ Thai food before.

① she has tried   ② tried she
③ has she tried   ④ she tried
⑤ she had tried

3

> Liam doesn't like hot weather, and _____ .

① so am I   ② so do I
③ neither am I   ④ neither do I
⑤ neither did I

4 다음 중 어법상 바른 것은?

① Here the host of this event comes.
② Amy loves not only swimming but also to hike.
③ Never I dreamed that I would see you again.
④ That was last Sunday when I finally finished reading the book.
⑤ We were best friends when in elementary school.

서술형 [5-6] 다음 문장에서 어법상 어색한 부분을 찾아 쓰고 바르게 고쳐 쓰시오.

5

> Jessie does knows how to use this device.

_____ → _____

6

> On the top of the hill a beautiful castle is.

_____ → _____

7 다음 빈칸에 들어갈 말이 순서대로 짝지어진 것은?

> • This refrigerator has the problem _____ making too much noise.
> • I support the idea _____ every child needs to exercise regularly.

① that – that   ② of – that
③ that – of   ④ of – which
⑤ which – of

8 다음 중 어법상 어색한 것은?

① There he goes with his older brother.
② Julie likes drawing, and so does Tyler.
③ Little I could sleep because of the mosquito.
④ It was Sam that shared snacks with his classmates.
⑤ Into the forest disappeared the deer.

[9-10] 다음 대화의 빈칸에 들어갈 알맞은 것을 고르시오.

9

> A: I go to bed late on Saturdays.
> B: _____.

① So do I　　　　② So I am
③ So am I　　　　④ Neither I do
⑤ Neither did I

10

> A: Are Jeff and Paul still here?
> B: _____ of them is here. They have already gone home.

① Both　　　　② All
③ Every　　　　④ No
⑤ Neither

고난도

[11-12] 다음 중 밑줄 친 부분의 쓰임이 나머지 넷과 다른 것을 고르시오.

11　① We <u>do</u> love our parents.
② I <u>did</u> wash the dishes yesterday.
③ Josh <u>did</u> his homework, but didn't bring it.
④ Mary <u>does</u> look nervous right now.
⑤ I <u>do</u> hang out with Tim every day.

12　① We had to face the fact <u>that</u> we lost the match.
② The promise <u>that</u> she made was not kept.
③ There was a rumor <u>that</u> the festival would be canceled.
④ The thought <u>that</u> I did my best calmed me down.
⑤ Jamie heard the news <u>that</u> an earthquake occurred in his hometown.

[13-14] 다음 우리말을 알맞게 영작한 것을 고르시오.

13

> 모든 비싼 것이 좋은 품질을 가진 것은 아니다.

① Every expensive thing doesn't have a good quality.
② All expensive things have a good quality.
③ All expensive things don't have a good quality.
④ Not all expensive things have a good quality.
⑤ None of the expensive things has a good quality.

14

> 그 학생들 중 아무도 수업에 지각하지 않았다.

① None of the students was late for class.
② All the students were late for class.
③ Not every student was late for class.
④ Both of the students were not late for class.
⑤ Neither of the students was not late for class.

서술형

[15-16] 다음 문장을 밑줄 친 부분을 강조하는 문장으로 바꿔 쓰시오.

15

> I <u>wrote</u> a birthday card for you, but I lost it.
> → _____
> _____.

16

> <u>Kate</u> won the award in the contest last year.
> → _____
> _____.

[17-19] 우리말과 같도록 괄호 안의 말을 활용하여 문장을 완성하시오.

17
> 온라인으로 쇼핑하는 것이 항상 더 저렴한 것은 아니다. (be, always, cheap)

= Shopping online _____.

18
> 바닥 위에 퍼즐 조각들이 있었다. (be, the puzzle pieces)

= On the floor _____.

19
> 그는 그가 실수를 했다는 것을 좀처럼 인정할 수 없다. (can, admit)

= Hardly _____ that he made a mistake.

20 다음 중 어법상 바른 것끼리 묶인 것은?

> ⓐ It was my sister which took my necklace.
> ⓑ Rarely Olivia goes outside on weekends.
> ⓒ We can either cook or ordering some food for dinner.
> ⓓ No one has visited Mr. Brown's flower shop for days.
> ⓔ On the blanket lay the dog.

① ⓐ, ⓑ   ② ⓐ, ⓒ   ③ ⓑ, ⓒ
④ ⓑ, ⓓ   ⑤ ⓓ, ⓔ

21 다음 두 문장의 의미가 같도록 빈칸에 알맞은 말을 쓰시오.

> I have never thought that I could meet my favorite singer.
> → Never _____ _____ _____ that I could meet my favorite singer.

22 다음 중 밑줄 친 부분을 생략할 수 <u>없는</u> 것은?

> ① Laura went to the market and <u>Laura</u> bought some eggs.
> ② My mother came into my room when <u>I was</u> talking on the phone.
> ③ They sang a song because they were asked to <u>sing a song</u>.
> ④ Although <u>he is</u> young, he is intelligent.
> ⑤ I didn't want to go to school, but I had to <u>go to school</u>.

[23-24] 우리말과 같도록 괄호 안의 말을 알맞게 배열하시오.

23
> 어제 나에게 그 선물을 준 사람은 바로 Tom이었다. (me, that, Tom, yesterday, the, gave, was, gift)

= It _____.

24
> 그녀는 그 슬픈 소식을 좀처럼 믿을 수 없었다. (she, news, the, could, sad, believe)

= Hardly _____.

해커스북 중·고등
www.HackersBook.com

불규칙 동사 변화표

1. A-A-A형 원형-과거형-과거분사형이 모두 같은 경우

원형	과거형	과거분사형
cost 비용이 들다	cost	cost
hit 치다, 때리다	hit	hit
hurt 다치게 하다	hurt	hurt
let ~하게 하다	let	let

원형	과거형	과거분사형
put 놓다	put	put
read[ri:d] 읽다	read[red]	read[red]
shut 닫다	shut	shut
spread 펼치다	spread	spread

2. A-B-A형 원형-과거분사형이 같은 경우

원형	과거형	과거분사형
become ~이 되다	became	become
come 오다	came	come

원형	과거형	과거분사형
overcome 극복하다	overcame	overcome
run 달리다	ran	run

3. A-B-B형 과거형-과거분사형이 같은 경우

원형	과거형	과거분사형
bring 가져오다	brought	brought
build 짓다, 만들다	built	built
feed 먹이를 주다	fed	fed
feel 느끼다	felt	felt
find 찾다	found	found
get 얻다	got	got(ten)
have 가지다	had	had
hear 듣다	heard	heard
keep 유지하다	kept	kept
lay 놓다, 낳다	laid	laid
lead 이끌다	led	led

원형	과거형	과거분사형
leave 떠나다	left	left
lose 잃다, 지다	lost	lost
make 만들다	made	made
meet 만나다	met	met
send 보내다	sent	sent
sleep 자다	slept	slept
spend 쓰다	spent	spent
tell 말하다	told	told
think 생각하다	thought	thought
understand 이해하다	understood	understood
win 이기다	won	won

4. A-B-C형 원형-과거형-과거분사형이 모두 다른 경우

원형	과거형	과거분사형	원형	과거형	과거분사형
be ~이다, ~하다	was/were	been	hide 숨다	hid	hidden
bear 낳다	bore	born	know 알다	knew	known
begin 시작하다	began	begun	lie 눕다	lay	lain
bite 물다	bit	bitten	mistake 실수하다	mistook	mistaken
blow 불다	blew	blown	ride 타다	rode	ridden
break 깨다	broke	broken	ring 울리다	rang	rung
choose 선택하다	chose	chosen	rise 오르다	rose	risen
do 하다	did	done	see 보다	saw	seen
draw 그리다	drew	drawn	shake 흔들다	shook	shaken
drink 마시다	drank	drunk	show 보여주다	showed	showed shown
drive 운전하다	drove	driven	sing 노래하다	sang	sung
eat 먹다	ate	eaten	sink 가라앉다	sank	sunk sunken
fall 떨어지다, 넘어지다	fell	fallen	sow (씨를) 뿌리다	sowed	sowed sown
fly 날다	flew	flown	speak 말하다	spoke	spoken
forbid 금지하다	forbade	forbidden	steal 훔치다	stole	stolen
forget 잊다	forgot	forgotten	swell 붓다, 부풀다	swelled	swelled swollen
forgive 용서하다	forgave	forgiven	swim 수영하다	swam	swum
freeze 얼다	froze	frozen	take 가지고 가다	took	taken
give 주다	gave	given	throw 던지다	threw	thrown
go 가다	went	gone	wear 입고 있다	wore	worn
grow 자라다	grew	grown	write 쓰다	wrote	written

문법 사항	세부 내용	Starter	Level 1	Level 2	Level 3
be동사	be동사	O	O		
	There + be동사	O	O		
일반동사	일반동사	O	O		
시제	현재시제	O	O	O	
	과거시제	O	O	O	
	미래시제	O	O	O	
	현재진행시제	O	O	O	
	과거진행시제		O	O	
	현재완료시제			O	p.16
	과거완료시제				p.18
	미래완료시제				p.18
조동사	can	O	O	O	p.26
	may	O	O	O	p.26
	will	O	O	O	
	must	O	O	O	p.26
	have to	O	O	O	p.26
	should		O	O	p.26
	would like to			O	
	had better			O	p.28
	used to			O	p.28
	would rather				p.28
	may as well				p.28
	조동사 + have + p.p.				p.30
수동태	수동태			O	p.38
	수동태의 다양한 형태			O	p.38
	4형식/5형식 문장의 수동태			O	p.40
	by 이외의 전치사를 쓰는 수동태			O	p.42
	목적어가 that절인 문장의 수동태				p.42
	구동사의 수동태				p.42
부정사	to부정사		O	O	p.50, 52
	부정사를 목적격 보어로 쓰는 동사		O		p.54
	to부정사의 의미상 주어			O	p.56
	to부정사의 시제, 태				p.56
	to부정사 구문		O	O	p.58
	독립 부정사				p.58
동명사	동명사		O	O	p.66
분사	현재분사, 과거분사			O	p.76
	분사구문			O	p.78
	주의해야 할 분사구문				p.80
동사의 종류	주격 보어가 필요한 동사		O		
	감각동사	O	O	O	
	두 개의 목적어가 필요한 동사(수여동사)	O	O	O	
	목적격 보어가 필요한 동사		O	O	

문법 사항	세부 내용	Starter	Level 1	Level 2	Level 3
문장의 종류	명령문, 청유문, 감탄문	O	O		
	의문사 의문문	O	O		
	부정의문문, 선택의문문, 부가의문문		O		
명사와 관사	셀 수 있는 명사, 셀 수 없는 명사	O	O		
	관사		O		
대명사	인칭대명사	O	O		
	재귀대명사		O	O	
	지시대명사	O	O		
	비인칭 주어 it	O	O		
	부정대명사		O	O	
형용사와 부사	형용사, 부사	O	O		
비교구문	원급/비교급/최상급 비교		O	O	p.124
	비교구문을 이용한 표현			O	p.126
전치사	장소 전치사	O	O		
	시간 전치사	O	O		
	기타 전치사		O		
접속사	등위접속사	O	O		
	시간 접속사	O	O	O	p.102
	이유 접속사	O	O	O	p.102
	결과 접속사			O	p.102
	조건 접속사		O	O	p.102
	양보 접속사			O	p.102
	that		O	O	
	명령문 + and/or		O	O	
	상관접속사		O	O	p.104
	간접의문문				p.104
관계사	관계대명사			O	p.88
	관계부사			O	p.90
	주의해야 할 관계사의 쓰임			O	p.92
	관계사의 계속적 용법				p.92
	복합관계사				p.94
가정법	가정법 과거, 가정법 과거완료			O	p.112
	혼합 가정법				p.112
	I wish 가정법			O	p.114
	as if 가정법			O	p.114
	It's time 가정법				p.114
	Without[But for] 가정법				p.116
	if를 생략한 가정법				p.116
일치와 화법	시제의 일치			O	p.136
	수의 일치				p.134
	화법			O	p.138
특수구문	강조, 도치, 병렬, 부정, 동격, 생략				p.146, 148

MEMO

Smart, Useful, and Essential Grammar

HACKERS
GRAMMAR
SMART

3
LEVEL

초판 4쇄 발행 2023년 12월 4일
초판 1쇄 발행 2022년 1월 3일

지은이	해커스 어학연구소
펴낸곳	㈜해커스 어학연구소
펴낸이	해커스 어학연구소 출판팀
주소	서울특별시 서초구 강남대로61길 23 ㈜해커스 어학연구소
고객센터	02-537-5000
교재 관련 문의	publishing@hackers.com
	해커스북 사이트(HackersBook.com) 고객센터 Q&A 게시판
동영상강의	star.Hackers.com
ISBN	978-89-6542-457-4 (53740)
Serial Number	01-04-01

중고등영어 1위,
해커스북 HackersBook.com

· 깊은 이해로 이끄는 **예문/문제 해석**
· 불규칙 동사의 확실한 암기를 돕는 **불규칙 동사 테스트**
· 학습한 단어의 암기 여부를 쉽게 점검할 수 있는 **단어 리스트 및 단어 테스트**
· 교재의 단어를 언제 어디서나 들으면서 외우는 **단어암기 MP3**
· 서술형 시험을 완벽하게 대비할 수 있는 **영작/해석 워크시트**

한경비즈니스 선정 2020 한국품질만족도 교육(온·오프라인 중·고등영어) 부문 1위 해커스

HACKERS
GRAMMAR
SMART
LEVEL **3**

WORKBOOK

HACKERS
GRAMMAR
SMART
LEVEL **3**

WORKBOOK

HACKERS

UNIT 01 현재완료시제

Answers p.21

A 밑줄 친 부분이 어법상 맞으면 O를 쓰고, 틀리면 바르게 고쳐 쓰시오.

1 I have been listening to the radio <u>for</u> this morning. → _____

2 Sarah <u>has been</u> to Italy, so she doesn't live here now. → _____

3 The baby <u>slept</u> on the sofa since 2 o'clock. → _____

4 Ryan <u>has received</u> a scholarship for three years. → _____

B <보기>의 동사를 현재완료시제나 과거시제 형태로 바꿔 문장을 완성하시오.

<보기>	stay	graduate	complete	post

1 Anna _____ her diary on the blog for two years.

2 My brother _____ from middle school in 2017.

3 I _____ in Jejudo since last month.

4 The researchers _____ the science project a few months ago.

C 현재완료시제나 현재완료진행시제를 이용하여 다음 두 문장을 한 문장으로 연결하시오.

1 Mr. Shaw fixed my computer. It's working now.
→ Mr. Shaw _____.

2 They started to eat dinner an hour ago. They're still eating dinner.
→ They _____.

3 The athletes started to prepare for the Olympics last year. They're still preparing for it.
→ The athletes _____.

D 우리말과 같도록 괄호 안의 말을 알맞게 배열하시오.

1 그 밴드는 최근에 새로운 앨범을 발매했다. (album, has, the, released, new, band, a)
= _____ recently.

2 도보 여행자들은 몇 시간 동안 해안을 따라 걷고 있다. (the, been, along, have, walking, coast)
= The hikers _____ for hours.

3 나는 그 유명한 작가의 최신작 소설을 이미 읽었다. (read, latest, I, novel, have, already, the)
= _____ by the famous author.

4 선생님은 미국 역사에 대해 30분 동안 이야기하고 계신다. (talking, history, has, about, American, been)
= The teacher _____ for 30 minutes.

UNIT 02 과거완료시제와 미래완료시제

A 괄호 안의 동사를 활용하여 완료진행시제 문장을 완성하시오.

1 By next month, I _____ Spanish for a year. (learn)

2 Ethan _____ with his friends when I went to see him. (chat)

3 Ms. Dean _____ for hours by the time she arrives at the airport. (drive)

4 The girl _____ her father until he finished washing his car. (help)

B 밑줄 친 부분이 어법상 맞으면 O를 쓰고, 틀리면 바르게 고쳐 쓰시오.

1 In 30 minutes, I <u>had been studying</u> for two hours. → _____

2 They <u>had not known</u> each other before they met at the party. → _____

3 It's 11 A.M. now. He <u>had been swimming</u> for an hour by noon. → _____

4 Mia <u>will have been taking</u> a shower when I called her. → _____

C 우리말과 같도록 괄호 안의 말을 활용하여 문장을 완성하시오.

1 내년이면 그들은 역사 박물관을 3년째 짓고 있을 것이다. (build the history museum)

= They _____ for three years by next year.

2 모든 학생들이 앉은 후에 강의가 시작됐다. (sit down)

= The lecture started after all the students _____.

3 Olivia가 도착할 때쯤, 직원들은 상점을 닫았을 것이다. (close the shop)

= By the time Olivia arrives, the employees _____.

4 비가 오기 시작했을 때 그 소년들은 두 시간 동안 축구를 하고 있었다. (play soccer)

= The boys _____ for two hours when it started to rain.

D 우리말과 같도록 괄호 안의 말을 알맞게 배열하시오.

1 내가 집에 도착했을 때 그 TV 쇼는 이미 끝났었다. (had, the, ended, already, TV, show)

= _____ when I got home.

2 만약 그가 롤러코스터를 다시 탄다면, 그는 그것을 다섯 번째 탔을 것이다. (five, have, ridden, he, times, will, it)

= If he rides the roller coaster again, _____.

3 Linda는 그곳으로 이사하기 전에 부산을 여러 번 방문했었다. (many, had, Busan, times, visited, Linda)

= _____ before she moved there.

4 알람이 울릴 때쯤 그 소년은 일어났을 것이다. (will, up, the, woken, boy, have)

= _____ by the time the alarm goes off.

Chapter Test +

Answers p.21

[1-3] 다음 빈칸에 들어갈 알맞은 것을 고르시오.

1

| Joyce _____ to Spain once. |

① travels   ② has traveled
③ will be traveled   ④ is traveling
⑤ will have traveled

2

| The soccer match _____ before we arrived at the stadium. |

① starts   ② is starting
③ has started   ④ had started
⑤ will have started

3

| Henry _____ in line for an hour when he finally purchased the ticket. |

① stands
② is standing
③ has been standing
④ had been standing
⑤ will have been standing

4 다음 빈칸에 들어갈 말로 어색한 것은?

| Molly has studied at the city library _____. |

① two weeks ago   ② before
③ since last year   ④ for three months
⑤ five times

[5-6] 다음 대화의 빈칸에 들어갈 알맞은 것을 고르시오.

5

| A: Is Kate still in Korea?
B: No. She _____ to her home country. |

① is   ② goes
③ has been   ④ has gone
⑤ will have been

6

| A: We have already visited the art gallery twice.
B: You're right. If we go there one more time, we _____ the gallery three times. |

① visited   ② have visited
③ had visited   ④ had been visiting
⑤ will have visited

서술형

[7-8] 완료진행시제를 이용하여 다음 두 문장을 한 문장으로 연결하시오.

7

| Susan started to watch a movie two hours ago. She is still watching it.
→ Susan _____ a movie for two hours. |

8

| Alan has been exercising for five years. He will exercise next year, too.
→ Alan _____ for six years by next year. |

[9-10] 다음 문장의 밑줄 친 부분을 바르게 고쳐 쓰시오.

9

> Tina <u>has been</u> the leader of the debate team a year ago.

→ _____

10

> I <u>have been washing</u> the dishes when Sarah came over.

→ _____

[11-12] 다음 중 어법상 <u>어색한</u> 것을 고르시오.

11 ① Billy hasn't slept well for weeks.
② We have never been abroad before last summer.
③ My parents have been married for 20 years.
④ I have been waiting for him since 3 P.M.
⑤ Doris has just come back from a long holiday.

12 ① Jennifer felt better because she had taken a break.
② The flight will have landed by the time you call them.
③ Abigail has been knitting a sweater for over a month.
④ My dad had been watching TV when I got home.
⑤ Mr. Jones had been skiing for five years by next year.

13 다음 (A)~(C)에 들어갈 말이 바르게 짝지어진 것은?

> • I ___(A)___ in Seoul before I moved to Daegu.
> • We have been studying ___(B)___ 7 P.M.
> • They ___(C)___ in Europe for a month by tomorrow.

	(A)	(B)	(C)
①	have lived	for	have stayed
②	had lived	since	had stayed
③	had lived	since	will have stayed
④	have lived	since	have stayed
⑤	had lived	for	will have stayed

14 다음 중 밑줄 친 부분이 어법상 바른 것은?

① He realized that he <u>has forgotten</u> his mom's birthday.
② Danielle <u>has been taking</u> a shower when the package arrived.
③ I <u>have studied</u> for the math test yesterday.
④ Marilyn <u>had played</u> the violin until she was ten.
⑤ By tomorrow, it <u>has been snowing</u> for four days.

[15-16] 괄호 안의 동사를 활용하여 빈칸에 알맞은 말을 쓰시오.

15

> I read the novel three times. If I read it once more, I _____ _____ it four times. (read)

16

> Alex apologized to Emma because he _____ _____ a big mistake. (make)

[17-18] 우리말과 같도록 괄호 안의 말을 알맞게 배열하시오.

17
> 이 나무는 2001년 이후로 여기에 서 있어왔다.
> (been, 2001, here, has, since, standing)

= This tree _____.

18
> 그의 여동생이 문을 두드렸을 때 그는 40분 동안 씻고 있었다. (for, washing, had, minutes, 40, been)

= He _____ when his sister knocked on the door.

[19-20] 주어진 문장의 밑줄 친 부분과 용법이 같은 것을 고르시오.

19
> The kid has already eaten all of the cookies.

① It has been so cold for the whole week.
② Have you ever been to Germany?
③ I have never tried Mexican food.
④ My dad hasn't read today's newspaper yet.
⑤ The basketball player has broken his arm, so he can't play anymore.

20
> Charlotte has lost her favorite skateboard.

① I haven't visited the new museum before.
② Roy has seen the musical three times.
③ Diana has just arrived at the classroom.
④ We have been friends since kindergarten.
⑤ She has left her hometown, and she'll never come back.

고난도

21 다음 중 어법상 바른 것의 개수는?

> ⓐ Isabella has lost her ring last month.
> ⓑ We will have completed the assignment by next week.
> ⓒ Marcus has been playing PC games for hours, so he decided to stop.
> ⓓ The train had already left when I arrived at the station.
> ⓔ I have taken boxing classes since 2019.

① 1개   ② 2개   ③ 3개
④ 4개   ⑤ 5개

서술형

[22-24] 우리말과 같도록 괄호 안의 말을 활용하여 완료시제나 완료진행시제 문장을 완성하시오.

22
> Harry는 그 식당에 여섯 번 가본 적이 있다. (be, that restaurant)

= Harry _____ six times.

23
> 만약 Judy가 장미 한 송이를 더 심으면, 그녀는 장미를 다섯 송이 심게 될 것이다. (plant, roses)

= If Judy plants one more rose, _____.

24
> 내가 교실로 들어갔을 때, 선생님은 수업을 이미 시작하셨었다. (already, start, the lesson)

= When I entered the classroom, the teacher _____.

Chapter 02 조동사

UNIT 01   can, may, must, should

A 다음 빈칸에 알맞은 말을 <보기>에서 한 번씩만 골라 쓰시오.

<보기>   can't   may   don't have to   should

1 People _____ drink plenty of water for their health.

2 If you want, you _____ sit here. This seat is empty.

3 I know the news is just a rumor. It _____ be true.

4 You _____ pay a parking fee. It's free.

B 다음 두 문장의 의미가 같도록 빈칸에 알맞은 말을 쓰시오.

1 You may enter the building from 7 A.M. to 9 P.M.
→ You _____ _____ the building from 7 A.M. to 9 P.M.

2 We need not practice dancing. The show has been canceled.
→ We _____ _____ _____ _____ dancing. The show has been canceled.

3 You should water these flowers three times a week.
→ You _____ _____ _____ these flowers three times a week.

C <보기>의 말과 괄호 안의 말을 활용하여 대화를 완성하시오.

<보기>   can   can't   must

1 A: _____ me the pepper? (you, pass)
B: Sure. Here you go.

2 A: You _____ slowly in school zones. (drive)
B: OK. I'll slow down.

3 A: Is that boy Daniel?
B: That boy _____ Daniel. Daniel is resting at home. (be)

D 우리말과 같도록 괄호 안의 말을 알맞게 배열하시오.

1 오늘 밤에는 추울지도 모른다. 자기 전에 창문을 닫아라. (cold, be, tonight, may, it)
= _____. Close the window before you go to bed.

2 우리는 우리의 환경을 보호해야 한다. (protect, our, ought, to, we, environment)
= _____.

3 당신은 7세 미만의 아이들에 대한 비용을 지불할 필요가 없습니다. (to, have, pay, don't, you)
= _____ for children under the age of seven.

Chapter 02 조동사 **7**

A 밑줄 친 부분이 어법상 맞으면 O를 쓰고, 틀리면 바르게 고쳐 쓰시오.

1 I would rather <u>to go home</u> now as it's getting dark. → _____

2 There used to <u>being</u> a train station here. → _____

3 We may <u>well as</u> take a short walk to calm down. → _____

4 Emma <u>had</u> better find someone to give her advice. → _____

5 I would <u>not rather</u> blame others anymore. → _____

6 You may as well <u>stay</u> warm tonight. → _____

7 I used <u>hang</u> out with Mike in kindergarten. → _____

8 You had <u>rather</u> tell Julia that you are sorry. → _____

B 다음 빈칸에 알맞은 말을 <보기>에서 골라 쓰시오.

<보기> would rather used to may as well

1 Edward _____ be a soccer player in the past.

2 We _____ go somewhere before the holiday ends.

3 I _____ take the medicine than go to the hospital.

C 우리말과 같도록 괄호 안의 말을 알맞게 배열하시오.

1 우리는 Chris에게 수영하는 법을 가르쳐 달라고 요청하는 편이 좋겠다. (ask, to, as, may, Chris, teach, well, swimming, us)

= We _____.

2 Jones씨는 어렸을 때 런던에서 공부하곤 했다. (in, study, to, used, London)

= Mr. Jones _____ when he was young.

3 나는 치마를 입느니 차라리 바지를 입겠다. (would, pants, a, rather, wear, skirt, than)

= I _____.

4 너는 매일 산책하는 것이 낫겠다. (better, take, every, had, a, day, walk)

= You _____.

UNIT 03 조동사 + have + p.p.

A <보기>의 조동사와 괄호 안의 동사를 활용하여 빈칸에 쓰시오.

<보기>	can't	must	should

1 He forgot his password. He _____ _____ _____ it somewhere. (write)

2 Olivia _____ _____ _____ all the apples in the fridge. There's none left. (eat)

3 She _____ _____ _____ the car. She doesn't have a driver's license. (drive)

B 다음 두 문장의 의미가 비슷하도록 「조동사 + have + p.p.」를 활용하여 문장을 완성하시오.

1 It's not possible that you solved all the questions in 30 minutes.
→ You _____ all the questions in 30 minutes.

2 I am sorry that I didn't see a doctor before the symptoms got worse.
→ I _____ a doctor before the symptoms got worse.

3 I'm not sure whether they expected the business to succeed.
→ They _____ the business to succeed.

4 I'm sure that something burned in the oven.
→ Something _____ in the oven.

C 주어진 문장을 우리말로 해석하시오.

1 You should have taken public transportation on Monday morning.
= _____ .

2 We could have avoided the worst situation.
= _____ .

3 She may have been a ballerina in the past.
= _____ .

D 우리말과 같도록 괄호 안의 말을 알맞게 배열하시오.

1 나는 너에게 전화했어야 했지만, 나의 휴대폰을 충전하는 것을 잊어버렸다. (should, you, I, have, called)
= _____ , but I forgot to charge my cell phone.

2 그의 지갑이 사라졌다. 그것은 도둑맞은 것이 틀림없다. (have, stolen, it, been, must)
= His wallet has disappeared. _____ .

3 그들은 자러 갔을 리가 없다. 불이 켜져 있다. (gone, they, to, have, can't, bed)
= _____ . The lights are on.

Chapter Test ✛

Answers p.22

[1-3] 다음 빈칸에 들어갈 알맞은 것을 고르시오.

1

> You _____ eat the cupcake on the table if you want.

① may　　　　　　② must not
③ cannot　　　　　④ used to
⑤ have to

2

> I _____ hear Kelly's voice because of the noise.

① must not　　　　② should not
③ cannot　　　　　④ would rather not
⑤ had better not

3

> Jeff _____ PC games yesterday. I saw him working on his homework all day.

① must have played　　② can't have played
③ should have played　④ might have played
⑤ could have played

4 다음 우리말을 영작한 것 중 어색한 것을 모두 고르시오.

① 그녀는 그때 바빴던 것이 틀림없다.
　= She can't have been busy at that time.
② 너는 주스를 마시느니 차라리 물을 마시겠니?
　= Would you rather drink water than juice?
③ 우리는 여기서 조용히 대화할 필요가 없다.
　= We must not talk quietly here.
④ Ryan은 그의 친구를 만나서 기쁜 것이 틀림없다.
　= Ryan must be happy to meet his friend.
⑤ 그 아이는 길에서 넘어졌을 수도 있었다.
　= The kid could have fallen down on the street.

서술형

5 다음 두 문장의 의미가 같도록 빈칸에 알맞은 말을 쓰시오.

> Ms. Hill would drink three cups of coffee every day.
> → Ms. Hill _____ _____ _____ three cups of coffee every day.

6 주어진 문장의 밑줄 친 부분과 의미가 같은 것은?

> All players <u>should</u> follow the rules of the game.

① can　　　　　　② ought to
③ used to　　　　④ would
⑤ would rather

[7-8] 다음 중 어법상 어색한 것을 고르시오.

7 ① You had better throw away your old stuff.
② People should put on sunscreen in summer.
③ The machine could be dangerous to kids.
④ We don't need not worry about little things.
⑤ The singer on stage must be very popular.

8 ① We should have taken Jake's advice.
② Lucy can't have been in school on Saturday.
③ He might have cried after hearing the news.
④ They could have finished their work earlier.
⑤ The teacher must have see us running in the hallway.

[9-10] 다음 대화의 빈칸에 들어갈 알맞은 것을 고르시오.

9

A: Should I fill in every blank on this form?
B: You _____ write everything. We just need your name and phone number.

① can't   ② must   ③ could not
④ need not   ⑤ ought to

10

A: Timothy didn't show up at the meeting.
B: He _____ have woken up late. I heard he went to bed late last night.

① can   ② can't   ③ may
④ should   ⑤ would

[11-12] 다음 글의 빈칸에 들어갈 말이 순서대로 짝지어진 것을 고르시오.

11

In art class, the teacher provides brushes for the students. So, you _____ bring one. However, if you want, you _____ use your own brush.

① must – can
② must – used to
③ should – can
④ need not – can
⑤ need not – used to

12

I made Sharon angry yesterday. I _____ sorry to her right away, but I didn't. Since it was my fault, she _____ very angry at me. I'll call her and apologize today.

① should have said – must have been
② should have said – can't have been
③ can't have said – can't have been
④ can't have said – must have been
⑤ could have said – can't have been

[13-15] 다음 문장에서 어법상 어색한 부분을 찾아 쓰고 바르게 고쳐 쓰시오.

13

We ought to not be rude to one another.

_____ → _____

14

I must have had breakfast. I already feel hungry.

_____ → _____

15

My mom used to working as a history teacher in her 30s.

_____ → _____

16 다음 중 짝지어진 두 문장의 의미가 <u>다른</u> 것은?

① We should prepare for the speech contest.
   → We ought to prepare for the speech contest.
② You don't have to feel sorry for me.
   → You don't need to feel sorry for me.
③ I shouldn't have repeated the same error.
   → I can't have repeated the same error.
④ Samantha would go to ballet classes.
   → Samantha used to go to ballet classes.
⑤ They may have heard the song before.
   → They might have heard the song before.

[17-18] 다음 중 밑줄 친 조동사의 의미가 나머지 넷과 다른 것을 고르시오.

17 ① My sister can jump really high.
② Rachael can speak Chinese well.
③ I can climb the mountain in an hour.
④ You can borrow my laptop if you need it.
⑤ Benjamin can cook spaghetti well.

18 ① We must do our best in everything.
② The crying baby must be hungry.
③ I must take care of the dog today.
④ Passengers must wear seat belts.
⑤ You must come home early today.

19 다음 중 어법상 바른 것은?
① We had not better go out today.
② He would be short when he was young.
③ Ms. Smith may have be sad yesterday.
④ All visitors should to sign their names.
⑤ I might have caught a cold.

20 다음 우리말을 영작할 때 빈칸에 들어갈 알맞은 것은?

나는 수업에 늦느니 차라리 택시를 타겠다.
= I _____ take a taxi than be late to class.

① may
② could
③ had better
④ would rather
⑤ may as well

21 다음 중 어법상 바른 것끼리 묶인 것은?

ⓐ We must checking the door before we go.
ⓑ She is able to lift 30kg with just one arm.
ⓒ I should help her when she asked before.
ⓓ He could have told the truth, but he didn't.
ⓔ Joshua need not to go to school today.

① ⓐ, ⓑ
② ⓐ, ⓒ
③ ⓑ, ⓓ
④ ⓒ, ⓔ
⑤ ⓓ, ⓔ

22 우리말과 같도록 주어진 <조건>에 맞게 영작하시오.

나는 그 식물에 물을 줬어야 했다.

<조건>　1. water, plant를 활용하시오.
　　　　2. 6단어로 쓰시오.

= _____.

[23-24] 우리말과 같도록 괄호 안의 동사를 활용하여 빈칸에 쓰시오.

23
우리는 저 버스를 타는 편이 좋겠다. (take)

= We _____ _____ _____
_____ that bus.

24
그들은 강에서 함께 수영하곤 했다. (swim)

= They _____ _____ _____ in the river together.

UNIT 01 수동태의 쓰임

Answers p.23

A 밑줄 친 부분이 어법상 맞으면 O를 쓰고, 틀리면 바르게 고쳐 쓰시오.

1 Many exciting movies are <u>be shown</u> at the theater now. → _____

2 This machine <u>has to be tested</u> again before people use it. → _____

3 The terrible accident <u>was happened</u> last night. → _____

4 Some trees in the forest will <u>cut</u> by the carpenters. → _____

5 The flight to Tokyo has <u>been delayed</u> because of storm. → _____

B <보기>의 동사를 활용하여 문장을 완성하시오. (단, 현재시제로 쓰시오.)

<보기>	resemble	visit	deliver

1 The newspaper _____ every morning.

2 This website _____ by many people around the world.

3 The brothers _____ each other very much.

C 다음 능동태 문장을 수동태로 바꿔 쓰시오.

1 Amy has collected old coins since 2015.
→ Old coins _____ since 2015.

2 Jane's friends are preparing a surprise party.
→ A surprise party _____ .

3 The company will release the new smartwatch next month.
→ The new smartwatch _____ next month.

D 우리말과 같도록 괄호 안의 말을 알맞게 배열하시오.

1 Rachel이 보낸 이메일은 다음 주까지 확인되어도 된다. (by, week, may, next, checked, be)
= The e-mail from Rachel _____ .

2 그 마을은 지진에 의해 파괴되었다. (the, been, earthquake, has, destroyed, by)
= That town _____ .

3 그 재정 문제는 관리자들에 의해 논의되고 있다. (managers, the, discussed, being, is, by)
= The financial issue _____ .

4 이 스웨터는 차가운 물에서 세탁되어야 한다. (must, in, water, washed, be, cold)
= This sweater _____ .

UNIT 02   4형식/5형식 문장의 수동태

Answers p.23

A   다음 문장의 밑줄 친 부분을 바르게 고쳐 쓰시오.

1 The cat was seen chase a mouse.   → _____

2 The ball was passed for the soccer player by his teammate.   → _____

3 Nicole was made to angry by Scott's impolite behavior.   → _____

4 Some shelters were built to the homeless by the city.   → _____

5 The ticket should be shown of the clerk to enter the museum.   → _____

B   다음 능동태 문장을 수동태로 바꿔 쓰시오.

1 The flight attendants told the passengers to take a seat.
→ The passengers _____ .

2 Her grandfather gave Maria a beautiful watch.
→ Maria _____ .
→ A beautiful watch _____ .

3 The police officer made him get out of the car.
→ He _____ .

4 Luke heard Paul sing in the bathroom.
→ Paul _____ .

5 The club members elected Matthew president.
→ Matthew _____ .

C   우리말과 같도록 괄호 안의 말을 알맞게 배열하시오.

1 그 편지는 David에 의해 그의 친구에게 보내졌다. (was, to, his, sent, friend)
= The letter _____ by David.

2 Claire는 나에 의해 거리를 걷는 것이 보였다. (walking, was, seen, the, down, street)
= Claire _____ by me.

3 법정 안의 사람들은 판사에 의해 조용히 할 것이 요청되었다. (be, were, to, silent, asked)
= The people in the courtroom _____ by the judge.

4 Evan은 선생님에 의해 복도에 서있게 되었다. (made, in, to, stand, hallway, was, the)
= Evan _____ by the teacher.

A 밑줄 친 부분이 어법상 맞으면 O를 쓰고, 틀리면 바르게 고쳐 쓰시오.

1 My younger sister is often <u>looked by after</u> me. → _____

2 The playground is crowded <u>in</u> children on weekends. → _____

3 It <u>believes</u> that the dinosaurs existed millions of years ago. → _____

4 The African tribe's unique tradition is known <u>to</u> few people. → _____

B <보기>의 말을 활용하여 빈칸에 쓰시오. (단, 현재시제로 쓰시오.)

<보기>	fill	cover	worry

1 The stadium _____ _____ _____ baseball fans.

2 They _____ _____ _____ arriving late for the party.

3 The roads _____ _____ _____ snow after the heavy snowfall.

C 다음 능동태 문장을 수동태로 바꿔 쓰시오.

1 We should not put off the meeting.
→ The meeting _____.

2 In some cultures, people believe that 13 is an unlucky number.
→ In some cultures, it _____.
→ In some cultures, 13 _____.

3 People say that garlic is good for preventing cancer.
→ It _____.
→ Garlic _____.

D 우리말과 같도록 괄호 안의 말을 알맞게 배열하시오.

1 다리 하나를 건설하는 것은 수년이 걸린다고 생각된다. (bridge, that, thought, a, constructing, is)
= It _____ takes many years.

2 이 인기 있는 잼은 블루베리로 만들어진다. (from, made, blueberries, is)
= This popular jam _____.

3 Lena는 사회 문제에 흥미가 있다. (social, in, interested, is, issues)
= Lena _____.

Chapter Test ✛

Answers p.23

[1-3] 다음 빈칸에 들어갈 알맞은 것을 고르시오.

1

| A history film _____ to us during class. |

① shows   ② showed
③ is showing   ④ was shown
⑤ was showing

2

| Susan was made _____ to bed before 11 P.M. |

① go   ② going
③ to go   ④ to going
⑤ be gone

3

| The books _____ to the library by George tomorrow. |

① return   ② will return
③ were returned   ④ will be returned
⑤ will be returning

4 다음 빈칸에 들어갈 말이 나머지 넷과 다른 것은?

① Fred is expected _____ come back from his trip tomorrow.
② Instructions are being told _____ the visitors by the curator.
③ The opera singer was heard _____ sing on the stage by the audience.
④ A new backpack was bought _____ my sister by my mom.
⑤ A free coupon was given _____ every customer.

[5-6] 다음 우리말을 알맞게 영작한 것을 고르시오.

5

| 이 컴퓨터는 학생들에 의해 사용되면 안 된다. |

① This computer must not use by students.
② This computer must be used by students.
③ This computer must not be used by students.
④ This computer must not be using by students.
⑤ This computer must not been used by students.

6

| 그 문제는 Potter씨에 의해 다루어졌다. |

① The matter is dealing by Mr. Potter.
② The matter is dealt with Mr. Potter.
③ The matter was dealt by Mr. Potter.
④ The matter was dealing with by Mr. Potter.
⑤ The matter was dealt with by Mr. Potter.

서술형
[7-8] 다음 문장에서 어법상 어색한 부분을 찾아 쓰고 바르게 고쳐 쓰시오.

7

| This smartphone is belonged to Sally. |

_____ → _____

8

| The form should sign in order to get a new library card. |

_____ → _____

[9-10] 다음 중 어법상 어색한 것을 고르시오.

9　① This house was building three month ago.
　② The car accident happened yesterday.
　③ The knives must be kept away from children.
　④ A sharp question was asked of the speaker.
　⑤ A jazz song is being played on the radio.

10　① The new movie is said to be boring.
　② Generous people are looked up by others.
　③ It is believed that climate change was the cause of the flood.
　④ People were surprised at the discovery of DNA.
　⑤ All the furniture is covered with dust.

서술형

11 다음 능동태를 수동태로 바꾼 문장에서 어법상 어색한 부분을 찾아 쓰고 바르게 고쳐 쓰시오.

> I saw Kate walk with her dog last night.
> → Kate was seen walk with her dog last night by me.

_____ → _____

12 다음 대화의 빈칸에 들어갈 말이 순서대로 짝지어진 것은?

> A: I heard that you were joining the school baseball team. Is that true?
> B: Yes. I _____ onto the team by the coach yesterday.
> A: Wow! When is your first game?
> B: I'm not sure yet. I was told _____ on practicing for now.

① accepted – to focus
② am accepted – focus
③ am accepted – to focus
④ was accepted – focus
⑤ was accepted – to focus

[13-14] 다음 빈칸에 공통으로 들어갈 알맞은 것을 고르시오.

13
> • Graham Bell's new invention was shown _____ the public in 1876.
> • The Grand Canyon is known _____ many travelers as a tourist attraction.

① to　　　　② for　　　　③ of
④ with　　　⑤ at

14
> • The concert hall is crowded _____ fans.
> • The box was filled _____ lots of toys for babies.

① to　　　　② for　　　　③ of
④ with　　　⑤ at

서술형

[15-16] 다음 문장을 수동태로 바꿔 쓰시오.

15
> Dad taught us useful English expressions.
> → We _____
> _____ by Dad.

16
> My brother saw me dance in my room.
> → I _____
> _____ by my brother.

17 다음 중 문장의 태를 <u>잘못</u> 바꾼 것을 <u>모두</u> 고르시오.

① The experiment will be done by scientists.
  → Scientists will do the experiment.
② The artist was displaying the artworks.
  → The artworks were being displayed by the artist.
③ Reading books is thought to be helpful.
  → People think that reading books is helpful.
④ We must not look down on disabled people.
  → Disabled people must not be looked down by us.
⑤ Jessie bought Anthony a baseball cap.
  → A baseball cap was bought Anthony by Jessie.

[18-20] 우리말과 같도록 괄호 안의 말을 활용하여 문장을 완성하시오.

18
> 그 도시에 대한 어떤 질문이든 여행 가이드에게 물어질 수 있다. (can, ask)

= Any questions about the city _____ the tour guide.

19
> 나의 노트북은 Tiffany에 의해 사용되고 있다. (use)

= My laptop _____ by Tiffany.

20
> 파리는 프랑스의 수도라고 알려져 있다. (know, be)

= Paris _____ the capital city of France.

[21-22] 괄호 안의 말을 활용하여 빈칸에 알맞은 말을 쓰시오.

21
> These rooms _____ _____ _____ by students who want to study together. (may, reserve)

22
> The patient _____ _____ _____ _____ _____ by his family now. (take care of)

23 다음 (A)~(C)에 들어갈 말이 바르게 짝지어진 것은?

> Sam likes his bag because it is ___(A)___ fake leather. At school, he learned that many animals ___(B)___ to make leather products. He is interested ___(C)___ saving wild animals, so he is trying to avoid animal products.

	(A)	(B)	(C)
①	made of	killed	in
②	made by	killed	by
③	made by	are killed	of
④	made of	are killed	in
⑤	made of	killed	of

24 다음 중 어법상 바른 것은?

① The residents were stayed calm during the earthquake.
② The graduating students were given flowers.
③ Everyone was satisfied of the dessert.
④ K-pop songs are said to being popular these days.
⑤ A package was sent of Joyce by her cousin in New York.

Chapter 04 부정사

UNIT 01 to부정사의 명사적 용법

Answers p.24

A 다음 두 문장의 의미가 같도록 to부정사를 이용하여 문장을 완성하시오.

1 To breathe in space without any equipment is impossible.

→ It _____.

2 They are talking about where they should go for vacation.

→ They are talking about _____.

3 Can you tell me whom I should call in emergency?

→ Can you tell me _____?

4 To feel many different emotions is natural.

→ It _____.

5 I asked the doctor when I should take the medicine.

→ I asked the doctor _____.

B 우리말과 같도록 괄호 안의 말을 활용하여 빈칸에 쓰시오.

1 Luke는 나의 질문에 대답하는 것을 거부했다. (answer)

= Luke refused _____ _____ my question.

2 그는 금메달을 획득하는 것이 어렵다는 것을 알게 되었다. (win)

= He found _____ difficult _____ _____ a gold medal.

3 나는 음량을 어떻게 줄이는지 모른다. (turn down)

= I don't know _____ _____ _____ _____ the volume.

4 그 기관의 목표는 도시의 대기 오염을 줄이는 것이다. (reduce)

= The organization's goal _____ _____ _____ the air pollution in the city.

C 우리말과 같도록 괄호 안의 말을 알맞게 배열하시오.

1 우리는 주말 동안 무엇을 할지 계획하고 있다. (what, are, to, we, do, planning)

= _____ during the weekend.

2 현대 사회에서 법을 따르는 것은 중요하다. (important, the, is, follow, to, law, it)

= _____ in modern society.

3 설명서는 그 기계를 사용하는 것을 쉽게 해 준다. (it, use, makes, to, the, easy, machine)

= The manual _____.

4 나는 나의 친구들과 좋은 관계를 유지하기를 기대한다. (maintain, to, good, expect, a, relationship)

= I _____ with my friends.

A to부정사를 이용하여 다음 두 문장을 한 문장으로 연결하시오.

1 They have many issues. They are going to talk about the issues.
→ They have many issues _____.

2 Noah closed the window. He wanted to keep his room warm.
→ Noah closed the window _____.

3 Grace must be clever. She found a better solution.
→ Grace must be clever _____.

4 I have pens in different colors. I will write with the pens.
→ I have pens in different colors _____.

B 다음 두 문장의 의미가 같도록 「be동사 + to부정사」를 이용하여 문장을 완성하시오.

1 The prince was destined to become the king of the country.
→ The prince _____ the king of the country.

2 My family is going to travel across the country by car.
→ My family _____ across the country by car.

3 If they intend to win first prize, they need to cooperate with each other.
→ If they _____ first prize, they need to cooperate with each other.

C 주어진 문장을 우리말로 해석하시오.

1 We woke up early to see the sunrise.
= _____.

2 I was delighted to hear about the welcome event.
= _____.

3 There are many things to learn from mistakes.
= _____.

D 우리말과 같도록 괄호 안의 말을 알맞게 배열하시오.

1 그 여행자는 런던에서 머물 장소를 찾고 있다. (stay, for, is, London, a, to, place, searching, in)
= The tourist _____.

2 그들은 그 차 사고를 봐서 충격받았다. (see, to, car, shocked, were, the, accident)
= They _____.

UNIT 03 　부정사를 목적격 보어로 쓰는 동사

Answers p.25

A 밑줄 친 부분이 어법상 맞으면 O를 쓰고, 틀리면 바르게 고쳐 쓰시오.

1 I asked Jessica not <u>calling</u> late in the evening. → _____

2 Our teacher made us <u>memorize</u> a poem. → _____

3 The boss told the employee <u>send</u> the parcel. → _____

4 We saw the performers <u>marching</u> in the parade. → _____

5 Ella got her sister <u>buy</u> a cake for their mom. → _____

B 다음 빈칸에 알맞은 말을 <보기>에서 한 번씩만 골라 알맞은 형태로 바꿔 쓰시오.

<보기>	be	finish	wait

1 Logan helped me _____ my assignment.

2 Ms. Brown advised us _____ respectful to the elderly.

3 The doctor made the patient _____ for an hour.

<보기>	explore	swim	bring

4 The staff didn't let people _____ cameras inside the concert hall.

5 My father always encourages me _____ unfamiliar things.

6 The kids looked at some fish _____ in the pond.

C 우리말과 같도록 괄호 안의 말을 알맞게 배열하시오.

1 웹사이트 관리자는 내가 그 파일을 다운로드하는 것을 허락했다. (to, file, me, download, allowed, the)
= The website manager _____ .

2 Chloe는 초인종이 울리는 것을 들었고 문을 열기 위해 갔다. (doorbell, the, heard, ring)
= Chloe _____ and went to open the door.

3 나의 반 친구는 내가 그녀의 노트북을 사용하게 해줬다. (laptop, use, let, her, me)
= My classmate _____ .

4 그 트레이너는 우리가 열 번 더 팔굽혀펴기를 하라고 명령했다. (push-ups, to, ordered, us, do)
= The trainer _____ 10 times more.

UNIT 04 to부정사의 의미상 주어, 시제, 태

A 괄호 안의 말을 활용하여 빈칸에 쓰시오.

1 It is convenient _____ _____ to meet online for the group project. (we)

2 It is brave _____ _____ to speak up for the weak. (she)

3 It is impossible _____ _____ to run as fast as you. (I)

4 It is selfish _____ _____ to eat all the pizza by himself. (he)

B 밑줄 친 부분이 어법상 맞으면 O를 쓰고, 틀리면 바르게 고쳐 쓰시오.

1 The science homework needs <u>to finish</u> by tomorrow. → _____

2 It was fun <u>for us</u> to swim in the pool together. → _____

3 Steven seems <u>being honest</u> because I never saw him lie. → _____

4 It was kind <u>for you</u> to help the lost girl find her way. → _____

C 다음 두 문장의 의미가 같도록 문장을 완성하시오.

1 It seems that Isabel wants to go to the movies with you.
→ Isabel seems _____ to go to the movies with you.

2 It seems that the dog looked for a place to rest.
→ The dog seems _____ for a place to rest.

3 It seems that the girl left her umbrella on the train.
→ The girl seems _____ her umbrella on the train.

4 It seems that this bag is made of fake leather.
→ This bag seems _____ of fake leather.

D 우리말과 같도록 괄호 안의 말을 알맞게 배열하시오.

1 그들의 계획은 성공적이었던 것 같다. (have, successful, been, to, seems)
= Their plan _____.

2 나는 자고 있을 때 방해받는 것을 싫어한다. (be, hate, bothered, to)
= I _____ while I'm sleeping.

3 Lucy는 그녀의 팀 동료들에 의해 지지를 받아서 기뻤다. (supported, to, was, be, delighted)
= Lucy _____ by her teammates.

A 밑줄 친 부분이 어법상 맞으면 O를 쓰고, 틀리면 바르게 고쳐 쓰시오.

1 It took me years <u>to learn</u> to play the guitar. → _____

2 He was <u>enough lucky</u> to get the musical tickets. → _____

3 <u>Begin with</u>, I'll show you the latest models. → _____

4 The salmon steak is too salty for me <u>eat</u> without water. → _____

B 다음 두 문장의 의미가 같도록 문장을 완성하시오.

1 Luke is so tall that he can reach the cupboard.
→ Luke is _____ .

2 The sand was so hot that I couldn't walk on it.
→ The sand was _____ .

3 She was too scared to open her eyes.
→ She was _____ .

4 The pool was shallow enough for kids to swim in.
→ The pool was _____ .

C 주어진 문장을 우리말로 해석하시오.

1 To make matters worse, he had a fever.
= _____ .

2 It will take me three days to write the essay.
= _____ .

3 So to speak, the singer is a legend.
= _____ .

D 우리말과 같도록 괄호 안의 말을 알맞게 배열하시오.

1 저 오렌지들은 먹기에 너무 쓰다. (to, bitter, too, eat)
= Those oranges are _____ .

2 솔직히 말하면, 나는 네가 제시간에 올 것을 예상하지 않았다. (with, be, frank, to, you)
= _____ , I didn't expect you to come on time.

3 우리가 연을 날릴 만큼 충분히 바람이 불지 않는다. (fly, for, to, enough, a, windy, us, kite)
= It is not _____ .

Chapter Test ✛

Answers p.25

[1-3] 다음 빈칸에 들어갈 알맞은 것을 고르시오.

1

> I found it difficult _____ the plot of this novel.

① understand ② understood
③ to understand ④ to understanding
⑤ to be understood

2

> Mr. Smith made the students _____ on his lecture.

① focus ② focused
③ to focus ④ to focusing
⑤ focusing

3

> Josh saw an old man _____ the road slowly with his dog.

① crosses ② crossed
③ to cross ④ crossing
⑤ to crossing

4 다음 빈칸에 공통으로 들어갈 알맞은 것은?

> • It is easy _____ the marathoner to run two kilometers.
> • She brought a picture book _____ her brother to read.

① to ② for ③ of
④ with ⑤ from

서술형

[5-7] 다음 두 문장의 의미가 같도록 빈칸에 알맞은 말을 쓰시오.

5

> It seems that the chef closed his restaurant last week.
> → The chef _____ _____ _____ _____ his restaurant last week.

6

> I bought some brushes to paint the wall.
> → I bought some brushes _____ _____ _____ _____ the wall.

7

> The sofa is big enough for five people to sit on.
> → The sofa is _____ _____ _____ _____ _____ _____ _____ _____ .

8 다음 중 어법상 바른 것은?

① He got me book a plane ticket for him.
② We heard some people to fight outside.
③ She seems to been to New York many times.
④ David is to visit his uncle next week.
⑤ Shane decided to learning a new language.

서술형

[9-11] 괄호 안의 말을 활용하여 문장을 완성하시오.

9

Justin's dad encouraged him _____ a bigger dream. (have)

10

The wounded man heard his name _____ by the rescuers. (call)

11

We promised _____ our study schedule anymore. (not, put off)

12 다음 중 밑줄 친 부분을 바르게 고친 것은?

① It takes many years to becoming a doctor. (→ to become)

② My parents let me to ride the roller coaster again. (→ riding)

③ Samantha read a lot of books to being smarter. (→ be)

④ We watched the baseball players to be waited to go onto the field. (→ to wait)

⑤ My plan is to washed the dishes before Mom comes home. (→ to be washed)

[13-14] 다음 중 어법상 어색한 것을 고르시오.

13 ① Jenny wants her friends to sleep over at her house.

② Jamie stayed up late so as to play PC games.

③ We found that necessary to cancel our trip.

④ There aren't any nice houses for us to live in.

⑤ Tim wasn't sure what to buy at the shopping mall.

14 ① It took the genius only a minute to solve the problem.

② To tell the truth, I have never eaten kimchi.

③ The teacher had Jake continue his speech.

④ I listened to James singing popular pop songs.

⑤ It was careless for her to follow the stranger.

15 다음 빈칸에 들어갈 말로 어색한 것은?

My parents _____ me and my sister throw away the garbage.

① made   ② had   ③ let

④ helped   ⑤ got

서술형

16 우리말과 같도록 괄호 안의 말을 알맞게 배열하시오.

Ted는 차를 운전하기에 너무 어리다. (too, drive, young, Ted, a, is, car, to)

= _____ .

[17-18] 다음 중 밑줄 친 to부정사의 용법이 나머지 넷과 다른 것을 고르시오.

17 ① His goal is to watch ten movies this year.
② To go to outer space is one of my dreams.
③ We are to wear swimming suits in the pool.
④ It is difficult to remember everything from class.
⑤ The hikers found it impossible to walk on the icy trail.

18 ① You must buy a ticket to enter the theater.
② He lived to become a famous songwriter.
③ The fans were disappointed to hear that the soccer game was canceled.
④ Taekwondo is not easy to learn.
⑤ It is interesting to take cooking classes.

[19-20] 다음 빈칸에 들어갈 말이 순서대로 짝지어진 것을 고르시오.

19

> • Strange _____, I heard a noise in the empty house.
> • If you are _____ an ID card, you have to fill out a form.

① say – get
② to say – get
③ to say – to get
④ to saying – to get
⑤ to saying – getting

20

> • Jimmy felt a hand _____ his shoulder.
> • The citizens expected the mayor _____ the city's problems.

① grab – fix
② grab – to fix
③ to grab – fix
④ to grab – to fix
⑤ grabbing – fix

21 다음 중 짝지어진 두 문장의 의미가 <u>다른</u> 것은?

① Sophia is going to arrive at the airport soon.
→ Sophia is to arrive at the airport soon.
② I saved money to buy a laptop.
→ I saved money in order to buy a laptop.
③ Mr. Green is strong enough to lift a car.
→ Mr. Green is so strong that he can lift a car.
④ It is quite hard to grow a rose.
→ To grow a rose is quite hard.
⑤ It seems that Jay studied hard for the exam.
→ Jay seems to study hard for the exam.

[22-24] 우리말과 같도록 괄호 안의 말을 활용하여 문장을 완성하시오.

22

> 그 고양이는 우리가 안 보고 있을 때 몰래 무언가를 가져갔던 것 같다. (take, something)

= The cat seems _____ in secret when we were not watching.

23

> 우리는 Isaac의 생일을 위해 무엇을 살지 결정했다. (what, buy)

= We decided _____ for Isaac's birthday.

24

> 나의 친구는 내가 그 태국 음식을 먹어보게 했다. (try, the Thai dish)

= My friend got me _____.

Chapter 05 동명사

UNIT 01 동명사의 쓰임

Answers p.26

A 괄호 안의 말을 알맞은 형태로 바꿔 문장을 완성하시오.

1 You should avoid _____ a taxi during rush hour. (take)

2 He apologized for _____ rude to his parents. (be)

3 I don't mind _____ sitting next to me. (she)

4 Jacob's hobby is _____ rare postcards. (collect)

5 The toddler is afraid of _____ alone at night. (sleep)

B 밑줄 친 부분이 어법상 맞으면 O를 쓰고, 틀리면 바르게 고쳐 쓰시오.

1 Don't put off go to the gym.　　　　→ _____

2 Nancy helped her friends without been asked.　　　　→ _____

3 Performing on the stage makes me nervous.　　　　→ _____

4 Tyler said sorry for having been forgotten my birthday.　　　　→ _____

C 다음 두 문장의 의미가 같도록 동명사를 이용하여 문장을 완성하시오.

1 We were proud that he achieved his goal.
→ We were proud of _____ his goal.

2 Edward was angry that he was robbed of his luggage.
→ Edward was angry about _____ of his luggage.

3 Do you mind if I join your study group?
→ Do you mind _____ your study group?

D 우리말과 같도록 괄호 안의 말을 알맞게 배열하시오.

1 그 아이들은 아이스크림을 먹었던 것을 부인했다. (eaten, denied, ice cream, the, having)
= The kids _____.

2 나는 혼자서 나의 여동생들을 돌본 후에 피곤했다. (taking, of, was, after, tired, care)
= I _____ my younger sisters by myself.

3 Cindy는 상냥한 이웃으로 기억된 것에 만족했다. (with, was, being, satisfied, remembered)
= Cindy _____ as a friendly neighbor.

Chapter 05 동명사 Hackers Grammar Smart Level 3

UNIT 02 　동명사와 to부정사를 목적어로 쓰는 동사

A 　밑줄 친 부분이 어법상 맞으면 O를 쓰고, 틀리면 바르게 고쳐 쓰시오.

1 Please stop <u>to think</u> about the worst. 　　　　　→ _____

2 Brandon hopes <u>entering</u> the college in England. 　→ _____

3 The firefighters are trying <u>to put</u> out the fire. 　　→ _____

4 It is no use <u>complain</u> about small things. 　　　　→ _____

B 　괄호 안의 동사를 알맞은 형태로 바꿔 문장을 완성하시오.

1 Do you prefer not _____ hot sauce on your pizza? (put)

2 The doorbell rang, so I stopped _____ and went to the door. (eat)

3 My old computer was worth _____. It works well now. (fix)

4 The researchers expect _____ the vaccine this year. (develop)

C 　다음 두 문장의 의미가 같도록 문장을 완성하시오.

1 Mary began drawing the portrait of her mother.
　→ Mary began _____ the portrait of her mother.

2 Please remember that you should not leave the trash in the park.
　→ Please remember _____ the trash in the park.

3 My brother and I like cycling along the river.
　→ My brother and I like _____ along the river.

4 Ken forgot that he had met me before, so he asked my name again.
　→ Ken forgot _____ me before, so he asked my name again.

D 　우리말과 같도록 괄호 안의 말을 알맞게 배열하시오.

1 그들은 이 문제에 책임이 있다는 것을 인정했다. (admitted, for, responsible, this, being, matter)
　= They _____.

2 John은 그의 가장 친한 친구와 말다툼한 것을 후회했다. (with, his, regretted, friend, arguing, best)
　= John _____.

3 Emily는 그녀의 개가 웅덩이에 뛰어들지 못하게 했다. (dog, from, her, kept, jumping)
　= Emily _____ into the puddle.

[1-3] 다음 빈칸에 들어갈 알맞은 것을 고르시오.

1

> Jack felt like _____ ice cream after swimming.

① have   ② to have
③ having   ④ being had
⑤ to be had

2

> The book club members agreed _____ every Saturday.

① meet   ② to meet
③ meeting   ④ being met
⑤ to be met

3

> I wish to be alone right now without _____ by others.

① bother   ② to bother
③ bothering   ④ being bothered
⑤ having bothered

4 다음 우리말을 알맞게 영작한 것은?

> 나는 그녀가 금메달을 따는 것을 꿈꿨다.

① I dreamed of to win the gold medal.
② I dreamed of she winning the gold medal.
③ I dreamed of her winning the gold medal.
④ I dreamed of her to win the gold medal.
⑤ I dreamed of she having won the gold medal.

5 다음 빈칸에 들어갈 말로 어색한 것을 모두 고르시오.

> The girl _____ to tell a lie to her parents.

① avoids   ② hates
③ denies   ④ refuses
⑤ wants

서술형

[6-8] 다음 문장에서 어법상 어색한 부분을 찾아 쓰고 바르게 고쳐 쓰시오.

6

> Sandra is planning seeing a doctor for her injuries.

_____ → _____

7

> My wallet is at home because I forgot taking it with me.

_____ → _____

8

> Josh apologized for having been missed my call a few hours ago.

_____ → _____

Chapter 05

동명사

Hackers Grammar Smart **Level 3**

[9-10] 다음 중 어법상 어색한 것을 고르시오.

9
① We regret to tell you that all rooms are booked.
② I'm looking forward to go to the art center.
③ Mr. Ford tried to repair the copy machine, but failed.
④ The hikers began climbing up the mountain.
⑤ Larry keeps talking about his trip to Paris.

10
① The documentary is definitely worth watching.
② The boy is excited about having a birthday party.
③ Hannah is used to waking up early.
④ I was afraid of upsetting my teacher.
⑤ The mayor is considering to build a library.

서술형
[11-12] 괄호 안의 동사를 활용하여 문장을 완성하시오.

11
Diane injured her knee during the marathon, so she gave up _____ more. (run)

12
You should remember _____ your umbrella since it is going to rain in the afternoon. (take)

고난도
13 주어진 문장의 밑줄 친 부분과 쓰임이 같은 것은?

His job is analyzing the marketing data.

① Ms. Brown quit teaching because of her health.
② My goal is saving wild animals.
③ He left the country without saying goodbye.
④ Trying new food is always exciting.
⑤ I don't mind going to the theater alone.

서술형
[14-16] 우리말과 같도록 괄호 안의 말을 활용하여 문장을 완성하시오.

14
Emma는 지난주에 카메라를 산 것을 잊었다. (forget, buy)

= Emma _____ a camera last week.

15
그 의사는 환자들을 돌보느라 바쁘다. (busy, take care of)

= The doctor _____ the patients.

16
나의 언니는 내가 그녀의 코트를 입는 것에 대해 불평했다. (complain about, wear)

= My sister _____ her coat.

서술형

[17-18] 우리말과 같도록 괄호 안의 말을 알맞게 배열하시오.

17
> 나는 그 책을 읽는 데 두 시간을 썼다. (book, two, reading, spent, I, the, hours)

= _____
_____.

18
> 그 경비원은 낯선 사람들이 이 건물에 들어오지 못하게 했다. (entering, this, prevented, from, the, guard, building, strangers)

= _____
_____.

[19-20] 다음 빈칸에 들어갈 말이 순서대로 짝지어진 것을 고르시오.

19
> • My brother promised _____ me his backpack for the field trip.
> • The writer stopped _____ novels and started to write poems.

① lend – write   ② to lend – to write
③ to lend – writing   ④ lending – writing
⑤ lending – to write

20
> • Do you mind _____ turning some music on?
> • She feels ashamed of _____ selfish when she was younger.

① I – having been   ② I– to be
③ me – to have been   ④ my – having been
⑤ my – to have been

21 다음 중 어법상 바른 것은?

① She is good at speak both Korean and English.
② Don't forget bringing your laptop next time.
③ Frank couldn't help to fall in love with her.
④ We wished to see a rainbow, but we couldn't.
⑤ My grandmother is not used to drive a car.

22 다음 중 밑줄 친 부분을 바르게 고친 것은?

① Donna enjoys to watching TV drama series.
      → to watch
② The student is sure of passed the exam.
      → being passed
③ He denies to have been there yesterday.
      → have been
④ The runner expected to winning the race.
      → winning
⑤ I'll never forget having hugged by the actor.
      → having been hugged

서술형 고난도

[23-24] 동명사를 이용하여 다음 두 문장을 한 문장으로 연결하시오.

23
> Eva didn't submit her homework on time. She admits it.
> → Eva admits _____
> _____ on time.

24
> He was given many presents by friends on his birthday. He loved it.
> → He loved _____
> _____ by friends on his birthday.

UNIT 01　현재분사와 과거분사

A　밑줄 친 부분이 어법상 맞으면 O를 쓰고, 틀리면 바르게 고쳐 쓰시오.

1 Did you have your smartphone <u>fixing</u>?　→ _____

2 The teacher's explanation sounded <u>confused</u> to me.　→ _____

3 Dad bought an electric drill <u>making</u> in Germany.　→ _____

4 I went to the museum to see a picture <u>painted</u> by Monet.　→ _____

B　우리말과 같도록 <보기>의 말을 한 번씩만 골라 알맞은 형태로 바꿔 쓰시오.

<보기>　interest　disappoint　surprise

1 그의 무례한 태도는 매우 실망스러웠다.

= His rude attitude was very _____.

2 Helen은 천둥 소리에 의해 놀랐다.

= Helen was _____ by the sound of a thunder.

3 우리는 뇌세포에 대한 몇몇 흥미로운 사실들을 배웠다.

= We learned some _____ facts about brain cells.

C　분사를 이용하여 다음 두 문장을 한 문장으로 연결하시오.

1 The girl is my sister. She is wearing a white blouse.

→ The girl _____ is my sister.

2 There is some furniture. It was scratched by the cat.

→ There is some furniture _____.

3 Eric saw a horse. It was jumping over the fence.

→ Eric saw a horse _____.

D　우리말과 같도록 괄호 안의 말을 알맞게 배열하시오.

1 그 도둑은 경찰이 그를 향해 다가오는 것을 들었다. (towards, the, coming, heard, him, police)

= The thief _____.

2 나는 부엌에서 무언가가 타고 있는 것을 냄새 맡을 수 있었다. (burning, smell, something, could)

= I _____ in the kitchen.

3 Angela는 그녀의 치아가 치과의사에 의해 진찰되게 했다. (teeth, examined, had, her)

= Angela _____ by the dentist.

UNIT 02 분사구문

A 밑줄 친 부분이 어법상 맞으면 O를 쓰고, 틀리면 바르게 고쳐 쓰시오.

1 <u>Not had</u> my glasses, I couldn't read the sign on the road. → _____

2 <u>Following</u> the smell, the dog found his snack. → _____

3 <u>Shouted</u> loudly, the director made the actor focus. → _____

4 <u>Stay</u> in Paris, I visited the Eiffel Tower. → _____

B 다음 두 문장의 의미가 같도록 분사구문을 이용하여 문장을 완성하시오. (단, 접속사를 생략하시오.)

1 When she completed the puzzle, she felt satisfied.

→ _____, she felt satisfied.

2 If you buy two items, you can get another for free.

→ _____, you can get another for free.

3 Because I talked during class, I was scolded by my teacher.

→ _____, I was scolded by my teacher.

4 While he walked down the street, he ran into Betty.

→ _____, he ran into Betty.

C 다음 두 문장의 의미가 같도록 괄호 안의 접속사를 활용하여 문장을 완성하시오.

1 Eating dinner, she usually watches the news. (while)

→ _____, she usually watches the news.

2 Not having enough time, I had to skip lunch. (as)

→ _____, I had to skip lunch.

3 Coming into the classroom, he called my name. (as soon as)

→ _____, he called my name.

D 우리말과 같도록 괄호 안의 말을 활용하여 빈칸에 쓰시오.

1 만약 내가 그 배우를 본다면, 그의 사인을 요청할 것이다. (see, the actor)

= _____ _____ _____, I will ask for his autograph.

2 Julia는 제시간에 도착하지 않았기 때문에, 시험을 볼 수 없었다. (arrive, on time)

= _____ _____ _____ _____, Julia couldn't take the exam.

3 Sam은 방 안으로 걸어 들어오면서, 불을 켰다. (walk, into the room)

= _____ _____ _____, Sam turned the lights on.

UNIT 03   주의해야 할 분사구문

A   밑줄 친 부분이 어법상 맞으면 O를 쓰고, 틀리면 바르게 고쳐 쓰시오.

1 <u>Born</u> in Seoul, I've lived here all my life.   → _____

2 <u>It be</u> my birthday, Megan made me a cake.   → _____

3 <u>Having been saved</u> enough money, we're going to travel to Europe. → _____

4 He is reading a novel with his cat <u>slept</u> nearby.   → _____

B   다음 두 문장의 의미가 같도록 분사구문을 이용하여 문장을 완성하시오.

1 Because they were excited about their vacation, they couldn't sleep.

→ _____, they couldn't sleep.

2 Although the weather is cold, Tom isn't wearing a coat.

→ _____, Tom isn't wearing a coat.

3 Since we hadn't seen each other for ages, we had a lot to talk about.

→ _____, we had a lot to talk about.

C   다음 두 문장의 의미가 같도록 괄호 안의 접속사를 활용하여 문장을 완성하시오.

1 Picked up by her mother, she doesn't have to take the school bus. (as)

→ _____, she doesn't have to take the school bus.

2 Having sold their apartment, they have no place to stay. (because)

→ _____, they have no place to stay.

3 Our dad cooking dinner, we took care of our baby sister. (while)

→ _____, we took care of our baby sister.

D   우리말과 같도록 괄호 안의 말을 활용하여 빈칸에 쓰시오.

1 그녀는 밤에 혼자 남겨졌을 때, 두려움을 느꼈다. (leave alone, at night)

= _____ _____ _____ _____, she felt scared.

2 영화가 끝난 후에, 많은 사람들이 영화관 밖으로 나왔다. (the movie, be over)

= _____ _____ _____ _____, many people got out of the theater.

3 그 축구 선수는 팬들이 보는 채로 골을 넣었다. (the fans, watch)

= The soccer player scored a goal _____ _____ _____ _____.

Chapter Test ✛

Answers p.27

[1-3] 다음 빈칸에 들어갈 알맞은 것을 고르시오.

1

Look at the stars _____ in the sky.

① shine   ② shining

③ to shine   ④ shone

⑤ being shone

2

Bella was _____ to hear the noise from the attic.

① surprise   ② surprising

③ surprised   ④ to surprising

⑤ to surprised

3

_____ the school bus, Jason is late for class.

① Miss   ② Missed

③ To missed   ④ Being Missed

⑤ Having missed

4 다음 중 어법상 바른 것은?

① Carol was satisfying with her new hairstyle.

② Paul is sitting with his legs crossed.

③ Having praised by the teacher, he felt proud.

④ We had the speaker fixing last week.

⑤ Strictly spoken, it was your fault.

[5-6] 다음 빈칸에 들어갈 말이 순서대로 짝지어진 것을 고르시오.

5

• _____ hard, you will be able to achieve your goal. • We picked up the trash _____ on the street.

① Tried – leaving

② Tried – left

③ Trying – left

④ Trying – leaving

⑤ Having tried – leaving

6

• Going up the hill was _____ for the kids. • I love to watch my hamster _____ berries.

① exhausting – eating

② exhausting – eaten

③ exhausting – being eaten

④ exhausted – eating

⑤ exhausted – eaten

서술형

[7-8] 괄호 안의 말을 활용하여 빈칸에 알맞은 말을 쓰시오.

7

_____ _____ a cold last week, Brian still feels sick. (catch)

8

_____ _____ enough time for the report, I had to stay up late at night. (have, not)

9
① Who is the man staring at us?
② He had a satisfying time at the amusement park.
③ They stood waiting for the bus together.
④ Ashley had the spot on her dress removing.
⑤ I want to stop this boring conversation.

10
① Boarding the train, she said goodbye to us.
② Given many gifts, Kevin jumped with excitement.
③ Decorated with vanilla cream, the cake was white.
④ Having worked out for a long time, they felt tired.
⑤ Amazing by his acting, the audience gave applause.

서술형
[11-12] 다음 문장에서 어법상 어색한 부분을 찾아 쓰고 바르게 고쳐 쓰시오.

11
> Spoken of his personality, he is diligent and generous.

_____ → _____

12
> Knowing not the way to the station, the tourist was anxious.

_____ → _____

서술형
[13-15] 다음 문장의 밑줄 친 부분을 분사구문으로 바꿔 쓰시오.

13
> As it was cold, we stayed near the fireplace.
> → _____, we stayed near the fireplace.

14
> As soon as he had finished his painting, he started to work on another one.
> → _____, he started to work on another one.

15
> Since she is known to the public, she refuses to go to crowded places.
> → _____, she refuses to go to crowded places.

16 다음 중 어법상 바른 것의 개수는?

> ⓐ People helped to find the losing child.
> ⓑ She feels exciting about planning her vacation.
> ⓒ We searched for a restaurant serving Thai dishes.
> ⓓ A girl riding a bike accidentally ran into me.
> ⓔ There is somebody knocked on the door.

① 1개　　　　② 2개　　　　③ 3개
④ 4개　　　　⑤ 5개

17 다음 밑줄 친 부분과 바꿔 쓸 수 있는 것은?

> Walking slowly, you won't make it to the finish line quickly.

① And you walk slowly
② If you walk slowly
③ When you walked slowly
④ Unless you walk slowly
⑤ Although you walk slowly

고난도

18 다음 중 밑줄 친 부분의 쓰임이 나머지 넷과 다른 것은?

① Susan sat eating some snacks.
② The newspaper headline was shocking.
③ The man carving a statue is a famous sculptor.
④ The smiling baby made us feel happy.
⑤ I enjoy writing in a journal every day.

서술형 고난도

19 다음 글의 밑줄 친 ⓐ~ⓔ 중 어법상 어색한 것을 찾아 기호를 쓰고 바르게 고쳐 쓰시오.

> Last week, Mom wanted to go to the orchestra with me. ⓐBeing excited to watch the concert, Mom packed her bag in a hurry. ⓑArrived at the concert hall, Mom realized that she hadn't brought the tickets. She was very ⓒdisappointing, so I bought tickets for a movie ⓓplaying that day instead. Even though Mom couldn't see the concert, she said she was ⓔpleased to spend time with me.

(1) _____ → _____
(2) _____ → _____

20 다음 밑줄 친 부분을 부사절로 바꾼 것 중 어색한 것은?

① Visiting the website, you can download the coupon. (→ If you visit the website)
② Having come from another city, I know nothing about here. (→ Because I came from another city)
③ Taking a taxi, you won't be late to the appointment. (→ If you take a taxi)
④ Going up on stage, we felt nervous. (→ As we went up on stage)
⑤ Seeing the accident ahead, he suddenly stopped his car. (→ As he was seen the accident ahead)

서술형

[21-24] 우리말과 같도록 괄호 안의 말을 활용하여 빈칸에 쓰시오.

21

> 그 컵은 금으로 장식되었기 때문에, 꽤 비싸다. (decorate)

= _____ with gold, the cup is quite expensive.

22

> 그는 연설을 하는 동안, 많은 물을 마셨다. (give, a speech)

= _____ _____ _____, he drank a lot of water.

23

> 비록 나는 과거에 키가 작았지만, 지금은 키가 크다. (be, short)

= _____ _____ _____ _____ in the past, I'm tall now.

24

> 그녀의 행동으로 판단하건대, 그녀는 게으르다. (judge, behavior)

= _____ _____ _____ _____, she is lazy.

UNIT 01 관계대명사

Answers p.28

A 밑줄 친 부분이 어법상 맞으면 O를 쓰고, 틀리면 바르게 고쳐 쓰시오.

1 <u>That</u> I want to have for dessert is an apple pie. → _____

2 Jeremy fought with the girls <u>whose</u> made fun of his clothes. → _____

3 This is the maple tree <u>which</u> I planted with my father. → _____

4 There are many people <u>who</u> dream is to travel around the world. → _____

5 The city will inspect all buildings <u>that</u> were built before 2005. → _____

B 다음 두 문장을 밑줄 친 부분을 선행사로 하는 문장으로 연결하시오. (단, that은 쓰지 마시오.)

1 I can smell <u>the food</u>. My neighbors are cooking it.

→ _____.

2 The boys caught <u>the woman</u>. She stole Kyle's wallet.

→ _____.

3 Linda is carrying <u>a bag</u>. Its zipper is broken.

→ _____.

4 This is <u>a documentary</u>. It is about World War II.

→ _____.

5 <u>My uncle</u> lives in Indonesia. I visit him once a year.

→ _____.

C 우리말과 같도록 괄호 안의 말을 알맞게 배열하시오.

1 '게르니카'는 피카소에 의해 그려진 예술품이다. (which, the, painted, artwork, was)
= *Guernica* is _____ by Picasso.

2 내가 지금 당장 필요한 것은 시원한 물 한 잔이다. (need, now, I, right, what)
= _____ is a cup of cold water.

3 Nina는 그녀가 어제 입었던 같은 재킷을 입고 있다. (she, jacket, the, that, wore, same)
= Nina is wearing _____ yesterday.

4 Johnson씨는 테니스 선수였던 여자이다. (the, who, be, used, woman, to)
= Ms. Johnson is _____ a tennis player.

UNIT 02 관계부사

A 다음 빈칸에 알맞은 관계부사를 쓰시오.

1 Italy is the country _____ Betty spent her childhood.

2 Let me show you _____ you can make cheese from milk.

3 Mark explained the reason _____ he didn't like swimming.

4 January is the month _____ my younger brother was born.

B 다음 두 문장의 의미가 같도록 빈칸에 알맞은 관계부사를 쓰시오.

1 I hope to learn the way I can stay calm in stressful situations.
→ I hope to learn _____ I can stay calm in stressful situations.

2 Tomorrow is the day on which my sister comes home from the trip.
→ Tomorrow is the day _____ my sister comes home from the trip.

3 The shopping mall to which I used to go turned into a wedding hall.
→ The shopping mall _____ I used to go turned into a wedding hall.

4 The doctor told me the reason for which I had to get an injection.
→ The doctor told me the reason _____ I had to get an injection.

C 관계부사를 이용하여 다음 두 문장을 한 문장으로 연결하시오.

1 2015 is the year. I moved to another school in that year.
→ _____.

2 The police found the place. The evidence was hidden in that place.
→ _____.

3 This video teaches us the way. We can improve our speech skills in that way.
→ _____.

D 우리말과 같도록 괄호 안의 말을 알맞게 배열하시오.

1 너의 가족이 보스턴에서 살기로 정한 어떤 이유가 있니? (your, reason, family, any, chose, why)
= Is there _____ to live in Boston?

2 오후 10시는 슈퍼마켓이 문을 닫는 시간이다. (supermarket, when, the, closes, time, the)
= 10 P.M. is _____.

3 커피콩이 재배되는 몇몇의 지역들이 있다. (coffee, are, beans, where, regions, grown)
= There are a few _____.

UNIT 03 주의해야 할 관계사의 쓰임

A 밑줄 친 부분이 어법상 맞으면 O를 쓰고, 틀리면 바르게 고쳐 쓰시오.

1 The road on that Clara was walking was slippery. → _____

2 We used a little flour, what made the soup thicker. → _____

3 Ocarina is a musical instrument created by the Chinese. → _____

4 The boy to who I lent my notebook was Henry. → _____

B 다음 문장에서 생략된 부분을 넣어 완전한 문장을 쓰시오.

1 Mary took a picture with the singer she has liked for years.

→ _____ .

2 I still remember the party Paul threw two years ago.

→ _____ .

3 A gram is a unit used to measure mass.

→ _____ .

C 다음 두 문장의 의미가 같도록 접속사를 이용하여 문장을 완성하시오.

1 David fixed his smartphone, which still doesn't work.
   → David fixed his smartphone, _____ .

2 We found a nice place beside the river, where we had a picnic.
   → We found a nice place beside the river, _____ .

3 My favorite city is San Francisco, which is in northern California.
   → My favorite city is San Francisco, _____ .

D 우리말과 같도록 괄호 안의 말을 알맞게 배열하시오.

1 테레사 수녀는 많은 사람들에 의해 존경받는 수녀였다. (many, by, respected, nun, a, people)
   = Mother Teresa was _____ .

2 Brown씨는 내가 너에게 말했던 그 아나운서이다. (announcer, about, who, the, told, I, you)
   = Mr. Brown is _____ .

3 나는 지난 주말에 놀이공원에 갔는데, 그때 그곳은 아이들로 붐볐다. (with, was, when, kids, crowded, it)
   = I went to the amusement park last weekend, _____ .

UNIT 04 복합관계사

A 다음 빈칸에 알맞은 말을 <보기>에서 한 번씩만 골라 쓰시오.

<보기>	whichever	wherever	whenever

1 My father goes camping _____ he doesn't go to work.

2 _____ the teacher led, the students followed.

3 _____ bus the tourists take, they can get to the museum.

B 다음 두 문장의 의미가 같도록 문장을 완성하시오.

1 Anyone who comes to the charity event will be welcomed.

→ _____ will be welcomed.

2 Stay positive no matter what happens.

→ Stay positive _____ .

3 No matter how well you explain the rule, I can't understand it.

→ _____ , I can't understand it.

4 My dog barked at any time when someone knocked on the door.

→ My dog barked _____ .

C 주어진 문장을 우리말로 해석하시오.

1 There are mosquitoes wherever you go in summer.

→ _____ .

2 However long it takes, I will finish the marathon.

→ _____ .

3 Whatever plan we have, we have to cancel it because of rain.

→ _____ .

D 우리말과 같도록 괄호 안의 말을 알맞게 배열하시오.

1 Jeffrey는 집에 올 때는 언제나 그의 손을 먼저 씻는다. (Jeffrey, home, whenever, comes)

= _____ , he washes his hands first.

2 좌석을 원하는 누구든지 일찍 도착해야 한다. (seat, whoever, a, wants)

= _____ should arrive early.

3 네가 어느 모자를 쓰더라도, 그것은 너에게 잘 어울린다. (wear, hat, whichever, you)

= _____ , it looks good on you.

Chapter Test +

[1-3] 다음 빈칸에 들어갈 알맞은 것을 고르시오.

1

> Timmy is writing an e-mail to Amy, _____ lives in New York.

① which   ② that
③ who   ④ whom
⑤ what

2

> Did you take a picture of that tower _____ structure is unique?

① who   ② which
③ that   ④ whose
⑤ whom

3

> My mom tells me to be kind to _____ I meet.

① whomever   ② wherever
③ whenever   ④ however
⑤ whichever

4 다음 중 어법상 바른 것은?

① I'll be calm and brave what happens to me.
② We will visit Gwangju, when Dad was born.
③ That Mark said yesterday was not true at all.
④ The scientists developed the vaccine, that saved many lives.
⑤ Whichever activities you choose, you will enjoy it.

서술형

[5-6] 다음 문장에서 어법상 어색한 부분을 찾아 쓰고 바르게 고쳐 쓰시오.

5

> Let's go to a nice place when all of us can sit and talk.

_____ → _____

6

> The book describes the way how ancient people built their houses.

_____ → _____

서술형

[7-8] 다음 두 문장의 의미가 같도록 빈칸에 알맞은 말을 쓰시오.

7

> No matter where I shop, I can use this gift card.
> → _____ I shop, I can use this gift card.

8

> I went to the festival on Friday, and then I saw my favorite singer.
> → I went to the festival on Friday, _____ I saw my favorite singer.

고난도

9 다음 빈칸에 들어갈 관계대명사가 나머지 넷과 <u>다른</u> 것은?

① We must write down _____ the teacher is saying now.

② The parents told the police _____ their lost child was wearing.

③ Richard is not someone _____ likes to go swimming.

④ I don't know _____ happened when I was absent.

⑤ _____ Julie did made all of us angry.

서술형

[10-12] 알맞은 관계사를 이용하여 다음 두 문장을 한 문장으로 연결하시오.

10
> The child was given a box. It was filled with cookies.
> → The child was given a box _____ _____ _____ _____ _____ .

11
> My uncle has to fix his phone. Its camera is not working.
> → My uncle has to fix his phone _____ _____ _____ _____ _____ .

12
> You should apologize to Nicole for the thing. You did the thing yesterday.
> → You should apologize to Nicole for _____ _____ _____ _____ .

13 다음 빈칸에 공통으로 들어갈 알맞은 것은?

> • The man _____ I admire the most is King Sejong.
> • Sandra is my friend with _____ I take math classes.

① whom　　② who　　③ that
④ whose　　⑤ which

[14-15] 다음 중 어법상 <u>어색한</u> 것을 고르시오.

14 ① The company is trying to hire a person who can speak more than two languages.

② The film they watched is about the history of Egypt.

③ I have a friend who eyes are green.

④ Mr. Brown looked for a pen with which he could write.

⑤ Joseph went to his favorite artist's exhibition, which became a precious memory.

15 ① I'm looking for a speaker whose sound quality is great.

② Robert still remembers the day when he left his hometown.

③ The teacher gives some snacks to whoever comes to class first.

④ Whatever high she jumped, she couldn't reach the ceiling.

⑤ The record shop is the place I go to listen to jazz music.

16 다음 우리말을 알맞게 영작한 것은?

> 과학자들은 그 실험이 실패한 이유를 찾아냈다.

① Scientists found out the reason which the experiment failed.
② Scientists found out the reason for the experiment failed.
③ Scientists found out why for the experiment failed.
④ Scientists found out why the experiment failed.
⑤ Scientists found out the reason for why the experiment failed.

서술형

[17-19] 우리말과 같도록 괄호 안의 말을 활용하여 빈칸에 쓰시오.

17

> 그녀는 도서관에 갈 때는 언제나 읽을 책들을 빌려 온다. (go, the library)

= _____ _____ _____ _____
_____ _____, she borrows books to read.

18

> 장난감을 뺏긴 그 소년은 울기 시작했다. (toy, take away)

= The boy _____ _____ _____
_____ _____ started to cry.

19

> 나는 그가 말하는 것을 이해하지 못한다. (say)

= I don't understand _____ _____
_____.

고난도

20 다음 중 밑줄 친 부분이 어법상 바른 것은?

① That he hopes to do is to go camping on a sunny day.
② The computer was broken, that made me call the technician.
③ She is my aunt with that I'm taking a trip.
④ We met at 9 P.M., that all the stores on the street were closed.
⑤ Ryan has the same shoes that I bought before.

21 다음 중 밑줄 친 부분을 생략할 수 없는 것은?

① I'm sitting beside a girl whom I don't know.
② The boy who is dancing on the floor is Ted.
③ She is the very person that we saw at the bus stop yesterday.
④ Mars is a red planet that was named after a Roman god.
⑤ Mom likes the shop that has antique vases.

[22-23] 다음 빈칸에 들어갈 말이 순서대로 짝지어진 것은?

22

> • _____ made this sculpture can be called an artist.
> • _____ cold it is, Kevin never has hot drinks.

① Whoever – Whatever
② Whoever – However
③ Whichever – Whatever
④ Whichever – However
⑤ Whomever – However

23

> • I respect Admiral Yi Sun-shin, _____ is famous for winning tough battles.
> • Janet lived France, _____ she made many French friends.

① which – when
② which – where
③ who – when
④ who – where
⑤ whom – where

Chapter 08 접속사

UNIT 01 부사절을 이끄는 접속사

Answers p.30

A 괄호 안에서 알맞은 것을 고르시오.

1 The baby started to cry (as soon as / unless) he saw a stranger.

2 (Until / Because) the pizza was delivered late, it wasn't hot.

3 Nicole will take care of my dog while I (am / will be) gone.

4 The article is (as / so) difficult that the students can't understand it.

B 다음 빈칸에 가장 알맞은 말을 <보기>에서 골라 그 기호를 쓰시오.

<보기>	ⓐ until the storm passes
	ⓑ because it was too hot
	ⓒ as soon as you get my text message
	ⓓ because I hurt my arm
	ⓔ unless you know the password
	ⓕ although it is old

1 The printer still works well _____.

2 Everyone should stay inside _____.

3 Tim carried the box for me _____.

4 Please call me _____.

5 Matilda took her coat off _____.

6 You can't log in to the application _____.

C 우리말과 같도록 괄호 안의 말을 알맞게 배열하시오.

1 나는 이전에 파리에 가본 적이 없기 때문에, 그곳에 대한 약간의 정보가 필요하다. (been, I, Paris, before, haven't, to, as)

= _____, I need some information about it.

2 만약 네가 최선을 다하지 않는다면, 경주에서 우승하지 못할 것이다. (try, your, unless, best, you)

= _____, you won't win the race.

3 끔찍한 사고가 일어났던 이후로 6개월이 지났다. (accident, the, since, occurred, terrible)

= Six months have passed _____.

4 비록 그는 준비가 되지 않았지만 자신 있었다. (he, prepared, though, wasn't, even)

= _____, he felt confident.

A 밑줄 친 부분이 어법상 맞으면 O를 쓰고, 틀리면 바르게 고쳐 쓰시오.

1 Both the black cap and the white one <u>looks</u> good on you. → _____

2 I wonder whether <u>does Mark have</u> my phone number. → _____

3 She has not only a sore throat <u>but also</u> a headache. → _____

4 A sketchbook as well as pencils <u>are</u> needed for this class. → _____

B 괄호 안의 말을 활용하여 다음 두 문장을 한 문장으로 연결하시오.

1 Natalie didn't join the book club. Josh didn't join the book club, either. (neither)

→ _____.

2 The doctor is helping the patient. The nurses are also helping the patient. (not only)

→ _____.

3 I'm going to buy the shirt. I'm going to buy the pants, too. (both)

→ _____.

C 다음 두 문장을 한 문장으로 연결하시오.

1 Do you think? + Why are polar bears white?

→ _____?

2 I'm not sure. + Will Kelly agree with your suggestion?

→ _____.

3 He wants to know. + How was the city of Pompeii destroyed?

→ _____.

D 우리말과 같도록 괄호 안의 말을 알맞게 배열하시오.

1 나는 그들이 하키의 규칙을 알고 있는지 궁금하다. (rules, if, the, know, they)

= I wonder _____ of hockey.

2 Jack이나 나 둘 중 한 명이 결정을 내려야 한다. (have, Jack, to, either, I, or, make)

= _____ a decision.

3 너는 누가 진실을 말하고 있다고 생각하니? (who, is, you, do, telling, believe)

= _____ the truth?

[1-3] 다음 빈칸에 들어갈 가장 알맞은 것을 고르시오.

1

The wind was so strong _____ many trees fell down.

① if　　　　② unless　　　　③ though

④ that　　　⑤ as soon as

2

_____ you don't apologize to her, she will stay angry at you.

① Until　　　② If　　　　③ Although

④ Unless　　⑤ Even if

3

I want to learn not only skiing _____ snowboarding.

① or　　　　② nor　　　　③ also

④ but　　　⑤ and

4 다음 두 문장을 한 문장으로 연결한 것 중 어색한 것을 모두 고르시오.

① I wonder. + Why does he look so happy?

　→ Why I wonder he looks so happy.

② I don't know. + Who opened the door?

　→ I don't know who opened the door.

③ Do you think? + When can you come?

　→ When do you think can you come?

④ I'm not sure. + Will this TV drama end soon?

　→ I'm not sure if this TV drama will end soon.

⑤ Can you tell me? + How did the accident happen?

　→ Can you tell me how the accident happened?

5 다음 중 밑줄 친 if의 의미가 나머지 넷과 다른 것은?

① The outdoor event will be held if the weather is not bad.

② If one more person joins, we can play this board game.

③ You will get a discount if you bring a coupon.

④ If they have ID cards, they can enter the building.

⑤ I'm not sure if that sentence is correct.

서술형

[6-8] 우리말과 같도록 괄호 안의 말을 활용하여 빈칸에 쓰시오.

6

Molly와 Cathy 둘 다 서로의 옆에 앉기를 원한다. (want)

= _____ _____ _____ _____

_____ to sit next to each other.

7

Ben은 친절하기 때문에 인기가 많다. (kind)

= _____ _____ _____ _____ ,

he is popular.

8

나는 그가 제시간에 도착할지 아닐지 모른다. (arrive)

= I don't know _____ _____ _____

_____ on time.

Chapter 08

접속사

Hackers Grammar Smart　Level 3

[9-10] 다음 우리말을 알맞게 영작한 것을 고르시오.

9

> 그는 물이나 차 둘 중 하나를 마시고 싶다.

① He wants to drink neither water nor tea.
② He wants to drink either water or tea.
③ He wants to drink both water and tea.
④ He wants to drink not only water but tea.
⑤ He wants to drink water as well as tea.

10

> 너는 누가 정답을 안다고 생각하니?

① Do you think will who know the answer?
② Do you think who knows the answer?
③ Do you think who does know the answer?
④ Who do you think knows the answer?
⑤ Who you do think knows the answer?

[11-12] 다음 두 문장의 의미가 같도록 문장을 완성하시오.

11

> If I don't get the ticket, I can't go to the concert with you.
> → _____, I can't go to
>   the concert with you.

12

> The dessert as well as the main dish was delicious.
> → _____
>   was delicious.

[13-15] 다음 문장에서 어법상 어색한 부분을 찾아 쓰고 바르게 고쳐 쓰시오.

13

> Either Jane or Mason are going to be the leader of the debate team.

_____ → _____

14

> Do you know where can I buy the USB?

_____ → _____

15

> I'll wait for you until you will come back.

_____ → _____

16 다음은 세 가지 과일에 대한 정보를 나타낸 표이다. 상관접속사와 괄호 안의 동사를 활용하여 빈칸에 알맞은 말을 쓰시오.

	Price	Calories	Weight
Apple	$2	100 kcal	200 g
Pear	$4	200 kcal	400 g
Peach	$4	100 kcal	300 g

(1) _____ a pear _____ a peach
    _____ $4. (cost)

(2) _____ _____ an apple _____
    a peach _____ 100 kcal. (have)

(3) _____ an apple _____ a pear
    _____ 300 g. (weigh)

[17-18] 다음 빈칸에 공통으로 들어갈 알맞은 것을 고르시오.

17

> • _____ it snowed heavily, all flights were canceled.
> • I saw a huge sculpture _____ I entered the museum.

① as   ② even if   ③ until
④ though   ⑤ unless

18

> • Dave has exercised regularly _____ he was in elementary school.
> • _____ you are reliable, I'll tell you one of my secrets.

① if   ② since   ③ when
④ while   ⑤ although

[19-20] 다음 중 어법상 어색한 것을 고르시오.

19 ① Though they are twins, they don't look alike.
② As she was taking a shower, she sang a song.
③ We used to play baseball when we were young.
④ Unless you don't come to the party, he will be disappointed.
⑤ The man checked on his phone while he was waiting in line.

20 ① The math problem was difficult not only for me but for my friend.
② Both you and your brother has been kind to me.
③ I wonder whether Ryan remembers me.
④ Neither Alice nor I am listening to music now.
⑤ Where do you think we can spend time during the day?

서술형

21 알맞은 접속사를 이용하여 다음 두 문장을 한 문장으로 연결하시오.

> I don't like seafood. However, I like this spaghetti with salmon.
> → _____ I don't like seafood, I like this spaghetti with salmon.

[22-23] 다음 빈칸에 들어갈 말이 순서대로 짝지어진 것은?

22

> • The runner came in last in the race _____ she ran faster than ever.
> • My laptop was _____ at home nor at the library.

① since – neither   ② though – either
③ though – neither   ④ because – either
⑤ because – neither

23

> • I'm not sure _____ I will go to Thailand for vacation.
> • Study hard _____ you want to get a higher grade.

① where – unless   ② where – if
③ if – unless   ④ whether – unless
⑤ whether – if

24 다음 중 어법상 바른 것은?

① If you will explain it to me once more, I will understand better.
② The desk is too heavy that he can't lift it.
③ Let's have dinner as soon as Dad comes.
④ Please tell me what is the good news.
⑤ Do you suppose who has the key?

UNIT 01 가정법 과거/과거완료, 혼합 가정법

Answers p.31

A 밑줄 친 부분이 어법상 맞으면 O를 쓰고, 틀리면 바르게 고쳐 쓰시오.

1 If Mark weren't sleepy, he <u>can</u> focus on the class. → _____

2 If you <u>will soak</u> the bottle in water, the label will peel off easily. → _____

3 If Jason entered the competition, he <u>would have won</u>. → _____

4 If the party <u>had been</u> more exciting, she wouldn't have left so soon. → _____

B 다음 빈칸에 알맞은 말을 <보기>에서 골라 쓰시오.

<보기>	had planted the flowers	would have opened
	could send a letter	were in your situation

1 If he had quit his job, he _____ his own restaurant.

2 If I _____, I would apologize to your friend.

3 If I _____, I could have a beautiful garden now.

4 If she remembered David's address, she _____ to him.

C 다음 문장을 가정법 문장으로 바꿔 쓰시오.

1 As I didn't check my pocket, I couldn't find my ring.
  → If _____, I could have found my ring.

2 As we missed the bus, we aren't there now.
  → If we hadn't missed the bus, we _____.

3 As my father is busy, he can't spend more time with us.
  → If _____, he could spend more time with us.

D 우리말과 같도록 괄호 안의 말을 활용하여 문장을 완성하시오.

1 만약 내가 대통령이라면, 더 많은 휴일을 만들 텐데. (be, a president)
  = If _____, I would make more holidays.

2 만약 그가 그의 모자를 가져왔더라면, 지금 또 다른 것이 필요하지 않을 텐데. (bring, hat)
  = If _____, he wouldn't need another one now.

3 만약 내가 그의 생일이라는 것을 알았더라면, 그에게 전화했을 텐데. (will, call)
  = If I had known it was his birthday, _____.

UNIT 02   I wish/as if/It's time 가정법

A   괄호 안에서 알맞은 것을 고르시오.

1   It's time I (have / had) my hair cut. My hair is too long.

2   I wish we (could meet / could have met) the mayor, but we couldn't.

3   I'm not good at singing. I wish I (were / had been) a talented singer.

4   Eric talks as if he (knows / knew) American history, but he doesn't know it well.

B   <보기>의 말을 활용하여 가정법 문장을 완성하시오.

<보기>	be expensive	be on sale
	be much braver	think about the future

1   I wish this bag _____ . I don't have enough money.

2   It's time you _____ .

3   His watch looks as if it _____ , but it is actually cheap.

4   I couldn't try skydiving. I wish I _____ .

C   다음 문장을 가정법 문장으로 바꿔 쓰시오.

1   I'm sorry that I said those words to Justin.
   → I wish _____ .

2   In fact, Sharon didn't clean the kitchen.
   → Sharon talks as if _____ .

3   I'm sorry that I'm not as strong as superman.
   → I wish _____ .

D   우리말과 같도록 괄호 안의 말을 알맞게 배열하시오.

1   이 여배우가 더 많은 영화에서 주연을 맡으면 좋을 텐데. (actress, wish, would, I, this, star)
   = _____ in more movies.

2   우리가 했던 실수들을 잊어야 할 때이다. (forgot, time, it's, we, mistakes, the)
   = _____ we made.

3   그 요리사는 마치 요리 대회에서 1등을 했던 것처럼 행동했다. (won, he, prize, had, if, first, as)
   = The chef acted _____ in the cooking contest.

UNIT 03 · Without[But for] 가정법, if를 생략한 가정법

A 다음 빈칸에 알맞은 말을 <보기>에서 골라 쓰시오.

<보기>	were it not for computers	were my feet smaller
	without your jacket	had I played the drums well

1 _____, I could wear these shoes.

2 _____, I would have been really cold.

3 _____, our lives would be inconvenient.

4 _____, I could have joined the band.

B 다음 두 문장의 의미가 같도록 괄호 안의 말로 시작하는 가정법 문장을 완성하시오.

1 If it were not for a break, you would get exhausted. (without)

→ _____, you would get exhausted.

2 Were it not for the light, I couldn't read books at night. (if)

→ _____, I couldn't read books at night.

3 If it had not been for your advice, we would have wasted too much time. (but)

→ _____, we would have wasted too much time.

4 Without water, the flowers couldn't grow. (if)

→ _____, the flowers couldn't grow.

5 If it had not been for Tim, we wouldn't have known how to install this program. (had)

→ _____, we wouldn't have known how to install this program.

C 우리말과 같도록 괄호 안의 말을 알맞게 배열하시오.

1 코치님이 없었다면, 테니스를 배우는 것은 쉽지 않았을 텐데. (been, it, for, coach, not, had, the)

= _____, learning tennis wouldn't have been easy.

2 나의 친구들이 없다면, 나는 매우 외로울 텐데. (it, were, my, for, not, friends)

= _____, I would be very lonely.

3 만약 네가 전에 거짓말을 했었더라면, 그들은 너를 믿지 않았을 텐데. (lies, before, told, you, had)

= _____, they wouldn't have trusted you.

Chapter Test +

Answers p.31

[1-3] 다음 빈칸에 들어갈 알맞은 것을 고르시오.

1

> If you _____ on time, we wouldn't have waited so long.

① arrive ② arrived
③ have arrived ④ will arrive
⑤ had arrived

2

> If I had taken the medicine, I _____ sick now.

① am ② am not
③ will be ④ wouldn't be
⑤ wouldn't have been

3

> She never lived in Busan. But she talks as if she _____ in Busan before.

① live ② lives
③ had lived ④ lived
⑤ is living

서술형
4 다음 두 문장의 의미가 같도록 문장을 완성하시오.

> But for the roses, the garden wouldn't look so beautiful.
> → If _____, the garden wouldn't look so beautiful.

[5-6] 다음 중 밑줄 친 부분이 어법상 어색한 것을 고르시오.

5 ① If Carol had gotten the opportunity, she wouldn't have missed it.
② Had his phone worked, he would have called.
③ If my family lived near the sea, I could have gone to the beach every day.
④ Were I you, I would stop complaining.
⑤ If the teacher gives me more time, I will memorize more English vocabularies.

6 ① I wish I could make myself a dress.
② Jacob talks as if he had a lot of money.
③ It's time you went back to your class.
④ But for your help, I couldn't have passed the exam.
⑤ The cookies look as if they had been tasty, but they aren't.

7 다음 대화의 빈칸에 들어갈 말이 순서대로 짝지어진 것은?

> A: I wish I _____ how to play the piano when I was younger.
> B: Me too. If I _____ then, I could play my favorite songs now.

① learn – learned
② learned – learned
③ learned – had learned
④ had learned – learned
⑤ had learned – had learned

[8-10] 다음 문장을 가정법 문장으로 바꿔 쓰시오.

8

As the novel is sold out, I can't buy it.
→ If the novel _____,

_____.

9

I'm sorry that you didn't have time to exercise with me.
→ I wish _____

_____.

10

As I didn't bring the ball, we can't play soccer now.
→ Had I _____,

_____.

서술형

11 다음 문장의 밑줄 친 부분을 if를 생략하여 다시 쓰시오.

If it were not for flour, bread couldn't be made.

→ _____, bread couldn't be made.

고난도

12 다음 중 밑줄 친 부분을 바르게 고치지 못한 것은?

① I wish I haven't heard the bad news.
   (→ hadn't heard)

② Had it not for this flashlight, we couldn't have seen in the dark. (→ If it had not for)

③ If Amy got enough rest then, she would not feel tired now. (→ had gotten)

④ It's time he quits playing PC games. (→ quit)

⑤ Without your support, I couldn't had finished the essay. (→ couldn't have finished)

[13-14] 다음 빈칸에 들어갈 말이 순서대로 짝지어진 것을 고르시오.

13

• Without lifeguards, many lives _____.
• Thomas talks as if he _____ the leader of the debate team. In fact, he isn't.

① wouldn't be saved – were
② wouldn't be saved – had been
③ would be saved – were
④ would be saved – had been
⑤ wouldn't have been saved – had been

14

• If I had gone to eat lunch, I _____ here now.
• _____ a movie director, she would have made many films for children.

① would be – Had she been
② wouldn't be – Were she
③ wouldn't be – Had she been
④ wouldn't have been – Were she
⑤ wouldn't have been – Had she been

서술형

[15-16] 다음 문장에서 어법상 어색한 부분을 찾아 쓰고 바르게 고쳐 쓰시오.

15

If I were in Seoul last week, I could have met my cousins.

_____ → _____

16

I wish the singer released more songs before he died.

_____ → _____

17 다음 중 짝지어진 두 문장의 의미가 <u>다른</u> 것은?

① If you had been in my situation, you would have agreed with me.
→ As you weren't in my situation, you didn't agree with me.

② I wish I hadn't told a lie to my parents.
→ I'm sorry that I told a lie to my parents.

③ If I were a cat, I could sleep all day.
→ As I wasn't a cat, I can't sleep all day.

④ As there isn't a user's manual, we can't operate the machine.
→ If there were a user's manual, we could operate the machine.

⑤ Without glasses, I couldn't see things clearly.
→ Were it not for glasses, I couldn't see things clearly.

[18-20] 우리말과 같도록 괄호 안의 말을 활용하여 빈칸에 쓰시오.

18

Jeff는 마치 호랑이를 봤었던 것처럼 말했다. (see, a tiger)

= Jeff talked as if _____ _____

_____ _____ _____ .

19

내가 그 배우를 직접 만나면 좋을 텐데. (meet, the actor)

= I _____ _____ _____ _____

_____ in person.

20

만약 내가 너라면, 너무 많은 탄산음료를 마시지 않을 텐데. (be)

= _____ _____ _____ , I wouldn't

drink too much soda.

[21-22] 다음 우리말을 알맞게 영작한 것을 고르시오.

21

만약 내가 Josh라면, 시끄럽게 하지 않을 텐데.

① If I am Josh, I wouldn't make a noise.
② If I were Josh, I wouldn't make a noise.
③ If I were Josh, I wouldn't have made a noise.
④ If I had been Josh, I wouldn't make a noise.
⑤ If I had been Josh, I wouldn't have made a noise.

22

Sarah는 마치 좋은 소식을 들었던 것처럼 말했다.

① Sarah talked as if she hears good news.
② Sarah talked as if she have heard good news.
③ Sarah talked as if she has heard good news.
④ Sarah talked as if she had heard good news.
⑤ Sarah talked as if she will have heard good news.

23 다음 세 문장의 의미가 같도록 빈칸에 알맞은 말을 쓰시오.

Without rules, the world might be unstable.
→ _____ _____ rules, the world might be unstable.
→ _____ _____ _____ _____ rules, the world might be unstable.

24 다음 중 밑줄 친 부분이 어법상 바른 것은?

① It's time you <u>walk</u> the dog.
② If she <u>knew</u> your address, she would have sent you a package.
③ <u>Were Gary at the park</u>, he would have played with us.
④ Without music, our lives <u>would be</u> boring.
⑤ I wish I <u>could have talked</u> to her right now.

UNIT 01   원급/비교급/최상급 비교

Answers p.32

A   밑줄 친 부분이 어법상 맞으면 O를 쓰고, 틀리면 바르게 고쳐 쓰시오.

1 Today is <u>very</u> foggier than yesterday.   → _____

2 Ethan is the <u>more diligent</u> student in my class.   → _____

3 Victory is less <u>important</u> than fair play.   → _____

4 This laptop works as <u>better</u> as my desktop computer.   → _____

B   괄호 안의 말을 활용하여 다음 문장을 한 문장으로 바꿔 쓰시오.

1 The museum is a three-story building. The city hall is a five-story building. The department store is a nine-story building. (tall)
→ The department store is _____ of the three buildings.

2 Eagles live 55 years on average. Horses live 40 years on average. (long)
→ Eagles live _____ horses on average.

3 I go to the library once a week. Justin goes to the library twice a week. (often)
→ Justin goes to the library _____ me.

C   우리말과 같도록 괄호 안의 말을 활용하여 빈칸에 쓰시오.

1 그 운동화는 깃털만큼 가볍게 느껴졌다. (light)
= The sneakers felt _____ _____ _____ a feather.

2 이 옷 가게는 저곳보다 서비스가 더 우수하다. (superior)
= This clothes store is _____ _____ that one in terms of service.

3 일요일은 일곱 개의 요일 중 가장 편안한 날이다. (relaxing)
= Sunday is _____ _____ _____ of the seven days.

D   우리말과 같도록 괄호 안의 말을 알맞게 배열하시오.

1 Andrew는 그의 형만큼 천천히 먹으려고 노력한다. (brother, slowly, as, his, as)
= Andrew tries to eat _____.

2 Sally는 나의 모든 친구들 중에서 가장 노래를 잘하는 사람이다. (my, of, best, friends, all, the, singer)
= Sally is _____.

3 이 빵집에서 초콜릿 케이크는 딸기 케이크보다 더 인기 있다. (than, popular, cake, more, strawberry)
= Chocolate cake is _____ in this bakery.

A 밑줄 친 부분이 어법상 맞으면 O를 쓰고, 틀리면 바르게 고쳐 쓰시오.

1 He will give us as much information as <u>he possible</u>. → _____

2 The drama is getting <u>much and much</u> interesting. → _____

3 <u>The sunnier</u> it is, the more energetic I become. → _____

4 Water pollution is one of <u>more serious</u> problems of all. → _____

B 괄호 안의 말을 알맞은 형태로 바꿔 문장을 완성하시오.

1 No other restaurant in the city is _____ than this one. (good)

2 The longer the customers waited, _____ they got. (angry)

3 The boy has four times _____ than his friend. (many cookies)

4 Rebecca is _____ girl that I have ever known. (brave)

C 다음 문장들의 의미가 같도록 빈칸에 알맞은 말을 쓰시오.

1 Trust is the most important thing in our friendship.

→ No other thing in our friendship is as _____ _____ _____ .

→ Trust is _____ _____ _____ _____ _____ thing in our friendship.

2 Yesterday was the coldest day of the year.

→ No other day of the year was _____ than _____ .

→ Yesterday was _____ _____ _____ _____ _____ days of the year.

D 우리말과 같도록 괄호 안의 말을 알맞게 배열하시오.

1 인공지능은 점점 더 똑똑해지고 있다. (smarter, getting, and, is, smarter)

= Artificial intelligence _____ .

2 그것은 내가 봤던 것 중에서 가장 슬픈 영화였다. (have, the, watched, movie, ever, I, saddest)

= It was _____ .

3 그 섬은 유명해지면 질수록 더 혼잡해졌다. (more, island, the, popular, the, got)

= _____ , the more crowded it became.

Chapter Test +

Answers p.32

[1-3] 다음 빈칸에 들어갈 알맞은 것을 고르시오.

1

> The larger a house is, _____ cleaning it is.

① hard
② harder
③ more hard
④ the harder
⑤ the hardest

2

> Please send me the pictures as _____ as possible.

① quickly
② quicklier
③ more quickly
④ the quickliest
⑤ the most quickly

3

> Health is _____ of all things.

① valuable
② more valuable
③ valuable as
④ valuable than
⑤ the most valuable

4 다음 중 어법상 바른 것은?

① I can walk very faster than you.
② Dubai has the taller building in the world.
③ This model is more popular than that one.
④ This is the most big museum in the country.
⑤ She is one of the kindest adult I have met.

서술형

[5-7] 다음 문장에서 어법상 어색한 부분을 찾아 쓰고 바르게 고쳐 쓰시오.

5

> The symptom is getting worst and worst.

_____ → _____

6

> My new coffee machine is inferior than the old one.

_____ → _____

7

> Having a good personality is most important than being successful.

_____ → _____

8 다음 중 밑줄 친 부분을 바르게 고친 것은?

① This peach is as sweeter as honey.
   (→ sweetest)
② He is the more famous writer in Korea.
   (→ most)
③ I am more busier this week than last week.
   (→ more busy)
④ The black coat is much prettier as the brown one. (→ than)
⑤ Tim goes shopping as often than me. (→ so)

9 다음은 세 학생의 시험 점수를 비교하는 표이다. 괄호 안의 말을 활용하여 문장을 완성하시오.

	English	Math	Science
Betty	100	70	90
Mark	80	90	65
Emily	90	100	85

(1) Betty got _____ English score of the three students. (high)

(2) Mark's science score is _____ _____ student's. (low, any)

(3) No student did _____ as Emily on the math test. (well)

10 다음 빈칸에 들어갈 말로 어색한 것은?

> The field trip was _____ more exciting than we thought.

① very   ② much
③ far   ④ even
⑤ a lot

[11-12] 괄호 안의 말을 활용하여 다음 문장을 한 문장으로 바꿔 쓰시오.

11
> • The Nile River is 6,650 km long.
> • The Mississippi River is 3,730 km long.

→ The Mississippi River is _____ as the Nile River. (not, long)

12
> • A chicken burger is $5.
> • A cheeseburger is $3.
> • A mushroom burger is $7.

→ No other burger is _____ a cheeseburger. (cheap)

[13-14] 다음 중 어법상 어색한 것을 고르시오.

13 ① Today is as warmer as yesterday.
② It is the most wonderful view I have seen.
③ These peppers are far spicier than the others.
④ The higher we climb up the mountain, the colder it becomes.
⑤ His new novel is getting more and more popular.

14 ① Fred plays soccer better than Ted.
② To me, nothing is more important than love.
③ The airplane is one of the safest vehicles.
④ Lisa is wisest than any other girl in my class.
⑤ Reading a magazine is not so interesting as watching a documentary.

[15-16] 다음 빈칸에 공통으로 들어갈 알맞은 것을 고르시오.

15
> • This board game is less complicated _____ the last one.
> • I waited in line longer _____ I expected.

① as   ② so
③ and   ④ much
⑤ than

16
> • No other snack in the supermarket is _____ tasty as chocolate chip cookies.
> • Keep yourself as calm _____ you can during the interview.

① much   ② as
③ very   ④ too
⑤ more

[17-19] 다음 두 문장의 의미가 같도록 빈칸에 알맞은 말을 쓰시오.

17

When you speak more clearly, the listener understands you better.

→ _____ _____ _____ you speak, _____ _____ the listener understands you.

18

The table is five times as heavy as the chair.

→ The table is _____ _____ _____ _____ the chair.

19

The diamond is the hardest stone on the earth.

→ No other _____ on the earth _____ _____ _____ the diamond.

20 주어진 문장과 의미가 <u>다른</u> 것은?

No other star in the sky is as bright as Sirius.

① No star in the sky is so bright as Sirius.
② Sirius is the brightest star in the sky.
③ Sirius is one of the brightest stars in the sky.
④ Sirius is brighter than any other star in the sky.
⑤ Sirius is brighter than all the other stars in the sky.

21 다음 중 짝지어진 두 문장의 의미가 <u>다른</u> 것은?

① My younger brother is taller than me.
  → I'm shorter than my younger brother.
② Karen is less careful than Jason.
  → Jason is as careful as Karen.
③ Tyler is the funniest kid in the class.
  → No kid in the class is as funny as Tyler.
④ Sit on your chair as straight as possible.
  → Sit on your chair as straight as you can.
⑤ Einstein was the most intelligent scientist in the world.
  → Einstein was more intelligent than any other scientist in the world.

[22-24] 우리말과 같도록 괄호 안의 말을 활용하여 문장을 완성하시오.

22

캐나다는 인도보다 세 배 더 크다. (big)

= Canada is _____ India.

23

이것은 내가 본 것 중에서 가장 아름다운 정원이다. (beautiful garden, see)

= This is _____ _____.

24

시금치는 가장 건강에 좋은 채소들 중 하나이다. (healthy, vegetable)

= Spinach is _____.

Chapter 11 일치와 화법

UNIT 01 수의 일치

Answers p.33

A 밑줄 친 부분이 어법상 맞으면 O를 쓰고, 틀리면 바르게 고쳐 쓰시오.

1 Mathematics <u>are</u> interesting for Kevin. → _____

2 Listening to classical music <u>help</u> me relax. → _____

3 Each correct answer <u>is</u> worth ten points. → _____

4 Emily and Amy <u>have</u> been to Singapore before. → _____

5 A number of dolphins <u>is</u> swimming near the shore. → _____

B 다음 빈칸에 알맞은 형태의 be동사를 쓰시오. (단, 현재시제로 쓰시오.)

1 There _____ only five dollars in my wallet.

2 The injured _____ being carried to the hospital.

3 What we're looking at _____ the Statue of Liberty.

4 Someone _____ calling my name from outside.

5 Both a novel and a poem _____ fun to read.

C 우리말과 같도록 괄호 안의 말을 활용하여 빈칸에 쓰시오.

1 버터 바른 빵은 내가 가장 좋아하는 아침 식사이다. (bread and butter, be)

= _____ _____ _____ _____ my favorite breakfast.

2 그 그룹에 있는 누구도 나의 나이를 알지 못한다. (nobody, know)

= _____ _____ _____ _____ _____ my age.

3 3킬로미터는 걷기에 그렇게 멀지 않다. (kilometer, be)

= _____ _____ _____ not that far to walk.

4 고층 건물의 수는 증가하고 있다. (skyscraper, increase)

= _____ _____ _____ _____ _____ _____ .

UNIT 02 시제의 일치

A 밑줄 친 부분이 어법상 맞으면 O를 쓰고, 틀리면 바르게 고쳐 쓰시오.

1 The teacher said that water <u>boiled</u> at 100°C. → _____

2 They knew that I <u>have</u> been to Canada when I was a child. → _____

3 Mom told me that she <u>will</u> cook potato soup for dinner. → _____

4 Josh said that his sister <u>was</u> the best athlete in her school. → _____

B 다음 문장의 밑줄 친 부분을 과거시제로 바꿔 완전한 문장을 쓰시오.

1 They <u>say</u> that Laura volunteers every month.
→ They _____.

2 Nobody <u>knows</u> that a bird built a nest under our roof.
→ Nobody _____.

3 The teacher <u>explains</u> to the kids that the sun rises in the east.
→ The teacher _____.

4 Ashley <u>says</u> that she can help me with my homework.
→ Ashley _____.

5 We <u>learn</u> that dinosaurs existed on earth millions of years ago.
→ We _____.

6 Noah <u>tells</u> me that he saw a ghost in his dream last night.
→ Noah _____.

C 우리말과 같도록 괄호 안의 말을 활용하여 문장을 완성하시오.

1 Helen은 우리가 전통적인 무언가를 먹을 것이라고 말했다. (will, eat, something traditional)
= Helen said that _____.

2 나는 그 약국이 월요일마다 문을 닫는다는 것을 알지 못했다. (pharmacy, close, on Mondays)
= I didn't know that _____.

3 그는 우리에게 콜로세움이 서기 80년에 지어졌다고 말했다. (the Colosseum, build, AD 80)
= He told us that _____.

UNIT 03 화법

A 다음 직접 화법을 간접 화법으로 바꾼 문장에서 어법상 어색한 부분을 찾아 바르게 고쳐 완전한 문장을 쓰시오.

1 She said to me, "When will your parents arrive home?"
→ She asked me when my parents will arrive home.
→ _____ .

2 The dentist said to Mike, "Don't drink too much soda."
→ The dentist told Mike not drink too much soda.
→ _____ .

3 He said to me, "I received the package yesterday."
→ He said me that he had received the package the day before.
→ _____ .

B 다음 문장을 간접 화법으로 바꿔 쓰시오.

1 Linda said, "I want to order two slices of pizza."
→ Linda _____ .

2 Thomas said to me, "Who wrote this novel?"
→ Thomas _____ .

3 She said to me, "Were you the class president last year?"
→ She _____ .

4 The doctor said, "You have to come to the hospital tomorrow."
→ The doctor _____ .

5 The man said to the people, "Don't leave empty boxes here."
→ The man _____ .

C 우리말과 같도록 괄호 안의 말을 활용하여 문장을 완성하시오.

1 Sarah는 나에게 내가 그녀의 부탁을 들어줄 수 있는지 물었다. (can, do)
= Sarah _____ her a favor.

2 엄마는 내가 밖에서 놀기에 너무 늦었다고 말했다. (it, be, too, late, for)
= Mom _____ to play outside.

3 나는 그에게 나의 사진을 아무에게도 보여주지 말라고 말했다. (show, photos)
= I _____ to anyone.

Chapter Test +

Answers p.34

[1-4] 다음 빈칸에 들어갈 알맞은 것을 고르시오.

1

Sarah realized that her wallet _____ lost.

① be
② is
③ was
④ has been
⑤ is being

2

My grandmother always told me that actions _____ louder than words.

① speak
② spoke
③ has spoken
④ had spoken
⑤ were spoken

3

We were taught that cheetahs _____ the fastest land animals.

① will be
② are
③ would be
④ were
⑤ had been

4

Mr. Green asked _____ he could delay the appointment.

① unless
② what
③ that
④ if
⑤ which

5 다음 중 어법상 바른 것은?

① A hundred dollars are needed to buy the sneakers I want.
② He said he will start the research the next day.
③ We learned that Mars had lower gravity than Earth.
④ Luke told me that he exercises once a week.
⑤ Everyone in my family have brown eyes.

서술형

[6-8] 다음 문장에서 어법상 어색한 부분을 찾아 쓰고 바르게 고쳐 쓰시오.

6

I asked my sister that she had taken my laptop.

_____ → _____

7

Many of us didn't know that the First World War had ended in 1918.

_____ → _____

8

The rich is getting richer these days.

_____ → _____

서술형

[9-11] 다음 문장을 간접 화법으로 바꿔 쓰시오.

9
> John said, "Are you going to join the book club next week?"
> → John asked _____
> _____.

10
> Ms. Holland said to us, "Stay calm in any situation."
> → Ms. Holland advised us _____
> _____.

11
> Alice said to me, "Jeff left three hours ago."
> → Alice told me that _____
> _____.

고난도

12 다음 중 직접 화법을 간접 화법으로 <u>잘못</u> 바꾼 것을 <u>모두</u> 고르시오.

① My mom said to me, "Are you hungry now?"
　→ My mom asked me if I was hungry then.
② Louis said to us, "Bella is going back to her hometown tomorrow."
　→ Louis told us that Bella was going back to her hometown the next day.
③ Lily said, "Can I go to the mall with you?"
　→ Lily asked if she can go to the mall with me.
④ The trainer said to me, "Drink more water."
　→ The trainer told me to drink more water.
⑤ I said to Paul, "When did you cut your hair?"
　→ I asked Paul when you had cut your hair.

서술형

13 괄호 안의 동사를 활용하여 빈칸에 쓰시오.

> In art class, I learned that the *Mona Lisa* _____ once stolen in 1911. (be)

14 다음 대화의 빈칸에 들어갈 알맞은 것은?

> *A*: What did the teacher tell you?
> *B*: He told me _____.

① don't run in the hallway
② not to run in the hallway
③ not run in the hallway
④ to run not in the hallway
⑤ not to running in the hallway

15 다음 문장을 간접 화법으로 바르게 바꾼 것은?

> Mary said, "I'm going to the movies today."

① Mary said that I'm going to the movies today.
② Mary said I'm going to the movies that day.
③ Mary told she is going to the movies today.
④ Mary said she was going to the movies that day.
⑤ Mary told that she was going to the movies that day.

16 다음 문장을 과거시제로 바꿀 때 밑줄 친 부분이 어법상 <u>어색한</u> 것은?

> Many people know that London is the capital of England.
> → Many people <u>knew</u> that <u>London</u> <u>was</u>
> 　　　　　　　①　　　②　　　③　　④
> 　the <u>capital</u> of England.
> 　　　⑤

[17-18] 다음 중 어법상 어색한 것을 고르시오.

17 ① Ted said that he had been looking for his cell phone.
② I thought that no news is good news.
③ Ms. Rogers heard that the meeting could be delayed.
④ My friend told me that his soccer team lost the game.
⑤ The article said the first washing machine had been created in 1851.

18 ① Statistics is the science of collecting and analyzing data.
② Both Kate and Joshua were excited to visit Korea.
③ The number of thieves have been decreasing recently.
④ Slow and steady wins the race.
⑤ Each person needs to reduce waste.

[19-20] 다음 빈칸에 들어갈 말이 순서대로 짝지어진 것을 고르시오.

19
• What Kelly showed us _____ surprising.
• Ten kilograms _____ heavy for me to lift.

① was – is
② was – are
③ was – have been
④ were – is
⑤ were – are

20
• The historian said that the Leaning Tower of Pisa _____ in the 14th century.
• When I was a child, I learned that the Moon _____ around the Earth.

① is built – goes
② was built – goes
③ was built – went
④ had been built – goes
⑤ had been built – went

고난도
21 다음 중 어법상 바른 것끼리 묶인 것은?

ⓐ A number of boys are going to school together.
ⓑ Are there anyone feeling cold?
ⓒ I believed that Ella couldn't tell a lie.
ⓓ Mom told us not make too much noise.
ⓔ The kids learned that strawberries had seeds on the surface.

① ⓐ, ⓑ
② ⓐ, ⓒ
③ ⓑ, ⓒ
④ ⓑ, ⓓ
⑤ ⓓ, ⓔ

서술형
[22-24] 우리말과 같도록 괄호 안의 말을 활용하여 문장을 완성하시오.

22 새로운 사람들을 만나는 것은 나를 행복하게 만든다. (make, happy)

= Meeting new people _____.

23 Tom은 나의 취미가 무엇인지 물었다. (hobby, be)

= Tom asked _____.

24 선생님은 우리에게 아브라함 링컨이 1861년에 대통령이 되었다고 말씀해주셨다. (become, the president)

= The teacher told us that Abraham Lincoln _____ in 1861.

Chapter 12 특수구문

UNIT 01 강조, 도치

Answers p.35

A 밑줄 친 부분이 어법상 맞으면 O를 쓰고, 틀리면 바르게 고쳐 쓰시오.

1 On the branch a blue bird sat. → _____

2 We did waited in line to get a free coupon. → _____

3 Rarely Megan goes fishing with her father. → _____

4 It was Kyle who cooked some soup for me. → _____

B 다음 문장을 밑줄 친 부분을 강조하는 문장으로 바꿔 쓰시오.

1 This lemonade tastes sour.
→ _____ .

2 Mr. Clark lives in the biggest house in this town.
→ _____ .

3 The new shopping mall is located on Main Street.
→ _____ .

C 다음 두 문장의 의미가 같도록 문장을 완성하시오.

1 Lucy has hardly forgotten her promise.
→ Hardly _____ .

2 The tunnel was below the mountain.
→ Below the mountain _____ .

3 The rude students rarely show respect for their teachers.
→ Rarely _____ .

D 우리말과 같도록 괄호 안의 말을 알맞게 배열하시오.

1 모퉁이에 기타를 치는 남자 한 명이 서있었다. (the, playing, corner, a, man, stood)
= At _____ the guitar.

2 나의 부모님이 서로 만났던 때는 바로 20년 전이었다. (met, parents, when, 20 years, my, ago)
= It was _____ each other.

3 나는 일찍 일어나는 것에 익숙해질 수 없어. – 나도 그래. (I, can, neither)
= I can't get used to waking up early. – _____ .

UNIT 02 병렬, 부정, 동격, 생략

Answers p.35

A 밑줄 친 부분이 어법상 맞으면 O를 쓰고, 틀리면 바르게 고쳐 쓰시오.

1 History documentaries are boring but <u>usefully</u>.   → _____

2 <u>Not</u> every oil is bad for your health.   → _____

3 You should write your report and <u>handing</u> it in today.   → _____

4 Lena read a magazine <u>while was</u> waiting for the bus.   → _____

B 다음 두 문장의 의미가 같도록 빈칸에 알맞은 말을 쓰시오.

1 Both Tom and Brandon don't like playing outside.

→ _____ of the boys likes playing outside.

2 The director's movies are sometimes successful, but sometimes not.

→ The director's movies are not _____ successful.

3 Some of those pens on the desk are mine, but the others aren't.

→ Not _____ of those pens on the desk are mine.

C 다음 문장에서 생략된 부분을 넣어 완전한 문장을 쓰시오.

1 Martin hurt his arm when moving the desk.

→ _____.

2 You don't have to wear suits if you don't want to.

→ _____.

3 Though stressed, she tried to think positively.

→ _____.

D 우리말과 같도록 괄호 안의 말을 알맞게 배열하시오.

1 우리는 공원에서 자전거를 타거나 산책을 할 수 있다. (bicycle, take, a, either, or, can, a, walk, ride)

= We _____ at the park.

2 만약 네가 원한다면 너는 나의 수건을 사용해도 된다. (you, my, want, may, towel, to, if, use)

= You _____.

3 그 정보 중 아무것도 도움이 되지 않았다. (the, helpful, none, was, information, of)

= _____.

Chapter Test +

Chapter 12

특수구문

Hackers Grammar Smart Level 3

[1-4] 다음 빈칸에 들어갈 알맞은 것을 고르시오.

1

> Both swimming and _____ sound exciting to me.

① surf
② to surf
③ surfing
④ surfed
⑤ to surfing

2

> Never _____ such a beautiful painting before.

① I saw
② I have seen
③ I had seen
④ have I seen
⑤ have I saw

3

> My brother is an outgoing person, and _____.

① so am I
② so do I
③ so did I
④ neither am I
⑤ neither do I

4

> It was last weekend _____ the kids went to the aquarium.

① where
② whom
③ how
④ what
⑤ that

서술형

[5-6] 다음 문장에서 어법상 어색한 부분을 찾아 쓰고 바르게 고쳐 쓰시오.

5

> Little I imagined that I would be the class president.

_____ → _____

6

> James couldn't solve the problem, and neither I could.

_____ → _____

7 다음 빈칸에 들어갈 말이 순서대로 짝지어진 것은?

> • The rumor _____ he cheated on the test is not true.
> • His ability _____ memorizing words is surprising.

① that – that
② that – of
③ of – that
④ of – which
⑤ which – of

8 다음 중 어법상 바른 것은?

① Hardly we could see the stars in the sky.
② Jessie doesn't like watching horror movies, and neither I do.
③ That was yesterday when I went to the beach.
④ Though exhausted, Frank finished the race.
⑤ You can either go outside or to stay home.

Chapter 12 특수구문 **69**

[9-11] 우리말과 같도록 괄호 안의 말을 활용하여 문장을 완성하시오.

9

그 직원들 중 아무도 친절하지 않았다. (none, clerk)

= _____ was friendly.

10

물 속으로 수영 선수가 뛰어들었다. (dive, the swimmer)

= Into the water _____.

11

모든 게임이 아이들에게 해로운 것은 아니다. (every, game)

= _____ is harmful to children.

12 다음 두 문장의 의미가 같도록 빈칸에 알맞은 말을 쓰시오.

Josh hardly expected that Jane would come to his birthday party.

→ Hardly _____ _____ _____ that Jane would come to his birthday party.

[13-14] 다음 우리말을 알맞게 영작한 것을 고르시오.

13

우리 둘 다 시험 성적에 만족하지 않는다.

① All of us are satisfied with the test score.
② Either of us is satisfied with the test score.
③ Not both of us are satisfied with the test score.
④ Not all of us are satisfied with the test score.
⑤ Neither of us is satisfied with the test score.

14

나의 아버지가 항상 엄격하신 것은 아니다.

① My father is strict.
② My father is not strict.
③ My father is not always strict.
④ My father is always not strict.
⑤ My father isn't always not strict.

[15-16] 다음 대화의 빈칸에 들어갈 알맞은 것을 고르시오.

15

A: I haven't started to research my essay topic yet.
B: _____.

① So I have
② So I haven't
③ So haven't I
④ Neither have I
⑤ Neither I have

16

A: Did you watch the baseball game?
B: No, _____ of us watches baseball games. We are all more into football.

① none
② no
③ every
④ never
⑤ both

서술형

[17-18] 다음 문장을 밑줄 친 부분을 강조하는 문장으로 바꿔 쓰시오.

17

> Amy <u>looks</u> tired after taking care of her niece.
> → _____
> _____ .

18

> Timmy asked <u>Robert</u> for a favor yesterday.
> → _____
> _____ .

서술형

19 우리말과 같도록 주어진 <조건>에 맞게 영작하시오.

> 곰 한 마리가 나온 곳은 바로 숲에서였다.

> <조건>　1. 「It is[was] ~ that …」 구문을 사용하시오.
> 　　　　 2. from the woods, come out을
> 　　　　　　 활용하시오.

> = _____

고난도

20 다음 중 어법상 바른 것의 개수는?

> ⓐ That is during winter when many people
> 　 go skiing.
> ⓑ The movie was both long and boring.
> ⓒ Up the hill went the car.
> ⓓ Dan feels happy today, and so am I.
> ⓔ Not every student enjoys PE class.

> ① 1개　　　　② 2개　　　　③ 3개
> ④ 4개　　　　⑤ 5개

21 다음 중 어법상 어색한 것은?

> ① Here she comes carrying a fruit basket.
> ② Lily didn't know the answer, and neither I did.
> ③ The fact that the artwork was fake was shocking.
> ④ My friend is not only smart but also friendly.
> ⑤ Dad takes various kinds of vitamins when tired.

고난도

22 다음 중 밑줄 친 부분의 쓰임이 나머지 넷과 <u>다른</u> 것은?

> ① <u>It</u> was John who lost the new laptop.
> ② <u>It</u> was an honor for me to be invited here.
> ③ <u>It</u> was in the park where the child was lost.
> ④ <u>It</u> is this week when summer vacation begins.
> ⑤ <u>It</u> was an umbrella that Sue borrowed from Jane.

서술형

[23-24] 다음 문장에서 생략된 부분을 넣어 완전한 문장을 쓰시오.

23

> Ashley didn't call me because she forgot to.
> → _____
> _____ .

24

> Unless under the age of ten, you can't get a discount.
> → _____
> _____ .

MEMO

HACKERS
GRAMMAR SMART

LEVEL **3**

ANSWERS

HACKERS

HACKERS

GRAMMAR SMART 3

LEVEL

3

ANSWERS

HACKERS

Chapter 01 | 시제

UNIT 01 현재완료시제

Smart Check
p.16

1 ②　　2 ③

Practice
p.17

A 1 has rented　　2 has never heard
　　3 met　　4 has been trying

B 1 has worked　　2 bought
　　3 took　　4 has been

C 1 have been waiting　　2 has been practicing
　　3 has been drawing　　4 have been discussing

D 1 has been
　　2 have already sold
　　3 ever been to
　　4 have been searching for

UNIT 02 과거완료시제와 미래완료시제

Smart Check
p.18

1 ②　　2 ②　　3 ③

Practice
p.19

A 1 will have submitted　　2 had never ridden
　　3 had been　　4 will have been

B 1 had ended　　2 will have heard
　　3 will have arrived　　4 had exercised

C 1 had been talking
　　2 will have been snowing
　　3 had been practicing

D 1 had gotten enough sleep
　　2 will have been playing the piano
　　3 will have run away

Writing Exercise
p.20

A 1 have been to Dubai
　　2 had danced
　　3 has lost her doll
　　4 has been taking drawing classes
　　5 has owned an Italian restaurant
　　6 have been doing the research on penguins
　　7 will have read

B 1 he had not been careful
　　2 We have used solar energy
　　3 She has improved her English skills
　　4 I had missed the train
　　5 He will have gone to the library
　　6 Natalie had been playing tennis

C 1 Your phone has been ringing
　　2 I have already decided
　　3 Ms. Hill had been drinking coffee
　　4 He will have been running the gym
　　5 The dog had broken my glasses
　　6 She has been a member of the book club

D 1 had won the math competition
　　2 will have been friends

Chapter Test
p.22

1 ④　　2 ⑤　　3 ④　　4 ③　　5 has → had
6 had → will have　　　7 ④　　8 ②
9 has lost　　10 had written　　11 ⑤　　12 ③
13 ①　　14 ②　　15 have known　　16 had forgotten
17 ③　　18 ②　　19 Sarah will have packed her bag
20 Have you ever seen a tiger　　21 ③
22 have discussed the issue
23 had been taking a nap
24 will have been traveling around the world

---

1 과거부터 현재까지 계속되는 일을 나타내고 있으므로 현재완료시제를 쓴다.

2 미래의 특정 시점까지 완료되거나 계속될 일을 나타내는 미래완료시제를 쓴다.

3 과거의 특정 시점 이전에 발생한 일이 그 시점에도 계속 진행되고 있었음을 나타내는 과거완료진행시제를 쓴다.

4 현재완료시제는 특정한 과거 시점을 나타내는 표현과 함께 쓸 수 없다.

5 과거의 특정 시점 이전에 발생한 일을 나타내는 과거완료시제를 쓴다.

6 미래의 특정 시점까지 완료되거나 계속될 일을 나타내는 미래완료시제를 쓴다.

7 과거의 특정 시점 이전에 발생한 일을 나타내는 과거완료시제를 쓴다.

8 과거에 일어난 일이 현재에도 계속 진행되고 있음을 나타내는 현재완료진행시제를 쓴다.

9 차 열쇠를 잃어버렸고 여전히 찾지 못하고 있으므로 현재완료시제를 쓴다.

10 2017년에 은퇴한 일보다 50곡의 노래를 작곡한 일이 더 이전에 발생했으므로 과거완료시제를 쓴다.

11 주어진 문장과 ⑤: 경험

①②: 결과   ③: 계속   ④: 완료

12 주어진 문장과 ③: 계속
①⑤: 완료   ②: 경험   ④: 결과

13 • 현재완료시제 문장에서 빈칸 뒤에 일의 시작 시점을 나타내는 last year가 왔으므로 since를 쓴다.
• 현재완료진행시제 문장에서 빈칸 뒤에 일의 지속 기간을 나타내는 three hours가 왔으므로 for를 쓴다.

14 ① has already started → had already started
③ has had → had
④ has been → had been[was]
⑤ has been writing → will have been writing

15 「for + 지속 기간」이 있고 과거에 일어난 일이 현재까지 영향을 미치고 있으므로 현재완료시제를 쓴다.

16 과거의 특정 시점 이전에 발생한 일을 나타내는 과거완료시제를 쓴다.

17 ③ has visited → visited

18 ② have → had

19 미래의 특정 시점까지 완료되거나 계속될 일을 나타내는 미래완료시제 문장이므로 「will have + p.p.」를 쓴다.

20 과거부터 현재까지의 경험을 나타내는 현재완료시제 문장이므로 「have + p.p.」를 쓴다.

21 ⓑ be → have been
ⓔ has → had

22 과거에 일어난 일이 현재에 완료되었음을 나타내는 현재완료시제 문장이므로 「have + p.p.」를 쓴다.

23 과거의 특정 시점 이전에 발생한 일이 그 시점에도 계속 진행되고 있었음을 나타내는 과거완료진행시제 문장이므로 「had been + V-ing」를 쓴다.

24 미래의 특정 시점에도 계속 진행될 일을 나타내는 미래완료진행시제 문장이므로 「will have been + V-ing」를 쓴다.

Chapter 02 | 조동사

UNIT 01 can, may, must, should

Smart Check   p.26
1 ②   2 ①

Practice   p.27

A 1 may   2 must   3 can't
   4 be able to 5 must not

B 1 should   2 can   3 may

C 1 ought not to   2 is able to
   3 have to

D 1 doesn't have[need] to take
   2 must[should] be checked

3 must be   4 may not need

UNIT 02 had better, would rather, used to, may as well

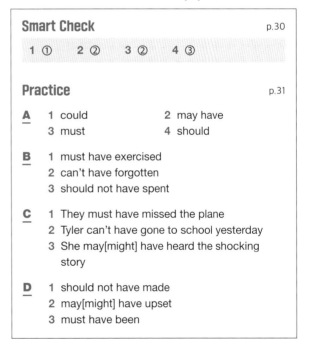

Smart Check   p.28
1 ③   2 ①   3 ②   4 ②

Practice   p.29

A 1 had better   2 take
   3 than   4 had better not
   5 used to   6 may as well

B 1 used to   2 would rather
   3 had better

C 1 used to buy
   2 would rather not answer
   3 had better not skip
   4 would visit
   5 may as well reserve

UNIT 03 조동사 + have + p.p.

Smart Check   p.30
1 ①   2 ②   3 ②   4 ③

Practice   p.31

A 1 could   2 may have
   3 must   4 should

B 1 must have exercised
   2 can't have forgotten
   3 should not have spent

C 1 They must have missed the plane
   2 Tyler can't have gone to school yesterday
   3 She may[might] have heard the shocking story

D 1 should not have made
   2 may[might] have upset
   3 must have been

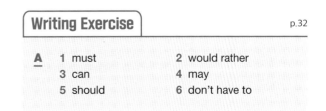

Writing Exercise   p.32

A 1 must   2 would rather
   3 can   4 may
   5 should   6 don't have to

B 1 used to be a bookstore
2 should not have yelled at my friend
3 had better add less salt
4 could have won the gold medal
5 can't be based on a true story
6 may as well call the restaurant

C 1 You ought to study harder
2 They can't have finished the research
3 You are not able to enter the museum
4 The bus must have been delayed
5 The doctor had to leave right away
6 The girl might have been Julie

D 1 Can I exchange   2 used to be
3 should have brought

Chapter Test
p.34

1 ⑤   2 ②   3 ④   4 ③
5 is able to speak   6 ④   7 ③   8 ⑤
9 ①   10 ④   11 used to   12 can't
13 ⑤   14 will be able to learn
15 must have known
16 would rather eat pizza than salad
17 ②   18 ④   19 ①   20 ④
21 rather → as well   22 has to → must
23 shouldn't → can't   24 ②

1 과거의 상태(전에는 ~이었다)를 나타내는 used to를 쓴다.

2 강한 부정의 추측(~일 리가 없다)을 나타내는 can't를 쓴다.

3 과거 사실에 대한 강한 추측(~했음이 틀림없다)을 나타내는 「must + have + p.p.」를 쓴다.

4 약한 추측(~일지도 모른다)을 나타내는 may를 쓴다.

5 can(능력·가능) = be able to

6 must(의무) = have to

7 ③ going → go

8 ⑤ had → have

9 ①: 약한 추측   주어진 문장과 ②③④⑤: 허가

10 ④: 강한 추측   주어진 문장과 ①②③⑤: 의무

11 • 과거의 반복적인 습관(~하곤 했다)을 나타내는 used to를 쓴다.
• 과거의 상태(전에는 ~이었다)를 나타내는 used to를 쓴다.

12 • 과거 사실에 대한 강한 추측(~했을 리가 없다)을 나타내는 「can't + have + p.p.」의 can't를 쓴다.
• 강한 부정의 추측(~일리가 없다)을 나타내는 can't를 쓴다.

13 ⑤ must → should

14 조동사는 두 개를 연속해서 쓸 수 없으므로 '~할 수 있다'라

는 의미의 can 대신 be able to를 will과 함께 쓴다.

15 과거 사실에 대한 강한 추측(~했음이 틀림없다)을 나타내는 「must + have + p.p.」를 쓴다.

16 would rather A than B 'B하느니 차라리 A하겠다'

17 ① would → used to
③ not would rather → would rather not
④ to follow → follow
⑤ to not → not to

18 충고·의무(~해야 한다)를 나타내는 ought to를 쓴다.

19 과거 사실에 대한 강한 추측(~했음이 틀림없다)을 나타내는 「must + have + p.p.」를 쓴다.

20 can't '~일 리가 없다'
must not '~하면 안 된다'

21 may as well '~하는 편이 좋다' (rather는 would와 함께 would rather((차라리) ~하겠다)의 형태로 쓰인다.)

22 강한 추측(~임이 틀림없다)을 나타내는 must를 쓴다.

23 과거 사실에 대한 강한 부정의 추측(~했을 리가 없다)을 나타내는 「can't + have + p.p.」를 쓴다.

24 ⓑ be → been
ⓓ had → would
ⓔ can → be able to

Chapter 03 | 수동태

UNIT 01 수동태의 쓰임

Smart Check
p.38

1 ③   2 ②

Practice
p.39

A 1 discovered   2 belongs to
3 be recycled   4 been repaired
5 are produced   6 appeared

B 1 was found   2 have been read
3 is being painted   4 might be seen
5 will be presented

C 1 is decorated   2 should be handed
3 have been inspected
4 are being installed

UNIT 02 4형식/5형식 문장의 수동태

Smart Check
p.40

1 ①   2 ②

Practice

p.41

A
1 for   2 to stop   3 to
4 flying

B
1 to   2 of   3 for
4 for

C
1 is called Milo by the children
2 was sent to the store by some customers
3 was heard knocking[to knock] on the door by Sandra
4 was advised to exercise regularly by the doctor

D
1 is expected to be   2 are kept tidy
3 were made to follow

UNIT 03 주의해야 할 수동태

Smart Check

p.42

1 ②   2 ②

Practice

p.43

A
1 to have   2 with
3 looked up to   4 is thought

B
1 with   2 in   3 to

C
1 are taken care of by doctors and nurses
2 was put off by my family
3 is expected to be a successful businessman
4 was looked down on by the people

D
1 It is said that   2 was surprised at
3 was dealt with

Writing Exercise

p.44

A
1 was broken by Harry
2 should be taken seriously by the company
3 were bought for me by my uncle
4 has been explained by the professor
5 is said that the temple is worth visiting, is said to be worth visiting

B
1 was seen sitting[to sit]
2 are satisfied with
3 can't be found
4 It is thought that
5 resembles
6 was looked down on

C
1 A decision may be made
2 is being learned by many students

3 was filled with tools
4 will be announced by the host
5 is taken care of by the gardener
6 was made to confess by the detective

D
1 was baked by my parents and me
2 were bought for her by them
3 was made to feel happy by the gifts

Chapter Test

p.46

1 ④   2 ③   3 ⑤   4 ⑤
5 the kid → to the kid
6 washing → being washed   7 ④   8 ③
9 ⑤   10 ②   11 ④   12 ③
13 had been prepared   14 is being heated
15 will be dealt with   16 ②, ④
17 He is said to be the best actor   18 ②
19 are looked up to   20 was put off
21 are being baked   22 ④
23 organize → to organize

1 건물이 설계하는 것이 아니라 설계되는 것이므로 수동태를 쓴다. 수동태의 동사는 「be동사 + p.p.」의 형태이므로 was designed를 쓴다.

2 가구가 옮기는 것이 아니라 옮겨지는 것이므로 수동태를 쓴다. 조동사가 있는 수동태는 「조동사 + be + p.p.」의 형태이므로 be moved를 쓴다.

3 시장이 존경하는 것이 아니라 존경받는 것이므로 수동태를 쓴다. 완료시제의 수동태는 「have/had been + p.p.」의 형태이므로 has been respected를 쓴다.

4 ⑤: of   ①②③④: to

5 직접 목적어가 주어인 수동태 문장은 간접 목적어 앞에 전치사 to/for/of 중 하나를 쓰며, 이때 tell은 to를 쓰는 동사이다.

6 접시들이 닦고 있는 것이 아니라 닦이고 있는 것이므로 수동태를 쓴다. 진행시제의 수동태는 「be동사 + being + p.p.」의 형태이고 현재 일어나고 있는 일을 나타내고 있으므로 are being washed를 쓴다.

7 ① is resembled → resembles
② watered → were watered
③ is called to → is called
⑤ in → at

8 첫 번째 빈칸: say의 목적어로 쓰인 that절의 주어를 수동태 문장의 주어로 쓸 때 「that절의 주어 + be동사 + said(p.p.) + to부정사 ~」의 형태로 쓴다.
두 번째 빈칸: be crowded with '~으로 붐비다'

9 ⑤ was appeared → appeared

10 ② of → in

11 • be satisfied with '~에 만족하다'
• be covered with '~으로 덮여 있다'

12 • be made of '~으로 만들어지다 (재료 성질이 변하지 않음)'
• take care of '~를 돌보다' (구동사를 수동태로 쓸 때 동사만 「be동사 + p.p.」의 형태로 쓰고, 나머지 부분은 동사 뒤에 그대로 쓴다.)

13 '준비되어 있었다'라는 과거의 의미이고 내가 도착한 시점보다 더 앞선 시점이므로 과거완료시제를 쓴다. 과거완료시제의 수동태는 「had been + p.p.」의 형태이므로 had been prepared를 쓴다.

14 '데워지고 있다'라는 현재진행의 의미이고 진행시제의 수동태는 「be동사 + being + p.p.」의 형태이므로 is being heated를 쓴다.

15 '다루어질 것이다'라는 미래의 의미이므로 조동사 will을 쓰며 조동사가 있는 수동태는 「조동사 + be + p.p.」의 형태이다. 구동사(deal with)를 수동태로 쓸 때 동사만 「be동사 + p.p.」의 형태로 쓰고, 나머지 부분은 동사 뒤에 그대로 쓰므로 will be dealt with를 쓴다.

16 지각동사가 쓰인 5형식 문장의 수동태에서 목적격 보어는 V-ing형이나 to부정사를 쓴다.

17 say의 목적어로 쓰인 that절의 주어를 수동태 문장의 주어로 쓸 때는 「that절의 주어 + be동사 + said(p.p.) + to부정사 ~」의 형태로 쓴다.

18 ② → Her opinion was looked down on by some members.

19 구동사(look up to)를 수동태로 쓸 때 동사만 「be동사 + p.p.」의 형태로 쓰고, 나머지 부분은 동사 뒤에 그대로 쓴다.

20 구동사(put off)를 수동태로 쓸 때 동사만 「be동사 + p.p.」의 형태로 쓰고, 나머지 부분은 동사 뒤에 그대로 쓴다. last week은 과거를 나타내는 표현이므로 was put off를 쓴다.

21 right now는 현재진행을 나타내는 표현이고, 진행시제의 수동태는 「be동사 + being + p.p.」의 형태이므로 are being baked를 쓴다.

22 첫 번째 빈칸: 내가 좋은 소식을 말한 것이 아니라 말해진 것이므로 수동태를 쓴다. 수동태의 동사는 「be동사 + p.p.」의 형태이므로 was told를 쓴다.
두 번째 빈칸: 그녀의 밴드가 허락한 것이 아니라 허락받은 것이므로 수동태를 쓴다. 완료시제의 수동태는 「have/had been + p.p.」의 형태이므로 had been allowed를 쓴다.

23 사역동사가 쓰인 5형식 문장을 수동태로 바꿀 때는 목적격 보어로 쓰인 동사원형을 to부정사로 바꾼다.

Chapter 04 | 부정사

UNIT 01 to부정사의 명사적 용법

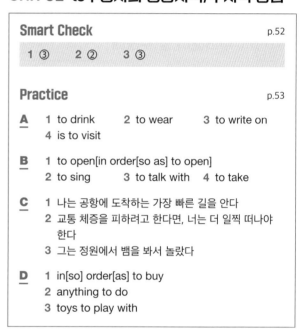

Smart Check p.50

1 ③   2 ①   3 ②

Practice p.51

A 1 to find   2 to use   3 to build
4 to hold[it should hold]

B 1 is not easy to see the stars in cities
2 is complicated to assemble a computer
3 is thrilling to camp in the forest

C 1 how to deal with   2 It, to spend
3 when to hand in

D 1 wish to make   2 is to design
3 it, to respect

UNIT 02 to부정사의 형용사적/부사적 용법

Smart Check p.52

1 ③   2 ②   3 ③

Practice p.53

A 1 to drink   2 to wear   3 to write on
4 is to visit

B 1 to open[in order[so as] to open]
2 to sing   3 to talk with   4 to take

C 1 나는 공항에 도착하는 가장 빠른 길을 안다
2 교통 체증을 피하려고 한다면, 너는 더 일찍 떠나야 한다
3 그는 정원에서 뱀을 봐서 놀랐다

D 1 in[so] order[as] to buy
2 anything to do
3 toys to play with

UNIT 03 부정사를 목적격 보어로 쓰는 동사

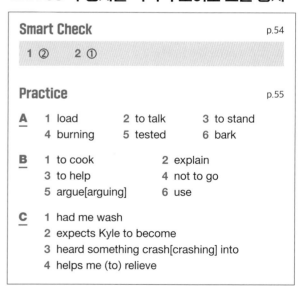

Smart Check p.54

1 ②   2 ①

Practice p.55

A 1 load   2 to talk   3 to stand
4 burning   5 tested   6 bark

B 1 to cook   2 explain
3 to help   4 not to go
5 argue[arguing]   6 use

C 1 had me wash
2 expects Kyle to become
3 heard something crash[crashing] into
4 helps me (to) relieve

UNIT 04 to부정사의 의미상 주어, 시제, 태

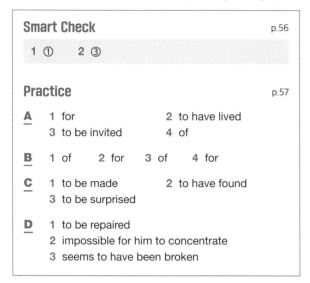

Smart Check   p.56

1 ①   2 ③

Practice   p.57

A 1 for   2 to have lived
3 to be invited   4 of

B 1 of   2 for   3 of   4 for

C 1 to be made   2 to have found
3 to be surprised

D 1 to be repaired
2 impossible for him to concentrate
3 seems to have been broken

UNIT 05 to부정사 구문, 독립부정사

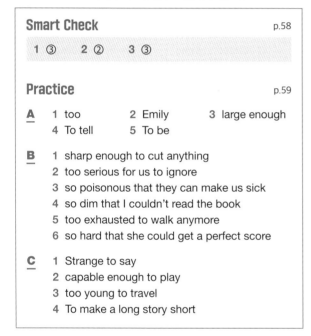

Smart Check   p.58

1 ③   2 ②   3 ③

Practice   p.59

A 1 too   2 Emily   3 large enough
4 To tell   5 To be

B 1 sharp enough to cut anything
2 too serious for us to ignore
3 so poisonous that they can make us sick
4 so dim that I couldn't read the book
5 too exhausted to walk anymore
6 so hard that she could get a perfect score

C 1 Strange to say
2 capable enough to play
3 too young to travel
4 To make a long story short

Writing Exercise   p.60

A 1 stay
2 (in order/so as) to improve
3 O
4 to be shocked[to have been shocked]
5 O   6 to be washed

B 1 ordered his dog to stop
2 is to increase taxes
3 is too cold to swim in
4 how to peel an apple
5 use their trunks (in order/so as) to drink water
6 is to return books

C 1 is talented enough to be
2 helps you to sleep well
3 To tell the truth
4 found it interesting to imagine
5 takes two hours to fly
6 got me to check the answers

D 1 to take   2 where to find
3 the fire alarm ring[ringing]

Chapter Test   p.62

1 ③   2 ④   3 ①   4 ③   5 ④
6 seems to have cried   7 too hot for us to play
8 when to hold   9 use   10 to be repaired
11 to complete   12 ②   13 ②   14 ④   15 ⑤
16 ③   17 friends to talk with
18 for my sister to drink
19 not to touch the exhibits
20 ④   21 ②   22 ④   23 ⑤
24 It was silly of you to trust him again

1 to부정사가 주어로 쓰일 때 주어 자리에 가주어 it을 쓰고 진주어 to부정사(구)를 뒤로 보낼 수 있다.

2 to부정사가 수식하는 명사 toy가 전치사의 목적어이므로 to부정사 뒤에 전치사 with를 쓴다.

3 have는 원형부정사를 목적격 보어로 쓰는 동사이므로 fix를 쓴다.

4 사람의 성격·성질을 나타내는 형용사(generous, foolish) 뒤에 오는 to부정사의 의미상 주어는 「of + 목적격」의 형태로 쓴다.

5 목적격 보어로 to부정사(to finish)가 왔으므로 원형부정사를 목적격 보어로 쓰는 make는 쓸 수 없다.

6 「It seems that + 주어 + 동사」는 「seem + to부정사」로 바꿔 쓸 수 있고, to부정사의 시제가 주절의 시제보다 앞서므로 「to have + p.p.」의 형태로 쓴다.

7 「so + 형용사/부사 + that + 주어 + can't + 동사원형」은 「too + 형용사/부사 + to부정사」로 바꿔 쓸 수 있다.

8 「의문사 + 주어 + should + 동사원형」은 「의문사 + to부정사」로 바꿔 쓸 수 있다.

9 let은 원형부정사를 목적격 보어로 쓰는 동사이므로 use를 쓴다.

10 need는 to부정사를 목적어로 쓰는 동사이고, 창문이 고쳐진다는 수동의 의미이므로 to부정사의 수동태 「to be + p.p.」를 쓴다.

11 「It takes + 목적어 + 시간 + to부정사」 '…가 ~하는 데 (시간)이 걸리다'

12 ① → to be   ③ → to write on
④ → to bring   ⑤ → cry[crying]

13 ① of → for
③ understand → to understand
④ enough big → big enough
⑤ to dealing → deal[to deal]

14 「so + 형용사/부사 + that + 주어 + can't + 동사원형」은
「too + 형용사/부사 + to부정사」로 바꿔 쓸 수 있다.
→ The sun is too bright for us to see with our bare
eyes.

15 • to부정사의 시제가 주절의 시제보다 앞설 때는 「to have
+ p.p.」의 형태로 쓴다.
• to부정사가 수동의 의미일 때는 「to be + p.p.」의 형태
로 쓴다.

16 • advise는 to부정사를 목적격 보어로 쓰는 동사이므로 to
eat을 쓴다.
• 사역동사 have의 목적어와 목적격 보어의 관계가 수동이
므로 과거분사 cut을 쓴다.

17 '대화할 친구들'이라는 의미로 명사 friends를 수식하는 형
용사적 용법의 to부정사를 쓴다.

18 '마실 차'라는 의미로 명사 tea를 수식하는 형용사적 용법의
to부정사를 쓰고, to부정사의 의미상 주어는 「for + 목적격」
의 형태로 to부정사 앞에 쓴다.

19 ask는 to부정사를 목적격 보어로 쓰는 동사이고 to부정사
의 부정형은 「not to + 동사원형」이다.

20 ④ to watch → watch

21 ② visiting → visit

22 주어진 문장과 ④: 명사적 용법
①③: 형용사적 용법   ②⑤: 부사적 용법

23 주어진 문장과 ⑤: 형용사적 용법
①③: 명사적 용법   ②④: 부사적 용법

24 '그를 또 믿다니 어리석다'라는 의미로 판단의 근거를 나타
내는 부사적 용법의 to부정사를 쓴다.

Chapter 05 | 동명사

UNIT 01 동명사의 쓰임

Smart Check   p.66

1 ③   2 ②   3 ③

Practice   p.67

A 1 Exploring   2 my
3 calling   4 being given

B 1 his[him]   2 living
3 her
4 missing[having missed]

C 1 my[me] spilling   2 having watched
3 being chosen

D 1 Gaining his trust takes
2 her keeping   3 being defeated

UNIT 02 동명사와 to부정사를 목적어로 쓰는 동사

Smart Check   p.68

1 ②

Practice   p.69

A 1 working   2 visiting
3 to move   4 seeing

B 1 hiding[having hidden]
2 eating   3 to sell
4 working[to work]

C 1 learning   2 respecting
3 to build   4 to charge

D 1 avoid wasting   2 tried using
3 is used to living   4 are busy dealing

Writing Exercise   p.70

A 1 Reading[To read] books
2 to pick me up
3 delivering[to deliver] pizzas
4 to join the volunteer program
5 going to Hanoi with my parents

B 1 regretted eating
2 having been treated unfairly
3 is considering working
4 deny having made
5 mind my[me] waiting
6 was worth listening to

C 1 began talking about the old times
2 Building a snowman in winter
3 remembered seeing the man
4 tried to move the large rock
5 could not help crying
6 hates being asked about his family

D 1 was busy preparing
2 are looking forward to going[look forward to
going]
3 On entering

p.72

1 ② **2** ③ **3** ④ **4** ③ **5** writing

6 to bring **7** ② **8** ③ **9** give → giving

10 taking → being taken **11** to buy → buying

12 ③ **13** ① **14** doesn't remember borrowing

15 denies having broken

16 is thinking of purchasing

17 ④ **18** ④ **19** ④ **20** ③, ④

21 his[him] being late **22** being disturbed

23 It is no use regretting the past **24** ③

---

1 consider는 동명사를 목적어로 쓰는 동사이므로 putting을 쓴다.

2 decide는 to부정사를 목적어로 쓰는 동사이므로 to book 을 쓴다.

3 「cannot help + V-ing」 '~하지 않을 수 없다'

4 동명사 going이 목적어이므로 to부정사를 목적어로 쓰는 plan은 쓸 수 없다.

5 finish는 동명사를 목적어로 쓰는 동사이므로 writing을 쓴 다.

6 '(미래에) ~할 것을 잊다'라는 의미이므로 동사 forget 뒤에 to부정사 to bring을 쓴다.

7 ② he → his[him]

8 ③ to read → reading

9 전치사(in)의 목적어 자리에 올 수 있는 것은 동명사이므로 giving을 쓴다.

10 아이들이 놀이공원에 데려가진다는 수동의 의미이므로 동 명사의 수동태 「being + p.p.」를 쓴다.

11 '(과거에) ~한 것을 후회하다'라는 의미이므로 동사 regret 뒤에 동명사 buying을 쓴다.

12 ③: 보어   주어진 문장과 ①②④⑤: 목적어

13 ① → persuading

14 '(과거에) ~한 것을 기억하다'라는 의미이므로 동사 remember 뒤에 동명사 borrowing을 쓴다.

15 deny는 동명사를 목적어로 쓰는 동사이고 동명사의 시제가 주절의 시제보다 앞서므로 deny 뒤에 완료 동명사 having broken을 쓴다.

16 전치사의 목적어 자리이므로 동명사 purchasing을 쓴다.

17 '(과거에) ~한 것을 잊다'라는 의미이므로 동사 forget 뒤에 동명사 watching을 쓴다.

18 • 「feel like + V-ing」 '~하고 싶다'
    • 「upon + V-ing」 '~하자마자'

19 • Paul이 비난을 받았다는 수동의 의미이고 동명사의 시제 가 주절의 시제보다 앞서므로 수동태의 완료형 「having been + p.p.」를 쓴다.
    • 「keep … from + V-ing」 '…가 ~하지 못하게 하다'

20 prefer는 동명사와 to부정사를 모두 목적어로 쓰는 동사이 므로 staying이나 to stay를 쓴다.

21 전치사의 목적어 자리이므로 동명사를 쓰고, 동명사의 의미 상 주어는 동명사 앞에 소유격이나 목적격을 써서 나타낸다.

22 내가 방해받는다는 수동의 의미이므로 동명사의 수동태 「being + p.p.」를 쓴다.

23 「It is no use + V-ing」 '~해도 소용없다'

24 ① waiting → to wait
    ② watch → watching
    ④ going → to go
    ⑤ to have → having

UNIT 01 현재분사와 과거분사

Smart Check p.76

1 ③ **2** ②

Practice p.77

A 1 flying 2 written
    3 practicing 4 exhausted

B 1 falling 2 confused
    3 wearing 4 caught

C 1 interested 2 amazing 3 pleased

D 1 the treasure hidden
    2 cracked mirror
    3 many houses damaged

UNIT 02 분사구문

Smart Check p.78

1 Turning **2** Not being **3** Though living

Practice p.79

A 1 Running 2 Not knowing
    3 Following 4 Graduating

B 1 Feeling 2 Reaching
    3 Going 4 Listening

C 1 Since he didn't have
    2 When I looked up
    3 If you turn right

D 1 Watching the scary movie
    2 Falling down on the ice
    3 Although[Though] being rich

UNIT 03 주의해야 할 분사구문

Smart Check   p.80

1 ③   2 ②

Practice   p.81

A 1 Watched   2 Today being Sunday
    3 Having taken   4 closed

B 1 speaking   2 crossed
    3 washing   4 Destroyed

C 1 Having had enough sleep last night
    2 (Being) Made of wood
    3 Having completed the work
    4 The snow starting to fall

D 1 Having lived here
    2 Considering the price
    3 with his dog following

Writing Exercise   p.82

A 1 Strictly speaking, this is not the best solution
    2 Walking along the lake, I listened to my favorite song
    3 He focused on the game with his arms folded
    4 Please avoid beverages containing a large amount of caffeine
    5 I bought a basket filled with lemon cookies
    6 The teacher's storytelling made the lecture more interesting

B 1 Crying loudly
    2 Not having learned French
    3 Seeing my old friend
    4 Having been born in Canada
    5 Climbing up the mountain
    6 The hotels being expensive

C 1 Blowing out the candles
    2 The boy carrying a parcel
    3 had the kitchen sink repaired
    4 Having visited Maldives before
    5 Judging from the gray clouds in the sky
    6 memos pinned to the bulletin board

D 1 kept in the closet
    2 Sitting on the bench
    3 with his computer turned on

Chapter Test   p.84

1 ③   2 ④   3 ③   4 ③   5 ④   6 ②

7 closing → closed   8 having been → having

9 ②   10 ③   11 Having been created

12 Calling   13 Winning the award

14 Having grown up here   15 Turning left   16 ②

17 Although[Though] he is young, Although[Though] being young

18 If you study hard, Studying hard

19 Because[As/Since] she climbed the mountain, Having climbed the mountain

20 While the dog was being washed, Being washed

21 ②   22 (1) ⓑ → Sitting   (2) ⓔ → pleased

23 ②

1 명사 man을 수식하고 명사와의 관계가 능동이므로 현재분사 standing을 쓴다.

2 '그녀의 학생들을 봤을 때'라는 의미의 부사절을 분사구문으로 나타낸 것이므로 Seeing을 쓴다.

3 I는 감정을 느끼는 대상이므로 과거분사 shocked를 쓴다.

4 ① surprising → surprised
   ② washing → washed
   ④ worn → wearing
   ⑤ interested → interesting

5 • The exhibits는 감정을 일으키는 원인이므로 현재분사 amazing을 쓴다.
   • Frank는 감정을 느끼는 대상이므로 과거분사 disappointed를 쓴다.

6 • '식물들에 물을 주면서'라는 의미의 부사절을 분사구문으로 나타낸 것이므로 Watering을 쓴다.
   • 목적어 wall을 보충 설명하고 목적어와의 관계가 수동이므로 과거분사 painted를 쓴다.

7 「with + (대)명사 + 분사」(~가 -한 채로/하면서)에서 명사 eyes와 분사의 관계가 수동이므로 과거분사 closed를 쓴다.

8 부사절의 시제가 주절의 시제보다 앞서므로 「having + p.p.」 형태의 완료형 분사구문을 쓴다.

9 ② run → running

10 ③ Having wiped → (Having been) Wiped

11 '피카소에 의해 그려졌기 때문에'라는 의미의 부사절을 분사구문으로 나타냈고, 부사절의 시제가 주절의 시제보다 앞서므로 Having been created를 쓴다.

12 '그의 딸의 이름을 부르면서'라는 의미의 부사절을 분사구문으로 나타낸 것이므로 Calling을 쓴다.

13 접속사 When과 주어 Lisa를 생략하고 동사 won을 Winning으로 바꾼다.

14 접속사 Because와 주어 Mark를 생략하고, 부사절의 시제가 주절의 시제보다 앞서므로 동사 grew를 Having grown으로 바꾼다.

15 접속사 If와 주어 you를 생략하고 동사 turn을 Turning으로 바꾼다.

16 ② → As I have enough money

17 첫 번째 문장: '비록 ~이지만'이라는 의미의 접속사 Although[Though]를 쓰고, 문장의 시제가 현재이므로 is 를 쓴다.
두 번째 문장: 주어 he를 생략하고 동사 is를 being으로 바꾼다. 양보를 나타내는 분사구문은 주로 접속사를 생략하지 않는다.

18 첫 번째 문장: '만약 ~한다면'이라는 의미의 접속사 If를 쓰고, 조건을 나타내는 부사절이므로 미래시제 대신 현재시제 study를 쓴다.
두 번째 문장: 접속사 If와 주어 you를 생략하고 동사 study 를 Studying으로 바꾼다.

19 첫 번째 문장: '~하기 때문에'라는 의미의 접속사 Because[As/Since]를 쓰고, 부사절의 시제가 과거이므로 climbed를 쓴다.
두 번째 문장: 접속사 Because[As/Since]와 주어 she를 생략하고, 부사절의 시제가 주절의 시제보다 앞서므로 동사 climbed를 Having climbed로 바꾼다.

20 첫 번째 문장: '~하는 동안'이라는 의미의 접속사 While을 쓰고, 부사절의 시제가 과거진행이므로 was being washed 를 쓴다.
두 번째 문장: 접속사 While과 주어 the dog를 생략하고 동사 was being washed를 Being washed로 바꾼다.

21 ②: 동명사 주어진 문장과 ①③④⑤: 현재분사

22 (1) '나의 새로운 반 친구 옆에 앉았을 때'라는 의미의 부사절을 분사구문으로 나타낸 것이므로 Sitting을 쓴다.
(2) I는 감정을 느끼는 대상이므로 과거분사 pleased를 쓴다.

23 ⓑ Having not → Not having
ⓒ stealing → stolen
ⓓ Felt → Feeling

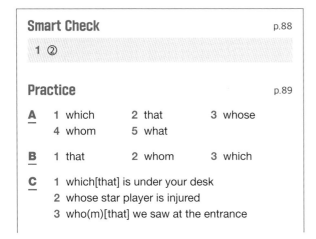

Chapter 07 | 관계사

UNIT 01 관계대명사

Smart Check p.88

1 ②

Practice p.89

A 1 which 2 that 3 whose 4 whom 5 what

B 1 that 2 whom 3 which

C 1 which[that] is under your desk
2 whose star player is injured
3 who(m)[that] we saw at the entrance

D 1 what Maria suggested
2 the books whose main character
3 a person who[that] maintains

UNIT 02 관계부사

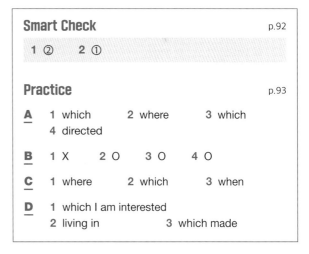

Smart Check p.90

1 ① 2 ② 3 ②

Practice p.91

A 1 when 2 why 3 how 4 where

B 1 how 2 why 3 when

C 1 how the copy machine works
2 where I always buy clothes
3 when the winter begins
4 why she decided to do volunteer work

D 1 the hall where
2 how Mexicans celebrate
3 the time when

UNIT 03 주의해야 할 관계사의 쓰임

Smart Check p.92

1 ② 2 ①

Practice p.93

A 1 which 2 where 3 which 4 directed

B 1 X 2 O 3 O 4 O

C 1 where 2 which 3 when

D 1 which I am interested
2 living in 3 which made

UNIT 04 복합관계사

Smart Check p.94

1 ① 2 ③

Practice p.95

A 1 Whoever 2 whichever 3 Wherever 4 Whatever

B 1 However 2 whomever 3 whenever

C 1 Wherever   2 Whatever
    3 Whoever   4 Whichever

D 1 However hot it is   2 Whatever I cook
    3 whichever way you go

Writing Exercise

p.96

A 1 who worked in the mines
  2 which likes to sleep in the sun
  3 whose roof was covered with snow
  4 who was driving too fast
  5 What Henry hates the most
  6 which was written by Hemingway

B 1 (why) Alice behaved strangely
  2 Whatever you buy
  3 where you grew up
  4 which is still in good shape
  5 however much it costs
  6 where I used to ride a bicycle

C 1 Fruits sold in this grocery store
  2 the first man that climbed
  3 whatever advice he needs
  4 different from what we expected
  5 a book which is about the tale
  6 whom he fell in love with[with whom he fell in love]

D 1 where   2 who(m)   3 which
  4 which   5 when

Chapter Test

p.98

1 ② 2 ① 3 ③ 4 ③ 5 ④ 6 ⑤
7 Whoever   8 what 9 However hard I tried
10 when Mark goes to bed
11 The way you solved this problem was creative
12 ④   13 ③   14 ①   15 that → who
16 which → what   17 ⑤
18 whose view is wonderful
19 which saved much time
20 why[for which] Tom looks excited   21 ⑤
22 ③ 23 ② 24 ④

1 선행사(The girl)가 사람이고 빈칸이 관계대명사절 안에서 주어 역할을 하므로 사람을 선행사로 하는 주격 관계대명사 who를 쓴다.

2 선행사(the city)가 장소를 나타내므로 관계부사 where를 쓴다.

3 앞에 나온 절(All ~ bloomed)을 선행사로 취하는 계속적 용법의 관계대명사 which를 쓴다.

4 ③: 주격 관계대명사 (주격 관계대명사는 생략할 수 없다.)
①②④: 목적격 관계대명사
⑤: 「주격 관계대명사 + be동사」

5 ④ that → which 또는 전치사 with를 관계대명사절의 맨 뒤로 보낸다.

6 ⑤ the way how → how[the way]

7 '그 건물에 들어가기를 원하는 누구든지 신분증이 필요하다.'라는 의미이며, anyone who는 복합관계대명사 whoever로 바꿔 쓸 수 있다.

8 '너는 네가 찾고 있던 것을 찾았니?'라는 의미이며, the thing that은 관계대명사 what으로 바꿔 쓸 수 있다.

9 '아무리 ~하더라도'라는 의미의 복합관계부사 however를 쓴다.

10 선행사(the time)가 시간을 나타내므로 관계부사 when을 쓴다.

11 방법을 나타내는 선행사 the way나 관계부사 how를 쓸 수 있지만, the way와 how는 둘 중 하나만 쓸 수 있다.

12 ① that → who
② which → when[at which]
③ Whatever → However
⑤ which → where

13 • 선행사(The new laptop)가 사물이므로 관계대명사 that 이나 which를 쓴다.
• 선행사(the season)가 사물이고 빈칸 앞에 전치사가 있으므로 관계대명사 which를 쓴다.

14 선행사가 없으므로 선행사를 포함하는 관계대명사 what을 쓴다.

15 관계대명사의 계속적 용법은 who나 which만 쓸 수 있고, 선행사(Steve)가 사람이므로 who를 쓴다.

16 선행사가 없으므로 선행사를 포함하는 관계대명사 what을 쓴다.

17 '어디서 공부하더라도'라는 의미이므로 장소와 관련하여 양보의 부사절을 이끄는 wherever를 쓴다.

18 두 번째 문장은 첫 번째 문장의 the hotel에 대해 보충 설명하고 있고, 두 번째 문장의 Its가 소유격의 역할을 하고 있으므로 소유격 관계대명사 whose를 쓴다.

19 두 번째 문장은 첫 번째 문장 전체에 대해 보충 설명하고 있으므로, 계속적 용법의 관계대명사 which를 쓴다.

20 두 번째 문장은 첫 번째 문장의 the reason에 대해 보충 설명하고 있고, 선행사가 이유를 나타내므로 관계부사 why나 for which를 쓴다.

21 ⑤: whose   ①②③④: what

22 ③ that → which

23 • 선행사(an exhibit)가 장소를 나타내므로 관계부사 where를 쓴다.
• 빈칸 앞에 콤마(,)가 있으므로 계속적 용법의 관계대명사 which를 쓴다.

24 • 선행사(the student)가 사람이고 빈칸 앞에 전치사가 있으므로 목적격 관계대명사 whom을 쓴다.

12 영어 실력을 높여주는 다양한 학습 자료 제공 HackersBook.com

- 선행사(the day)가 시간을 나타내므로 관계부사 when
  을 쓴다.

Chapter 08 | 접속사

UNIT 01 부사절을 이끄는 접속사

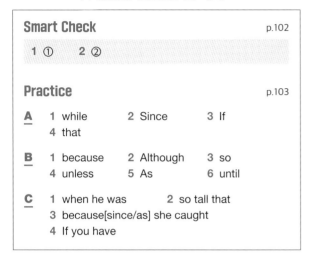

Smart Check p.102

1 ① **2** ②

Practice p.103

A 1 while 2 Since 3 If
4 that

B 1 because 2 Although 3 so
4 unless 5 As 6 until

C 1 when he was 2 so tall that
3 because[since/as] she caught
4 If you have

UNIT 02 상관접속사, 간접의문문

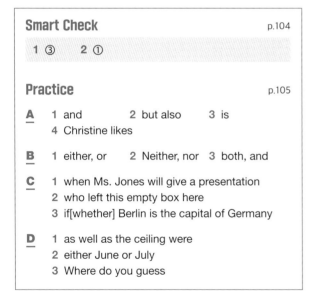

Smart Check p.104

1 ③ **2** ①

Practice p.105

A 1 and 2 but also 3 is
4 Christine likes

B 1 either, or 2 Neither, nor 3 both, and

C 1 when Ms. Jones will give a presentation
2 who left this empty box here
3 if[whether] Berlin is the capital of Germany

D 1 as well as the ceiling were
2 either June or July
3 Where do you guess

Writing Exercise p.106

A 1 because she was taking a shower
2 If you have a coupon
3 that she needs to wear a belt
4 until I find my lost wallet
5 Since it rained heavily
6 though the sun was shining

B 1 Neither Peter nor Noah threw away
2 while I am talking to you
3 either rice or noodles
4 bought both a novel and a magazine
5 Unless she does it herself
6 Not only Ron but also Fred remembers

C 1 They wonder how the pyramids were built
2 Do you know who found out the answer to the question
3 When do you think we should change the batteries
4 I'm not sure why Nathan disagrees with your idea
5 He doesn't know how much this picture is worth
6 Can you tell me where you saw Sally last night

D 1 because I had a fever
2 While I washed the dishes
3 Although I was exhausted

Chapter Test p.108

1 ① **2** ⑤ **3** ② **4** ②
5 participates → participate
6 will open → opens **7** very → so **8** ①, ④
9 either taxi or bus
10 Both my friend and I are
11 As soon as I get the letter, I will reply **12** ⑤
13 The movie as well as the original novel
14 If it doesn't rain on Sunday **15** ③ **16** ②
17 ④ **18** ③ **19** ③ **20** ①
21 Neither Luke nor I **22** ⑤
23 (1) Not only, but also (2) Neither, nor
(3) Both, and

1 '만약 네가 일찍 일어난다면 너는 일출을 볼 수 있을 것이다.'
라는 의미이므로 if(만약 ~한다면)를 쓴다.

2 'Jason은 그가 오늘 그의 독후감을 끝낼 수 있을지 확신하
지 못한다.'라는 의미이므로 의문사가 없는 간접의문문을 이
끄는 whether(~인지 아닌지)를 쓴다.

3 'Mary도 나도 탄산음료를 마시는 것을 좋아하지 않는다.'라
는 의미이므로 neither A nor B(A도 B도 아닌)를 쓴다.

4 ②: '~하고 있을 때, ~하면서'   ①③④⑤: '~하기 때문에'

5 both A and B 뒤에는 항상 복수동사를 쓴다.

6 시간을 나타내는 부사절에서는 미래시제 대신 현재시제를
쓴다.

7 '그 달걀은 너무 단단해서 내가 쉽게 깨뜨릴 수 없었다.'라는
의미이므로 「so ~ that …」(너무 ~해서 …한)을 쓴다.

8 ① → Can you tell me where the public toilet is?
④ → Lisa doesn't know if[whether] Kevin will join the band.

9 'A나 B 둘 중 하나'라는 의미의 either A or B를 쓴다.

10 'A와 B 둘 다'라는 의미의 both A and B를 쓰고, both A and B 뒤에는 항상 복수동사를 쓴다.

11 '~하자마자'라는 의미의 as soon as를 쓰고, 시간을 나타내는 부사절에서는 미래시제 대신 현재시제를 쓴다.

12 ① will arrive → arrives
② Unless you don't help → Unless you help[If you don't help]
③ am → are
④ Do you think where → Where do you think

13 not only A but also B(A뿐만 아니라 B도)는 B as well as A로 바꿔 쓸 수 있다.

14 unless(만약 ~하지 않는다면)는 if ~ not으로 바꿔 쓸 수 있다.

15 • '비록 우리는 자외선 차단제를 바를지라도 햇빛에 탈 수 있다.'라는 의미이므로 even if(비록 ~일지라도)를 쓴다.
• '나는 방금 점심을 먹었기 때문에 배고프지 않다.'라는 의미이므로 because(~하기 때문에)를 쓴다.

16 • '만약 우리가 지금 출발하지 않는다면, 우리는 행사를 놓칠 것이다.'라는 의미이므로 If(만약 ~한다면)를 쓴다.
• '비록 Evan은 더 나은 무용수가 되고 싶지만 열심히 연습하지 않는다.'라는 의미이므로 even though(비록 ~이지만)를 쓴다.

17 ④ will wait → wait[are waiting]

18 ③ were → was

19 • '나의 삼촌은 28살이었던 이후로 은행에서 근무해왔다.'라는 의미이므로 since(~한 이후로)를 쓴다.
• '나는 밀가루가 없기 때문에 지금 케이크를 구울 수 없다.'라는 의미이므로 since(~하기 때문에)를 쓴다.

20 • '네가 너의 어머니에게 장미를 사드린다면, 그녀는 매우 기뻐할 것이다.'라는 의미이므로 if(만약 ~한다면)를 쓴다.
• '나는 Parker 선생님이 올해에 나의 담임 선생님이 될지 아닐지 궁금하다.'라는 의미이므로 의문사가 없는 간접의문문을 이끄는 if(~인지 아닌지)를 쓴다.

21 'Luke도 나도 어제 무지개를 보지 않았다.'라는 의미이므로 Neither A nor B(A도 B도 아닌)를 쓴다.

22 의문사가 있는 간접의문문은 「의문사 + 주어 + 동사」의 어순인데, 간접의문문을 포함하는 문장의 동사가 생각이나 추측을 나타내는 guess인 경우 간접의문문의 의문사를 문장 맨 앞에 쓴다.

23 (1) Sarah뿐만 아니라 Emily도 16살이므로 not only A but also B(A뿐만 아니라 B도)를 쓴다.
(2) 수학도 미술도 Sarah가 가장 좋아하는 과목이 아니므로 neither A nor B(A도 B도 아닌)를 쓴다.
(3) Sarah와 Charles 둘 다 선생님이 되기를 원하므로 both A and B(A와 B 둘 다)를 쓴다.

Chapter 09 | 가정법

UNIT 01 가정법 과거/과거완료, 혼합 가정법

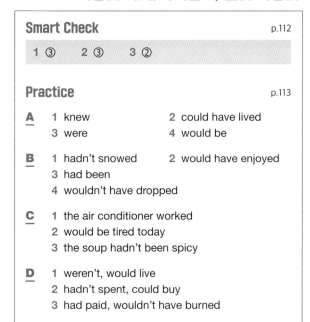

Smart Check p.112

1 ③   2 ③   3 ②

Practice p.113

A 1 knew   2 could have lived
3 were   4 would be

B 1 hadn't snowed   2 would have enjoyed
3 had been
4 wouldn't have dropped

C 1 the air conditioner worked
2 would be tired today
3 the soup hadn't been spicy

D 1 weren't, would live
2 hadn't spent, could buy
3 had paid, wouldn't have burned

UNIT 02 I wish/as if/It's time 가정법

Smart Check p.114

1 ③   2 ②   3 ①

Practice p.115

A 1 had seen   2 had been   3 started
4 had

B 1 were   2 shared   3 had seen
4 had been

C 1 didn't feel   2 hadn't known
3 had done

D 1 you visited your grandparents
2 she had saved a lot of money
3 you were careful

UNIT 03 Without[But for] 가정법, if를 생략한 가정법

Smart Check p.116

1 ③   2 ②   3 ②   4 ①

Practice p.117

A 1 Were   2 Had   3 Without

B
1 Were I you
2 Had I owned a hamster
3 Were it not for electricity

C
1 Without the map
2 But for the Wi-Fi
3 Had Tim brought his wallet

D
1 Were I in Rome
2 Had it not been for the donation
3 Were it not for the fridge

Writing Exercise

A
1 spoke
2 had run around for hours
3 had fixed   4 hadn't been ridden

B
1 the lake were frozen
2 he in Peru
3 you had cleaned the room
4 it were not for the Internet
5 Helen not been so nervous

C
1 Were it not for the telephone
2 they would not have been upset
3 It's time Amy got her laptop repaired
4 Had it not been for your effort
5 Were you interested in modern art

D
1 had another pen
2 were good at math
3 would buy a private plane

Chapter Test
p.120

1 ②   2 ④   3 ⑤
4 Without, If it had not been for   5 ⑤   6 ③
7 ④   8 ⑤   9 Had it not been for my family
10 ③   11 it had not been for your efforts
12 ⑤   13 ①   14 ate → had eaten
15 Without for → Without[But for]   16 ③
17 If it had rained
18 It's time people worried
19 had studied hard, she could have passed the
    exam   20 today were sunny
21 had taken the medicine, you wouldn't feel worse
    now   22 ①

1 현재의 사실과 반대되는 일을 가정하고 있으므로 가정법 과거를 쓰고, 가정법 과거에서 if절의 be동사는 주어에 상관없이 were를 쓴다.

2 과거의 사실과 반대되는 일이 현재까지 영향을 미치는 상황을 가정하고 있으므로 혼합 가정법을 쓴다.

3 주절이 「would + have p.p.」인 가정법 과거완료이고 if를 생략하면 주어와 동사의 위치가 바뀌므로 Had를 쓴다.

4 주절이 「would + have p.p.」인 가정법 과거완료이므로 「But for[Without] + 명사(구)」는 「If it had not been for + 명사(구)」로 바꿔 쓸 수 있다.

5 ⑤ has → had

6 ③ have been → be

7 '만약 ~했더라면 …했을 텐데'의 의미로 과거의 사실과 반대되는 일을 가정하는 가정법 과거완료이므로 「If + 주어 + had p.p. ~, 주어 + would, could, might + have p.p. …」를 쓴다.

8 과거의 사실과 반대되는 일을 가정하고 있으므로 가정법 과거완료 「If + 주어 + had p.p. ~, 주어 + would, could, might + have p.p. …」를 쓴다.

9 가정법에서 if를 생략하면 주어와 동사의 위치가 바뀐다.

10 ① saved → had saved   ② is → were
    ④ go → went
    ⑤ Were I sleepy → Had I been sleepy[If I had been sleepy]

11 주절이 「would + have p.p.」인 가정법 과거완료이므로 「But for + 명사(구)」는 「If it had not been for + 명사(구)」로 바꿔 쓸 수 있다.

12 • 주절의 시제(현재시제)보다 앞선 시점의 사실과 반대되는 일을 가정하는 「as if + 가정법 과거완료」를 써야 하므로 hadn't worn을 쓴다.
    • 과거의 사실과 반대되는 일을 가정하는 가정법 과거완료를 써야 하므로 would have read를 쓴다.

13 • 명사(구) 앞에 와서 if절을 대신하는 Without이나 But for를 쓴다.
    • 현재 이룰 수 없거나 실현 가능성이 매우 작은 일을 소망하는 「I wish + 가정법 과거」를 써야 하므로 could speak을 쓴다.

14 과거의 사실과 반대되는 일이 현재까지 영향을 미치는 상황을 가정하는 혼합 가정법이므로 if절에는 had eaten을 쓴다.

15 '~가 없(었)다면'이라는 의미의 가정법에서는 Without이나 But for를 쓴다.

16 ③ → If it had not been for the news, we wouldn't have known about the upcoming storm.

17 '만약 ~했더라면 …했을 텐데'의 의미로 과거의 사실과 반대되는 일을 가정하는 가정법 과거완료를 써야 하므로 If it had rained를 쓴다.

18 '~해야 할 때이다'의 의미로 했어야 하는 일을 하지 않은 것에 대한 유감을 나타내는 It's time 가정법을 써야 하므로 It's time people worried를 쓴다.

19 과거의 사실과 반대되는 일을 가정하는 가정법 과거완료 「If + 주어 + had p.p. ~, 주어 + would, could, might + have p.p. …」를 쓴다.

20 현재 이룰 수 없거나 실현 가능성이 거의 없는 일을 소망하는 「I wish + 가정법 과거」를 쓴다.

21 과거의 사실과 반대되는 일이 현재까지 영향을 미치는 상황

을 가정하는 혼합 가정법 「If + 주어 + had p.p. ~, 주어 + would, could, might + 동사원형 …」를 쓴다.

22　① → had come

Chapter 10 ｜ 비교구문

UNIT 01 원급/비교급/최상급 비교

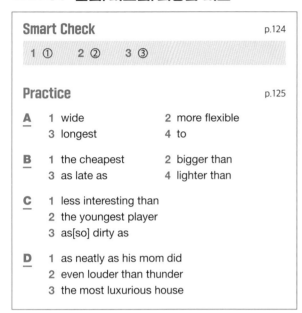

Smart Check　　　　　　　　　　p.124

1 ①　　2 ②　　3 ③

Practice　　　　　　　　　　　p.125

A　1 wide　　　　　2 more flexible
　　3 longest　　　 4 to

B　1 the cheapest　　2 bigger than
　　3 as late as　　　4 lighter than

C　1 less interesting than
　　2 the youngest player
　　3 as[so] dirty as

D　1 as neatly as his mom did
　　2 even louder than thunder
　　3 the most luxurious house

UNIT 02 비교구문을 이용한 표현

Smart Check　　　　　　　　　　p.126

1 ②

Practice　　　　　　　　　　　p.127

A　1 twice as high　　2 worse
　　3 cellists　　　　 4 colder and colder

B　1 as hard as I can　　2 heavier than
　　3 as honestly as he could
　　4 as[so] popular, more popular than any other
　　5 deeper than
　　6 hotter, hotter than all the other

C　1 as realistically as she could
　　2 The deeper, the darker
　　3 laziest boy I have met

Writing Exercise　　　　　　　p.128

A　1 333,000 times heavier than
　　2 The more people, the more exciting
　　3 (other) thing in my life is as[so] important
　　4 as soon as he can

B　1 the hottest day
　　2 superior to
　　3 as much as you can
　　4 more and more colorful
　　5 the busiest month
　　6 much more effectively

C　1 the instructions as carefully as you can
　　2 less expensive than last week
　　3 one of the tallest buildings
　　4 more interesting than documentaries
　　5 not as delicious as the one
　　6 hardest in the volleyball team

D　1 the oldest　　　 2 not as[so] cheap
　　3 better

Chapter Test　　　　　　　　　p.130

1 ③　　2 ④　　3 ②　　4 ①
5 three times as expensive as[three times more expensive than]
6 the lightest　　7 ⑤　　8 ②
9 more and more convenient
10 the more nervous you will feel
11 a lot easier than　　12 ⑤　　13 ④
14 animal → animals　　15 stronger → strong
16 softest → the softest　　17 three times as big as
18 animal, is as[so] tall as
19 The more exhausted, the more slowly
20 ③, ⑤　　　　21 ③　22 ①　23 ②　24 ④

1　'Jack은 Tina만큼 유창하게 불어를 말할 수 있다.'라는 의미이므로 부사의 원급 fluently를 쓴다. 형용사 fluent는 동사를 수식할 수 없다.

2　'피아노를 배우는 것은 내가 생각했던 것보다 더 어려웠다.'라는 의미이므로 비교급 more difficult를 쓴다.

3　「배수사 + as + 원급 + as」 '…보다 -배 더 ~한/하게'

4　② so → as　　　　③ most → the most
　　④ more and more good → better and better
　　⑤ deepest → deeper

5　노란색 가방이 갈색 가방보다 세 배 더 비싸므로 three times as expensive as[three times more expensive than]을 쓴다.

6 토끼가 가장 가벼우므로 최상급 비교 the lightest를 쓴다.

7 ⑤ → much

8 ②: 원급 비교 「as + 원급 + as」는 최상급 비교 「the + 최상급」과 바꿔 쓸 수 없다. any other는 비교급과 함께 쓰여 최상급을 표현할 수 있다.

9 '점점 더 ~한/하게'라는 의미의 「비교급 + and + 비교급」을 쓴다.

10 '~하면 할수록 더 …하다'라는 의미의 「the + 비교급, the + 비교급」을 쓴다.

11 '…보다 더 ~한/하게'라는 의미의 「비교급 + than」을 쓴다. 비교급 앞에 a lot을 써서 '훨씬'이라는 의미로 비교급을 강조할 수 있다.

12 ①: Brian이 Joshua보다 나이가 많으므로 'Brian은 Joshua보다 어리다.'는 적절하지 않다.
②: Aaron이 Brian보다 키가 크므로 'Aaron은 Brian만큼 키가 작다.'는 적절하지 않다.
③: Joshua는 Aaron보다 어리므로 'Joshua는 Aaron보다 나이가 더 많다.'는 적절하지 않다.
④: Joshua는 Brian보다 키가 작으므로 'Joshua는 Brian만큼 키가 크다.'는 적절하지 않다.

13 빈칸 뒤에 비교급(more boring)이 있으므로 '훨씬'이라는 의미로 비교급을 강조하는 even/much/far/a lot을 쓸 수 있다. very는 원급을 강조한다.

14 「one of the + 최상급 + 복수명사」 '가장 ~한 것들 중 하나'

15 「as + 원급 + as」 '…만큼 ~한/하게'

16 '가장 ~한/하게'라는 의미의 최상급 비교는 「the + 최상급」의 형태이므로 최상급 앞에 the를 쓴다.

17 「배수사 + 비교급 + than」은 「배수사 + as + 원급 + as」로 바꿔 쓸 수 있다.

18 「the + 최상급」은 「No (other) + 단수명사 ~ as[so] + 원급 + as」로 바꿔 쓸 수 있다.

19 '그 여행객은 지치면 지칠수록 더 천천히 걸었다.'라는 의미의 문장이므로 '~하면 할수록 더 …하다'라는 의미의 「the + 비교급, the + 비교급」을 쓴다.

20 ③ → Math is the most difficult subject.
⑤ → No (other) flower in the garden is as pretty as the rose.

21 ③ better → well

22 ① best → better

23 • '그녀는 원어민이 하는 것만큼 영어로 글을 잘 쓴다.'라는 의미의 원급 비교이므로 as를 쓴다.
• 'Simon은 그의 반에서 다른 어떤 학생보다 훨씬 더 재치 있다.'라는 의미의 비교급 비교이므로 than을 쓴다.

24 • 빈칸 뒤에 비교급(healthier)이 있으므로 비교급을 강조하는 even/a lot/much를 쓴다.
• 「배수사 + as + 원급 + as」의 형태이므로 원급 much를 쓴다.

Chapter **11** 일치와 화법

UNIT 01 수의 일치

Smart Check p.134

1 ③   2 ①   3 ②

Practice p.135

A 1 is   2 were   3 is
4 was

B 1 get   2 like   3 support
4 increases

C 1 trains   2 is   3 creates
4 have

D 1 Two hours was spent
2 A number of soldiers fight
3 What Jacob ordered was

UNIT 02 시제의 일치

Smart Check p.136

1 ②   2 ③   3 ①

Practice p.137

A 1 wouldn't   2 had   3 travels
4 is

B 1 was   2 expands   3 is
4 practices

C 1 would like   2 visits   3 had heard

D 1 she would be   2 knowledge is
3 Alaska became

UNIT 03 화법

Smart Check p.138

1 ②

Practice p.139

A 1 told   2 that
3 not to forget   4 I liked

B 1 asked my dad   2 where she could
3 to participate

C   1   told me (that) he had had

       2   asked the police officer if[whether] there was

       3   told[asked/ordered/advised] me to practice

D   1   when I had changed

       2   not to touch   3   who was talking

Writing Exercise
p.140

A   1   Both green and blue look

       2   Fifty dollars is

       3   Each item is shipped

       4   a number of flowers bloom

       5   What Robert said was

       6   the young enjoy

B   1   said that she might arrive late

       2   told me that a bad workman blames his tools

       3   said that the *Titanic* sank on April 15, 1912

       4   didn't know that the package had been delivered to me

       5   knew that a koala spends most of its time sleeping

       6   thought that it would be hard to reach the top of the mountain

C   1   told me (that) he preferred classical music to rock music

       2   asked him how long she could borrow that magazine

       3   told[asked/ordered/advised] my brother to turn off his phone

       4   told me (that) she would look after my dog the next[the following] day

       5   asked me if[whether] I could get a towel for her

       6   told[asked/ordered/advised] Anna to translate those English sentences into Korean

D   1   A number of fans want

       2   Five kilometers is

       3   Each runner wears

Chapter Test
p.142

1 ③   2 ②   3 ①   4 ⑤

5 when I would call her back

6 not to use the air conditioner until the next[the following] day

7 he had enjoyed the fireworks the previous day[the day before]   8 ⑤   9 are → is

10 decreased → decreases   11 had I → I had

12 ④   13 ③   14 ③

---

15 A number of students take the cooking class

16 ③   17 ②   18 ④   19 is   20 strikes

21 is increasing   22 if[whether] I could lend

23 ④

---

1   주절이 과거시제이므로 종속절에는 과거시제 joined를 쓴다.

2   역사적 사실을 말할 때는 주절의 시제와 상관없이 종속절에 항상 과거시제를 쓰므로 과거시제 was built를 쓴다.

3   일반적 사실을 말할 때는 주절의 시제와 상관없이 종속절에 항상 현재시제를 쓰므로 현재시제 is를 쓴다.

4   의문사가 없는 의문문의 간접 화법은 if나 whether로 주절과 종속절을 연결한다.

5   의문사가 있는 의문문의 간접 화법은 「ask (+ 목적어) + 의문사 + 주어 + 동사」의 어순으로 쓴다. 전달동사가 과거시제이므로 종속절의 will을 과거형 would로 바꾼다. 전달하는 사람의 입장에 맞게 인칭대명사 you를 I로 바꾸고 me를 her로 바꾼다.

6   부정명령문 Don't use를 not to use로 바꾸고, 전달하는 사람의 입장에 맞게 부사 tomorrow를 the next[the following] day로 바꾼다.

7   전달동사가 과거시제이므로 종속절의 과거시제 enjoyed를 과거완료시제 had enjoyed로 바꾼다. 전달하는 사람의 입장에 맞게 인칭대명사 I를 he로 바꾸고 부사 yesterday를 the previous day[the day before]로 바꾼다.

8   ① had been → was   ② are → is

     ③ is → are   ④ was → is

9   학과명 주어 뒤에는 항상 단수동사를 쓰므로 is를 쓴다.

10   과학적 사실을 말할 때는 주절의 시제와 상관없이 종속절에 항상 현재시제를 쓰므로 현재시제 decreases를 쓴다.

11   의문사가 없는 의문문의 간접 화법은 「ask (+ 목적어) + if[whether] + 주어 + 동사」의 어순이므로 I had를 쓴다.

12   ④ → Mr. Brown advised us not to go into the water without warm-up exercises.

13   의문사가 없는 의문문의 간접 화법은 「ask (+ 목적어) + if[whether] + 주어 + 동사」의 어순으로 쓴다. 전달동사가 과거시제이므로 종속절에 과거시제 saw를 쓰고, 전달하는 사람의 입장에 맞게 인칭대명사 you를 I로 바꾼다.

14   • 역사적 사실을 말할 때는 주절의 시제와 상관없이 종속절에 항상 과거시제를 쓰므로 과거시제 occurred를 쓴다.

     • 주절이 과거시제이므로 종속절에는 will의 과거형 would를 쓴다.

15   「a number of + 복수명사」(많은 ~) 뒤에는 항상 복수동사를 쓰므로 동사는 take를 쓴다.

16   ③ will → would

17   ② was → were

18   ④ was → is

19   every가 포함된 주어 뒤에는 항상 단수동사를 쓰므로 is를 쓴다.

20   과학적 사실을 말할 때는 주절의 시제와 상관없이 종속절에

항상 현재시제를 쓰므로 현재시제 strikes를 쓴다.

21 「the number of + 복수명사」(~의 수) 뒤에는 항상 단수동사를 쓰므로 is increasing을 쓴다.

22 의문사가 없는 의문문의 간접 화법은 「ask (+ 목적어) + if[whether] + 주어 + 동사」의 어순이고, 전달동사가 과거시제이므로 can의 과거형 could를 쓴다.

23 ⓐ are → is
ⓒ told → said
ⓔ had been → was

Chapter 12 | 특수구문

UNIT 01 강조, 도치

Smart Check
p.146

1 ②　　2 ③

Practice
p.147

A 1 did　　　　2 stood a cabin
3 that　　　　4 did I dream

B 1 Nick did win the lottery last month
2 It is a glass of milk that[which] she drinks every morning
3 It was an hour ago that[when] they felt the ground shaking

C 1 jumped the white horse
2 does lightning strike the same place twice
3 have I been to the movie theater alone

D 1 the chair hid a small cat
2 It was last week that
3 So do I

UNIT 02 병렬, 부정, 동격, 생략

Smart Check
p.148

1 ③

Practice
p.149

A 1 send　　2 had　　3 interesting
4 hitting

B 1 Not　　2 None　　3 no

C 1 winning the award
2 a winter sport
3 the climate is changing
4 throwing a party at the restaurant

D 1 I am　　　　2 bring friends here
3 he was　　　4 Eva

Writing Exercise
p.150

A 1 It was a deer that[which] Jenny saw in the forest
2 Rarely does the teacher finish his class early
3 Not all of my friends laughed at my joke
4 Into the room came my mother
5 It is on Saturday that[when] the football team has a big match

B 1 Steven is a hardworking student, and so am I
2 O
3 Hardly have I played tennis since I was a child
4 In the deep ocean lives the octopus
5 Ron is good at both dancing and singing
6 Emily didn't spread the rumors, and neither did I

C 1 front of the campfire gathered the kids
2 It is not always fun to meet
3 It was in the 18th century when
4 have I seen such a beautiful sight
5 had a fear of being injured
6 the idea that it is worth experiencing failure

D 1 Neither of the girls
2 Not every rose
3 None of the shoes

Chapter Test
p.152

1 ⑤　　2 ③　　3 ④　　4 ⑤　　5 knows → know
6 a beautiful castle is → is a beautiful castle
7 ②　　8 ③　　9 ①　　10 ⑤　　11 ③　　12 ②
13 ④　　14 ①
15 I did write a birthday card for you, but I lost it
16 It was Kate that[who] won the award in the contest last year
17 is not always cheaper　18 were the puzzle pieces
19 can he admit　20 ⑤　　21 have I thought
22 ②　　23 was Tom that gave me the gift yesterday
24 could she believe the sad news

---

1 과거시제이므로 동사원형 앞에 동사를 강조하는 did를 쓴다.

2 부정어 Never가 강조되어 문장의 맨 앞으로 올 때, 주어와 동사를 도치시켜 「부정어 + 조동사 + 주어」의 어순으로 쓴다.

3 '~도 아니다'라는 의미로 neither를 사용할 때 주어와 동사를 도치시켜 「neither + 동사 + 주어」의 어순으로 쓴다. 앞 절의 동사가 일반동사이므로 do를 쓴다.

4 ① the host of this event comes → comes the host of this event
② to hike → hiking 또는 swimming → to swim
③ I dreamed → did I dream
④ That → It

5 동사를 강조할 때는 동사원형 앞에 do/does/did를 쓴다.

6 장소의 부사구 On the top of the hill이 강조되어 문장의 맨 앞으로 올 때, 주어와 동사를 도치시켜 「장소의 부사(구) + 동사 + 주어」의 어순으로 쓴다.

7 • 명사(the problem)와 동명사구(making too much noise) 사이에 동격의 of를 쓴다.
• 명사(the idea)와 절(every ~ regularly) 사이에 동격의 that을 쓴다.

8 ③ I could → could I

9 '~도 그렇다'라는 의미로 so를 사용할 때 주어와 동사를 도치시켜 「so + 동사 + 주어」의 어순으로 쓴다. 앞 절의 동사가 일반동사이므로 do를 쓴다.

10 '그들 둘 다 여기에 없어.'라는 의미로 전체 부정을 나타내는 Neither를 쓴다.

11 ③: 일반동사 do   ①②④⑤: 동사를 강조하는 do

12 ②: 관계대명사 that   ①③④⑤: 동격의 that

13 '모두 ~인 것은 아니다'라는 의미로 부분 부정을 나타내는 「not + all」을 쓴다.

14 '아무도 ~ 않다'라는 의미로 전체 부정을 나타내는 none을 쓴다.

15 동사 wrote를 강조할 때는 동사원형 write 앞에 did를 쓴다.

16 주어 Kate를 It was와 that 사이에 써서 강조할 수 있다. 강조하는 대상이 사람이므로 that 대신 who를 쓸 수 있다.

17 '항상 ~인 것은 아니다'라는 의미로 부분 부정을 나타내는 「not + always」를 쓴다.

18 장소의 부사구 On the floor가 강조되어 문장의 맨 앞으로 올 때, 주어와 동사를 도치시켜 「장소의 부사(구) + 동사 + 주어」의 어순으로 쓴다.

19 부정어 Hardly가 강조되어 문장의 맨 앞으로 올 때, 주어와 동사를 도치시켜 「부정어 + 조동사 + 주어」의 어순으로 쓴다.

20 ⓐ which → that[who]
ⓑ Olivia goes → does Olivia go
ⓒ ordering → order

21 부정어 Never가 강조되어 문장의 맨 앞으로 올 때, 주어와 동사를 도치시켜 「부정어 + 조동사 + 주어」의 어순으로 쓴다.

22 ②: 주절과 부사절의 주어가 다르기 때문에 생략할 수 없다.

23 주어 Tom을 It was와 that 사이에 써서 강조할 수 있다.

24 부정어 Hardly가 강조되어 문장의 맨 앞으로 올 때, 주어와 동사를 도치시켜 「부정어 + 조동사 + 주어」의 어순으로 쓴다.

Chapter 01 시제

UNIT 01 현재완료시제

p.2

A 1 since 2 has gone
3 has slept 4 O

B 1 has posted 2 graduated
3 have stayed 4 completed

C 1 has fixed my computer
2 have been eating dinner for an hour
3 have been preparing for the Olympics since last year

D 1 The band has released a new album
2 have been walking along the coast
3 I have already read the latest novel
4 has been talking about American history

UNIT 02 과거완료시제와 미래완료시제

p.3

A 1 will have been learning
2 had been chatting
3 will have been driving
4 had been helping

B 1 will have been studying 2 O
3 will have been swimming
4 had been[was] taking

C 1 will have been building the history museum
2 had sat down
3 will have closed the shop
4 had been playing soccer

D 1 The TV show had already ended
2 he will have ridden it five times
3 Linda had visited Busan many times
4 The boy will have woken up

Chapter Test ✦

p.4

1 ② 2 ④ 3 ④ 4 ① 5 ④ 6 ⑤
7 has been watching 8 will have been exercising
9 was 10 had been[was] washing 11 ②
12 ⑤ 13 ③ 14 ④ 15 will have read
16 had made
17 has been standing here since 2001
18 had been washing for 40 minutes

19 ④ 20 ⑤ 21 ③
22 has been to that restaurant
23 she will have planted five roses
24 had already started the lesson

---

1 once가 있고 과거부터 현재까지의 경험을 나타내고 있으므로 현재완료시제를 쓴다.

2 과거의 특정 시점 이전에 발생한 일을 나타내는 과거완료시제를 쓴다.

3 과거의 특정 시점 이전에 발생한 일이 그 시점에도 계속 진행되고 있었음을 나타내는 과거완료진행시제를 쓴다.

4 현재완료시제는 특정한 과거 시점을 나타내는 표현과 함께 쓸 수 없다.

5 과거에 일어난 일의 결과가 현재까지 영향을 미치고 있음을 나타내므로 현재완료시제 has gone을 쓴다. 빈칸에 ③을 넣으면 has been to가 되어 '~에 가본 적이 있다'라는 의미가 되므로 어색하다.

6 미래의 특정 시점까지 완료되거나 계속될 일을 나타내는 미래완료시제를 쓴다.

7 2시간 전에 영화를 보기 시작했고 여전히 보고 있으므로 현재완료진행시제를 쓴다.

8 5년 동안 운동을 해오고 있었고 내년이면 6년째가 되므로 미래완료진행시제를 쓴다.

9 현재완료시제는 특정한 과거 시점을 나타내는 표현과 함께 쓸 수 없다.

10 'Sarah가 집에 들렀을 때 나는 설거지를 하고 있었다.'라는 의미이므로 과거완료진행시제나 과거진행시제를 쓴다.

11 ② have → had

12 ⑤ had → will have

13 (A): 과거의 특정 시점 이전에 발생한 일을 나타내는 과거완료시제를 쓴다.
(B): 현재완료진행시제 문장에서 빈칸 뒤에 일의 시작 시점을 나타내는 7 P.M.이 왔으므로 since를 쓴다.
(C): 미래의 특정 시점까지 완료되거나 계속될 일을 나타내는 미래완료시제를 쓴다.

14 ① has forgotten → had forgotten[forgot]
② has been taking → had been taking[was taking]
③ have studied → studied
⑤ has been snowing → will have been snowing

15 미래의 특정 시점까지 완료되거나 계속될 일을 나타내는 미래완료시제를 쓴다.

16 과거의 특정 시점 이전에 발생한 일을 나타내는 과거완료시제를 쓴다.

17 과거에 일어난 일이 현재에도 계속 진행되고 있음을 나타내는 현재완료진행시제 문장이므로 「have been + V-ing」를 쓴다.

18 과거의 특정 시점 이전에 발생한 일이 그 시점에도 계속 진행되고 있었음을 나타내는 과거완료진행시제 문장이므로 「had been + V-ing」를 쓴다.

19 주어진 문장과 ④: 완료
①: 계속　②③: 경험　⑤: 결과

20 주어진 문장과 ⑤: 결과
①②: 경험　③: 완료　④: 계속

21 ⓐ has lost → lost
ⓒ has → had

22 과거부터 현재까지의 경험을 나타내는 현재완료시제 문장이므로 「have + p.p.」를 쓴다.

23 미래의 특정 시점까지 완료되거나 계속될 일을 나타내는 미래완료시제 문장이므로 「will have + p.p.」를 쓴다.

24 과거의 특정 시점 이전에 발생한 일을 나타내는 과거완료시제 문장이므로 「had + p.p.」를 쓴다.

Chapter 02 조동사

UNIT 01 can, may, must, should

p.7

A 1 should　　2 may　　3 can't
4 don't have to

B 1 can enter
2 don't have[need] to practice
3 ought to water

C 1 Can you pass　　2 must drive
3 can't be

D 1 It may be cold tonight
2 We ought to protect our environment
3 You don't have to pay

UNIT 02 had better, would rather, used to, may as well

p.8

A 1 go home　　2 be　　3 as well
4 O　　5 rather not　　6 O
7 to hang　　8 better

B 1 used to　　　　2 may as well
3 would rather

C 1 may as well ask Chris to teach us swimming
2 used to study in London
3 would rather wear pants than a skirt
4 had better take a walk every day

UNIT 03 조동사 + have + p.p.

p.9

A 1 should have written　2 must have eaten
3 can't have driven

B 1 can't have solved　　2 should have seen
3 may[might] have expected
4 must have burned

C 1 너는 월요일 아침에 대중교통을 이용했어야 했다
2 우리는 최악의 상황을 피했을 수도 있었다
3 그녀는 과거에 발레리나였을지도 모른다

D 1 I should have called you
2 It must have been stolen
3 They can't have gone to bed

Chapter Test ✚

p.10

1 ①　　**2** ③　　**3** ②　　**4** ①, ③
5 used to drink　**6** ②　**7** ④　**8** ⑤　**9** ④
10 ③　　**11** ④　　**12** ①
13 ought to not → ought not to　　**14** must → should
15 working → work　　**16** ③　　**17** ④　　**18** ②
19 ⑤　　**20** ④　　**21** ③
22 I should have watered the plant
23 may as well take　　**24** used to swim

---

1 허가(~해도 된다)를 나타내는 may를 쓴다.

2 능력·가능(~할 수 있다)을 나타내는 can을 쓴다.

3 과거 사실에 대한 강한 부정의 추측(~했을 리가 없다)을 나타내는 「can't + have + p.p.」를 쓴다.

4 ① can't → must
③ must not → don't have to[don't need to/need not]

5 would(과거의 반복적인 습관) = used to

6 should(충고·의무) = ought to

7 ④ don't need not → don't have to[don't need to/ need not]

8 ⑤ see → seen

9 불필요(~할 필요가 없다)를 나타내는 need not을 쓴다.

10 과거 사실에 대한 약한 추측(~했을지도 모른다)을 나타내는 「may + have + p.p.」를 쓴다.

11 첫 번째 빈칸: 불필요(~할 필요가 없다)를 나타내는 need not을 쓴다.
두 번째 빈칸: 허가(~해도 된다)를 나타내는 can을 쓴다.

12 첫 번째 빈칸: 과거 사실에 대한 후회나 유감(~했어야 했다(하지만 하지 않았다))을 나타내는 「should + have + p.p.」를 쓴다.
두 빈째 빈칸: 과거 사실에 대한 강한 추측(~했음이 틀림없다)을 나타내는 「must + have + p.p.」를 쓴다.

13 ought to의 부정형은 ought not to이다.

14 과거 사실에 대한 후회나 유감(~했어야 했다(하지만 하지 않았다))을 나타내는 「should + have + p.p.」를 쓴다.

15 과거의 반복적인 습관(~하곤 했다)을 나타내는 used to 뒤에는 동사원형이 온다.

16 「should + have + p.p.」 '~했어야 했다(하지만 하지 않았다)'
「can't + have + p.p.」 '~했을 리가 없다'

17 ④: 허가 ①②③⑤: 능력·가능

18 ②: 강한 추측 ①③④⑤: 의무

19 ① had not better → had better not
② would → used to
③ be → been
④ to sign → sign

20 would rather A than B 'B하느니 차라리 A하겠다'

21 ⓐ checking → check
ⓒ help → have helped
ⓔ need not to → doesn't have to[doesn't need to/need not]

22 과거 사실에 대한 후회나 유감(~했어야 했다(하지만 하지 않았다))을 나타내는 「should + have + p.p.」를 쓴다.

23 「may as well + 동사원형」 '~하는 편이 좋다'

24 「used to + 동사원형」 '~하곤 했다'

Chapter 03 수동태

UNIT 01 수동태의 쓰임

p.13

A 1 being shown[shown] 2 O
3 happened 4 be cut 5 O

B 1 is delivered 2 is visited 3 resemble

C 1 have been collected by Amy
2 is being prepared by Jane's friends
3 will be released by the company

D 1 may be checked by next week
2 has been destroyed by the earthquake
3 is being discussed by the managers
4 must be washed in cold water

UNIT 02 4형식/5형식 문장의 수동태

p.14

A 1 chasing[to chase] 2 to
3 angry 4 for 5 to

B 1 were told to take a seat by the flight attendants
2 was given a beautiful watch by her grandfather, was given to Maria by her grandfather
3 was made to get out of the car by the police officer
4 was heard singing[to sing] in the bathroom by Luke
5 was elected president by the club members

C 1 was sent to his friend
2 was seen walking down the street
3 were asked to be silent
4 was made to stand in the hallway

UNIT 03 주의해야 할 수동태

p.15

A 1 looked after by 2 with
3 is believed 4 O

B 1 is filled with 2 are worried about
3 are covered with

C 1 should not be put off (by us)
2 is believed that 13 is an unlucky number, is believed to be an unlucky number
3 is said that garlic is good for preventing cancer, is said to be good for preventing cancer

D 1 is thought that constructing a bridge
2 is made from blueberries
3 is interested in social issues

Chapter Test ✛

p.16

1 ④ 2 ③ 3 ④ 4 ④ 5 ③ 6 ⑤
7 is belonged to → belongs to
8 sign → be signed 9 ① 10 ②
11 walk → walking[to walk] 12 ⑤ 13 ①
14 ④
15 were taught useful English expressions
16 was seen dancing[to dance] in my room
17 ④, ⑤ 18 can be asked of
19 is being used 20 is known to be
21 may be reserved 22 is being taken care of
23 ④ 24 ②

---

1 역사 영화가 보여주는 것이 아니라 보여지는 것이므로 수동태를 쓴다. 수동태의 동사는 「be동사 + p.p.」의 형태이므로

was shown을 쓴다.

2 사역동사가 쓰인 5형식 문장의 수동태에서 목적격 보어는 to부정사를 쓰므로 to go를 쓴다.

3 책들이 반납하는 것이 아니라 반납되는 것이므로 수동태를 쓴다. tomorrow는 미래를 나타내는 표현이고, 미래시제의 수동태는 「will be + p.p.」의 형태이므로 will be returned 를 쓴다.

4 ④: for   ①②③⑤: to

5 조동사가 있는 수동태의 부정문은 「주어 + 조동사 + not + be + p.p.」의 형태로 쓴다.

6 구동사(deal with)를 수동태로 쓸 때 동사(deal)만 「be동사 + p.p.」의 형태로 쓰고, 나머지 부분(with)은 동사 뒤에 그 대로 쓴다.

7 belong to는 목적어를 가지지만 상태를 나타내는 동사이므로 수동태로 쓸 수 없다.

8 조동사가 있는 수동태는 「조동사 + be + p.p.」의 형태로 쓴다.

9 ① building → built

10 ② are looked up → are looked up to

11 지각동사가 쓰인 5형식 문장을 수동태로 바꿀 때는 목적격 보어로 쓰인 동사원형을 V-ing형이나 to부정사로 바꾼다.

12 첫 번째 빈칸: 내가 팀을 받아들인 것이 아니라 팀에 받아들 여진 것이므로 수동태를 쓴다. 수동태의 동사는 「be동사 + p.p.」의 형태이고 yesterday는 과거를 나타내는 표현이므 로 was accepted를 쓴다.
두 번째 빈칸: 목적격 보어가 to부정사인 5형식 문장의 수동 태에서 목적격 보어는 to부정사를 그대로 쓴다.

13 • 직접 목적어가 주어인 수동태 문장에서 show는 간접 목 적어 앞에 전치사 to를 쓰는 동사이다.
   • be known to '~에게 알려져 있다'

14 • be crowded with '~으로 붐비다'
   • be filled with '~으로 가득 차 있다'

15 4형식 문장을 간접 목적어가 주어인 수동태 문장으로 바꿀 때는 「be동사 + p.p.」 바로 뒤에 직접 목적어를 쓴다.

16 지각동사가 쓰인 5형식 문장을 수동태로 바꿀 때는 목적격 보어로 쓰인 동사원형을 V-ing형이나 to부정사로 바꾼다.

17 ④ → Disabled people must not be looked down on by us.
   ⑤ → A baseball cap was bought for Anthony by Jessie.

18 조동사가 있는 수동태는 「조동사 + be + p.p.」의 형태이고, 직접 목적어가 주어인 수동태 문장에서 ask는 간접 목적어 앞에 전치사 of를 쓰는 동사이므로 can be asked of를 쓴 다.

19 '사용되고 있다'라는 현재진행의 의미이고 진행시제의 수 동태는 「be동사 + being + p.p.」의 형태이므로 is being used를 쓴다.

20 know의 목적어로 쓰인 that절의 주어를 수동태 문장의 주 어로 쓸 때 「that절의 주어 + be동사 + known(p.p.) + to부 정사 ~」의 형태로 쓴다.

21 조동사가 있는 수동태는 「조동사 + be + p.p.」의 형태이므 로 may be reserved를 쓴다.

22 now는 현재진행을 나타내는 표현이고 진행시제의 수동태 는 「be동사 + being + p.p.」의 형태이다. 구동사(take care of)를 수동태로 쓸 때 동사만 「be동사 + p.p.」의 형태로 쓰 고, 나머지 부분은 동사 뒤에 그대로 쓰므로 is being taken care of를 쓴다.

23 (A): be made of '~으로 만들어지다(재료 성질이 변하지 않음)'
   (B): 많은 동물이 죽이는 것이 아니라 죽임을 당하는 것이므 로 수동태를 쓴다. 수동태는 「be동사 + p.p.」의 형태이 므로 are killed를 쓴다.
   (C): be interested in '~에 흥미가 있다'

24 ① were stayed → stayed
   ③ of → with
   ④ being → be
   ⑤ of → to

Chapter 04 부정사

UNIT 01 to부정사의 명사적 용법

p.19

A
1 is impossible to breathe in space without any equipment
2 where to go for vacation
3 who(m) to call in emergency
4 is natural to feel many different emotions
5 when to take the medicine

B
1 to answer   2 it, to win
3 how to turn down   4 is to reduce

C
1 We are planning what to do
2 It is important to follow the law
3 makes it easy to use the machine
4 expect to maintain a good relationship

UNIT 02 to부정사의 형용사적/부사적 용법

p.20

A
1 to talk about
2 (in order/so as) to keep his room warm
3 to find a better solution
4 to write with

B
1 was to become   2 is to travel
3 are to win

C
1 우리는 일출을 보기 위해 일찍 일어났다
2 나는 환영 행사에 대해 들어서 기뻤다
3 실수로부터 배울 많은 것들이 있다

D
1 is searching for a place to stay in London
2 were shocked to see the car accident

UNIT 03 부정사를 목적격 보어로 쓰는 동사

A p.21
1 to call   2 O   3 to send
4 O   5 to buy

B
1 finish[to finish]   2 to be
3 wait   4 bring
5 to explore   6 swim[swimming]

C
1 allowed me to download the file
2 heard the doorbell ring
3 let me use her laptop
4 ordered us to do push-ups

UNIT 04 to부정사의 의미상 주어, 시제, 태

A p.22
1 for us   2 of her   3 for me
4 of him

B
1 to be finished   2 O
3 to be honest   4 of you

C
1 to want   2 to have looked
3 to have left   4 to be made

D
1 seems to have been successful
2 hate to be bothered
3 was delighted to be supported

UNIT 05 to부정사 구문, 독립부정사

A p.23
1 O   2 lucky enough
3 To begin with   4 to eat

B
1 tall enough to reach the cupboard
2 too hot for me to walk on
3 so scared that she couldn't open her eyes
4 so shallow that kids could swim in it

C
1 설상가상으로, 그는 열이 있었다
2 내가 그 에세이를 쓰는 데 3일이 걸릴 것이다
3 말하자면, 그 가수는 전설이다

D
1 too bitter to eat
2 To be frank with you
3 windy enough for us to fly a kite

Chapter Test + p.24

1 ③   2 ①   3 ④   4 ②
5 seems to have closed   6 in[so] order[as] to paint
7 so big that five people can sit on it   8 ④

9 to have   10 called   11 not to put off
12 ①   13 ③   14 ⑤   15 ⑤
16 Ted is too young to drive a car
17 ③   18 ⑤   19 ③   20 ②   21 ⑤
22 to have taken something
23 what to buy[what we should buy]
24 to try the Thai dish

---

1 to부정사가 5형식 문장의 목적어로 쓰일 때 목적어 자리에 가목적어 it을 쓰고 진목적어 to부정사(구)를 뒤로 보낸다.

2 make는 원형부정사를 목적격 보어로 쓰는 동사이므로 focus를 쓴다.

3 see는 원형부정사나 현재분사를 목적격 보어로 쓰는 동사이므로 crossing을 쓴다.

4 to부정사의 의미상 주어는 「for + 목적격」의 형태로 쓴다.

5 「It seems that + 주어 + 동사」는 「seem + to부정사」로 바꿔 쓸 수 있고, to부정사의 시제가 주절의 시제보다 앞서므로 「to have + p.p.」의 형태로 쓴다.

6 목적의 의미를 강조하기 위해 to를 in order to나 so as to 로 바꿔 쓸 수 있다.

7 「형용사/부사 + enough + to부정사」는 「so + 형용사/부사 + that + 주어 + can + 동사원형」으로 바꿔 쓸 수 있다. 주어 (The sofa)가 to부정사(to sit on)의 목적어이므로 that절에 반드시 목적격 it(=the sofa)을 쓴다.

8 ① book → to book
② to fight → fight[fighting]
③ been → have been
⑤ learning → learn

9 encourage는 to부정사를 목적격 보어로 쓰는 동사이므로 to have를 쓴다.

10 지각동사의 목적어와 목적격 보어의 관계가 수동이면 목적격 보어 자리에 과거분사를 쓰므로 called를 쓴다.

11 promise는 to부정사를 목적어로 쓰는 동사이고 to부정사의 부정형은 「not to + 동사원형」이므로 not to put off를 쓴다.

12 ② → ride
③ → to be
④ → wait[waiting]
⑤ → to wash

13 ③ that → it

14 ⑤ for → of

15 목적격 보어로 원형부정사(throw)가 왔으므로 to부정사를 목적격 보어로 쓰는 get은 쓸 수 없다.

16 「too + 형용사/부사 + to부정사」 '…하기에 너무 ~한/하게'

17 ③: 형용사적 용법   ①②④⑤: 명사적 용법

18 ⑤: 명사적 용법   ①②③④: 부사적 용법

19 • strange to say '이상한 얘기지만'
• 「be동사 + to부정사」 '~하려고 하다(의도)'

20 • feel은 원형부정사나 현재분사를 목적격 보어로 쓰는 동 사이므로 grab이나 grabbing을 쓴다.
• expect는 to부정사를 목적격 보어로 쓰는 동사이므로 to fix를 쓴다.

21 「It seems that + 주어 + 동사」는 「seem + to부정사」로 바 꿔 쓸 수 있지만, to부정사의 시제가 주절의 시제보다 앞설 때는 to부정사를 「to have + p.p.」의 형태로 쓴다.
→ Jay seems to have studied hard for the exam.

22 to부정사의 시제가 주절의 시제보다 앞설 때는 「to have + p.p.」의 형태로 쓴다.

23 '무엇을 ~할지'라는 의미의 「what + to부정사」를 쓴다. 「what + to부정사」는 「what + 주어 + should + 동사원형」 으로 바꿔 쓸 수 있다.

24 get은 to부정사를 목적격 보어로 쓰는 동사이다.

Chapter 05 동명사

UNIT 01 동명사의 쓰임

p.27

A
1 taking
2 being[having been]
3 her
4 collecting[to collect]
5 sleeping

B
1 going
2 being asked[having been asked]
3 O
4 having forgotten

C
1 his[him] achieving
2 being robbed
3 my[me] joining

D
1 denied having eaten the ice cream
2 was tired after taking care of
3 was satisfied with being remembered

UNIT 02 동명사와 to부정사를 목적어로 쓰는 동사

p.28

A
1 thinking
2 to enter
3 O
4 complaining

B
1 putting[to put]
2 eating
3 fixing
4 to develop

C
1 to draw
2 not to leave
3 to cycle
4 having met

D
1 admitted being responsible for this matter
2 regretted arguing with his best friend
3 kept her dog from jumping

Chapter Test ✚

p.29

1 ③ **2** ② **3** ④ **4** ③ **5** ①, ③
6 seeing → to see **7** taking → to take
8 having been → having **9** ② **10** ⑤
11 running **12** to take **13** ②
14 forgot buying **15** is busy taking care of
16 complained about my[me] wearing
17 I spent two hours reading the book
18 The guard prevented strangers from entering this building **19** ③ **20** ④ **21** ④ **22** ⑤
23 not having submitted her homework
24 being given many presents

---

1 「feel like + V-ing」 '~하고 싶다'

2 agree는 to부정사를 목적어로 쓰는 동사이므로 to meet을 쓴다.

3 전치사의 목적어 자리이고 내가 방해받지 않는다는 수동의 의미이므로 동명사의 수동태 being bothered를 쓴다.

4 전치사의 목적어 자리에 동명사를 쓰고, 동명사의 의미상 주 어는 동명사 앞에 소유격이나 목적격을 써서 나타낸다.

5 to부정사 to tell이 목적어이므로 동명사를 목적어로 쓰는 avoid와 deny는 쓸 수 없다.

6 plan은 to부정사를 목적어로 쓰는 동사이므로 to see를 쓴 다.

7 '(미래에) ~할 것을 잊다'라는 의미이므로 동사 forget 뒤에 to부정사 to take를 쓴다.

8 동명사의 시제가 주절의 시제보다 앞서고 동명사가 능동의 의미이므로 완료 동명사 「having + p.p.」를 쓴다.

9 ② go → going

10 ⑤ to build → building

11 give up은 동명사를 목적어로 쓰는 동사이므로 running을 쓴다.

12 '(미래에) ~할 것을 기억하다'라는 의미이므로 동사 remember 뒤에 to부정사 to take를 쓴다.

13 주어진 문장과 ②: 보어 ①③⑤: 목적어 ④: 주어

14 '(과거에) ~한 것을 잊다'라는 의미이므로 동사 forget 뒤에 동명사 buying을 쓴다.

15 「be busy + V-ing」 '~하느라 바쁘다'

16 전치사의 목적어 자리에 동명사를 쓰고, 동명사의 의미상 주 어는 동명사 앞에 소유격이나 목적격을 써서 나타낸다.

17 「spend + 시간/돈 + V-ing」 '~하는 데 시간/돈을 쓰다'

18 「prevent … from + V-ing」 '…가 ~하지 못하게 하다'

19 • promise는 to부정사를 목적어로 쓰는 동사이므로 to lend를 쓴다.
• stop은 동명사를 목적어로 쓰는 동사이므로 writing을 쓴 다. stop 뒤에 to부정사가 오면 '~하기 위해 멈추다'라는 의미로, 이때 to부정사는 부사적 용법으로 쓰여 목적을

나타낸다.

20 • 동명사의 의미상 주어는 동명사 앞에 소유격이나 목적격을 써서 나타내므로 my나 me를 쓴다.
   • 전치사의 목적어 자리이므로 동명사 having been을 쓴다.

21 ① speak → speaking
   ② bringing → to bring
   ③ to fall → falling
   ⑤ drive → driving

22 ① → watching
   ② → passing[having passed]
   ③ → having been
   ④ → to win

23 동명사의 시제가 주절의 시제보다 앞서므로 완료 동명사 「having + p.p.」를 쓴다. 동명사 앞에 not을 붙여 부정형을 만든다.

24 그가 많은 선물을 받았다는 수동의 의미이므로 동명사의 수동태 「being + p.p.」를 쓴다.

Chapter 06 분사

UNIT 01 현재분사와 과거분사

p.32

A　1 fixed　　　　　2 confusing
　　　3 made　　　　　4 O

B　1 disappointing　　2 surprised
　　　3 interesting

C　1 wearing a white blouse
　　　2 scratched by the cat
　　　3 jumping over the fence

D　1 heard the police coming towards him
　　　2 could smell something burning
　　　3 had her teeth examined

UNIT 02 분사구문

p.33

A　1 Not having　　2 O
　　　3 Shouting　　　4 Staying

B　1 Completing the puzzle
　　　2 Buying two items
　　　3 Talking during class
　　　4 Walking down the street

C　1 While she eats dinner
　　　2 As I didn't have enough time
　　　3 As soon as he came into the classroom

D　1 Seeing the actor　　2 Not arriving on time
　　　3 Walking into the room

UNIT 03 주의해야 할 분사구문

p.34

A　1 O　　　　　　　　2 It being
　　　3 Having saved　　4 sleeping

B　1 (Being) Excited about their vacation
　　　2 Although the weather being cold
　　　3 Not having seen each other for ages

C　1 As she is picked up by her mother
　　　2 Because they sold their apartment
　　　3 While our dad cooked dinner

D　1 Left alone at night
　　　2 The movie being over
　　　3 with the fans watching

Chapter Test ✚

p.35

1 ②　　2 ③　　3 ⑤　　4 ②　　5 ③　　6 ①

7 Having caught　　8 Not having　　9 ④

10 ⑤　　11 Spoken → Speaking

12 Knowing not → Not knowing　　13 It being cold

14 Having finished his painting

15 (Being) Known to the public　　16 ②　　17 ②

18 ⑤　　19 (1) ⓑ → Arriving　(2) ⓒ → disappointed

20 ⑤　　21 Decorated　　22 Giving a speech

23 Although[Though] having been short

24 Judging from her behavior

---

1 명사 stars를 수식하고 명사와의 관계가 능동이므로 현재분사 shining을 쓴다.

2 Bella는 감정을 느끼는 대상이므로 과거분사 surprised를 쓴다.

3 '통학 버스를 놓쳤기 때문에'라는 의미의 부사절을 분사구문으로 나타냈고, 부사절의 시제가 주절의 시제보다 앞서므로 Having missed를 쓴다.

4 ① satisfying → satisfied
   ③ Having praised → (Having been) Praised
   ④ fixing → fixed
   ⑤ spoken → speaking

5 • '만약 열심히 노력한다면'이라는 의미의 부사절을 분사구문으로 나타낸 것이므로 Trying을 쓴다.
   • 명사 trash를 수식하고 명사와의 관계가 수동이므로 과거분사 left를 쓴다.

6 • Going up the hill은 감정을 일으키는 원인이므로 현재분

사 exhausting을 쓴다.
- 목적어 hamster를 보충 설명하고 목적어와의 관계가 능동이므로 현재분사 eating을 쓴다.

7 '지난주에 감기에 걸렸기 때문에'라는 의미의 부사절을 분사구문으로 나타냈고, 부사절의 시제가 주절의 시제보다 앞서므로 Having caught을 쓴다.

8 '보고서를 위한 충분한 시간이 없기 때문에'라는 의미의 부사절을 분사구문으로 나타냈고, 분사구문의 부정형은 분사 앞에 not을 붙여 만들므로 Not having을 쓴다.

9 ④ removing → removed

10 ⑤ Amazing → (Being) Amazed

11 Speaking of '~에 대해 말하자면'

12 분사구문의 부정형은 분사 앞에 not을 붙여 만들므로 Not knowing을 쓴다.

13 접속사 As를 생략하고 동사 was를 being으로 바꾼다. 부사절의 주어와 주절의 주어가 다르므로 부사절의 주어를 생략하지 않는다.

14 접속사 As soon as와 주어 he를 생략하고, 부사절의 시제가 주절의 시제보다 앞서므로 동사 had finished를 Having finished로 바꾼다.

15 접속사 Since와 주어 she를 생략하고 동사 is known을 Being known으로 바꾼다. 이때 Being은 생략할 수 있다.

16 ⓐ losing → lost
ⓑ exciting → excited
ⓔ knocked → knocking

17 '만약 네가 천천히 걷는다면, 결승선에 빨리 도착하지 않을 것이다.'라는 의미이므로 조건을 나타내는 If you walk slowly를 쓴다.

18 ⑤: 동명사   주어진 문장과 ①②③④: 현재분사

19 (1) '콘서트 홀에 도착했을 때'라는 의미의 부사절을 분사구문으로 나타낸 것이므로 Arriving을 쓴다.
(2) She는 감정을 느끼는 대상이므로 과거분사 disappointed를 쓴다.

20 ⑤ → As he saw the accident ahead

21 '그 컵은 금으로 장식되었기 때문에'라는 의미의 부사절을 분사구문으로 나타낸 것이므로 Decorated를 쓴다. 수동형 분사구문에서 being은 생략할 수 있다.

22 '그는 연설을 하는 동안'이라는 의미의 부사절을 분사구문으로 나타낸 것이므로 Giving을 쓴다.

23 '비록 나는 과거에 키가 작았지만'이라는 의미의 부사절을 분사구문으로 나타냈고, 부사절의 시제가 주절의 시제보다 앞서므로 having been을 쓴다. 양보를 나타내는 분사구문은 주로 접속사를 생략하지 않는다.

24 Judging from '~으로 판단하건대'

Chapter 07 관계사

UNIT 01 관계대명사

p.38

A
1 What
2 who[that]
3 O
4 whose
5 O

B
1 I can smell the food which my neighbors are cooking
2 The boys caught the woman who stole Kyle's wallet
3 Linda is carrying a bag whose zipper is broken
4 This is a documentary which is about World War II
5 My uncle who(m) I visit once a year lives in Indonesia

C
1 the artwork which was painted
2 What I need right now
3 the same jacket that she wore
4 the woman who used to be

UNIT 02 관계부사

p.39

A
1 where
2 how
3 why
4 when

B
1 how
2 when
3 where
4 why

C
1 2015 is the year when I moved to another school
2 The police found (the place) where the evidence was hidden
3 This video teaches us how we can improve our speech skills

D
1 any reason why your family chose
2 the time when the supermarket closes
3 regions where coffee beans are grown

UNIT 03 주의해야 할 관계사의 쓰임

p.40

A
1 which
2 which
3 O
4 whom

B
1 Mary took a picture with the singer who(m) [that] she has liked for years
2 I still remember the party which[that] Paul threw two years ago

3 A gram is a unit which[that] is used to measure mass

C 1 but it still doesn't work
2 and there we had a picnic
3 and it is in northern California

D 1 a nun respected by many people
2 the announcer who I told you about
3 when it was crowded with kids

UNIT 04 복합관계사

p.41

A 1 whenever 2 Wherever 3 Whichever

B 1 Whoever comes to the charity event
2 whatever happens
3 However well you explain the rule
4 whenever someone knocked on the door

C 1 여름에 네가 가는 곳은 어디든지 모기들이 있다
2 아무리 오래 걸리더라도, 나는 마라톤을 완주할 것이다
3 우리가 무슨 계획을 가지고 있더라도, 우리는 비 때문에 그것을 취소해야 한다

D 1 Whenever Jeffrey comes home
2 Whoever wants a seat
3 Whichever hat you wear

Chapter Test +

p.42

1 ③　　2 ④　　3 ①　　4 ⑤　　5 when → where
6 the way how → how[the way]　　7 Wherever
8 when　　　　9 ③
10 which[that] was filled with cookies
11 whose camera is not working
12 what you did yesterday　　13 ①　　14 ③
15 ④　　16 ④　　17 Whenever she goes to the library
18 whose toy was taken away　　19 what he says
20 ⑤　　21 ⑤　　22 ②　　23 ④

---

1 선행사(Amy)가 사람이고 빈칸 앞에 콤마(,)가 있으므로 계속적 용법의 관계대명사 who를 쓴다.

2 빈칸 뒤에 선행사(that tower)가 소유하는 대상인 명사(structure)가 있으므로 소유격 관계대명사 whose를 쓴다.

3 '나의 엄마는 내가 만나는 누구든지에게 친절히 하라고 내게 말씀하신다.'라는 의미이므로 명사절을 이끄는 복합관계대명사 whomever를 쓴다.

4 ① what → whatever　　② when → where
③ That → What　　④ that → which

5 선행사(a nice place)가 장소를 나타내므로 관계부사 where를 쓴다.

6 the way와 how는 둘 중 하나만 쓸 수 있다.

7 '나는 어디서 쇼핑을 하더라도, 이 기프트 카드를 사용할 수 있다.'라는 의미이며, no matter where는 복합관계부사 wherever로 바꿔 쓸 수 있다.

8 '나는 금요일에 축제에 갔는데, 그때 내가 가장 좋아하는 가수를 봤다.'라는 의미이며, and then은 계속적 용법의 관계부사 when으로 바꿔 쓸 수 있다.

9 ③: who[that]　　①②④⑤: what

10 두 번째 문장은 첫 번째 문장의 a box에 대해 보충 설명하고 있고, 두 번째 문장의 It이 주어 역할을 하고 있으므로 사물을 선행사로 하는 주격 관계대명사 which나 that을 쓴다.

11 두 번째 문장은 첫 번째 문장의 his phone에 대해 보충 설명하고 있고, 두 번째 문장의 Its가 소유격의 역할을 하고 있으므로 소유격 관계대명사 whose를 쓴다.

12 두 번째 문장은 첫 번째 문장의 the thing에 대해 보충 설명하고 있고, '너는 네가 어제 한 것에 대해 Nicole에게 사과해야 한다.'라는 의미이므로 관계대명사 what을 쓴다.

13 • 선행사(The man)가 사람이고 관계대명사가 관계대명사절 안에서 목적어 역할을 하므로 목적격 관계대명사 who(m)이나 that을 쓴다.
• 선행사(my friend)가 사람이고 빈칸 앞에 전치사가 있으므로 목적격 관계대명사 whom을 쓴다.

14 ③ who → whose

15 ④ Whatever → However

16 '그 실험이 실패한 이유'라고 했으므로 선행사는 the reason이고, 선행사가 이유를 나타내므로 관계부사 why를 쓴다. 선행사가 the reason과 같은 일반적인 명사인 경우 선행사를 생략할 수 있다.

17 '도서관에 갈 때는 언제나'라는 의미이므로 시간의 부사절을 이끄는 복합관계부사 whenever를 쓴다.

18 toy는 선행사(The boy)가 소유하는 대상인 명사이므로 소유격 관계대명사 whose를 쓴다.

19 선행사가 없으므로 선행사를 포함하는 관계대명사 what을 쓴다.

20 ① That → What　　　　② that → which
③ that → whom　　　　④ that → when

21 ⑤: 주격 관계대명사 (주격 관계대명사는 생략할 수 없다.)
①③: 목적격 관계대명사
②④: 「주격 관계대명사 + be동사」

22 • '이 조각상을 만든 누구든지 예술가라고 불릴 수 있다.'라는 의미이므로 복합관계대명사 Whoever를 쓴다.
• '아무리 춥더라도, Kevin은 절대로 뜨거운 음료를 마시지 않는다.'라는 의미이므로 복합관계부사 However를 쓴다.

23 • 선행사(Admiral Yi Sun-shin)가 사람이고 관계대명사가 관계대명사절 안에서 주어 역할을 하므로 주격 관계대명사 who를 쓴다.
• 선행사(France)가 장소를 나타내므로 관계부사 where를 쓴다.

Chapter 08 접속사

UNIT 01 부사절을 이끄는 접속사

> p.45
>
> **A** 1 as soon as   2 Because
>   3 am   4 so
>
> **B** 1 ⓕ   2 ⓐ   3 ⓓ
>   4 ⓒ   5 ⓑ   6 ⓔ
>
> **C** 1 As I haven't been to Paris before
>   2 Unless you try your best
>   3 since the terrible accident occurred
>   4 Even though he wasn't prepared

UNIT 02 상관접속사, 간접의문문

> p.46
>
> **A** 1 look   2 Mark has
>   3 O   4 is
>
> **B** 1 Neither Natalie nor Josh joined the book club
>   2 Not only the doctor but (also) the nurses are
>   helping the patient
>   3 I'm going to buy both the shirt and the pants
>
> **C** 1 Why do you think polar bears are white
>   2 I'm not sure if[whether] Kelly will agree with
>   your suggestion
>   3 He wants to know how the city of Pompeii
>   was destroyed
>
> **D** 1 if they know the rules
>   2 Either Jack or I have to make
>   3 Who do you believe is telling

Chapter Test ✚

> p.47
>
> 1 ④   2 ②   3 ④   4 ①, ③ 5 ⑤
>
> 6 Both Molly and Cathy want
>
> 7 Because[Since/As] Ben is kind
>
> 8 if[whether] he will arrive   9 ②   10 ④
>
> 11 Unless I get the ticket
>
> 12 Not only the main dish but (also) the dessert
>
> 13 are → is   14 can I → I can
>
> 15 will come → come
>
> 16 (1) Both, and, cost (2) Not only, but also, has
>   (3) Neither, nor, weighs   17 ① 18 ②
>
> 19 ④   20 ②   21 Although[Though/Even though]
>
> 22 ③   23 ⑤   24 ③

1 '바람이 너무 세서 많은 나무들이 쓰러졌다.'라는 의미이므로 「so ~ that …」(너무 ~해서 …한)을 쓴다.

2 '만약 네가 그녀에게 사과하지 않는다면, 그녀는 네게 계속 화가 나 있을 것이다.'라는 의미이므로 If(만약 ~한다면)를 쓴다.

3 '나는 스키뿐만 아니라 스노보드도 배우고 싶다.'라는 의미이므로 not only A but (also) B(A뿐만 아니라 B도)를 쓴다.

4 ① → I wonder why he looks so happy.
  ③ → When do you think you can come?

5 ⑤: '~인지 아닌지'   ①②③④: '만약 ~한다면'

6 'A와 B 둘 다'라는 의미의 both A and B를 쓰고, both A and B 뒤에는 항상 복수동사를 쓴다.

7 '~하기 때문에'라는 의미의 Because[Since/As]를 쓴다.

8 '~인지 아닌지'라는 의미로 의문사가 없는 간접의문문을 이끄는 if[whether]를 쓴다.

9 'A나 B 둘 중 하나'라는 의미의 either A or B를 쓴다.

10 의문사가 있는 간접의문문은 「의문사 + 주어 + 동사」의 어순인데, 간접의문문을 포함하는 문장의 동사가 생각이나 추측을 나타내는 think인 경우 간접의문문의 의문사를 문장 맨 앞에 쓴다.

11 if ~ not(만약 ~하지 않는다면)은 unless로 바꿔 쓸 수 있다.

12 B as well as A(A뿐만 아니라 B도)는 not only A but (also) B로 바꿔 쓸 수 있다.

13 Either A or B 뒤에 오는 동사는 B(Mason)에 수일치시킨다.

14 의문사가 있는 간접의문문은 「의문사 + 주어 + 동사」의 어순이다.

15 시간을 나타내는 부사절에서는 미래시제 대신 현재시제를 쓴다.

16 (1) 배와 복숭아 둘 다 4달러이므로 both A and B(A와 B 둘 다)를 쓰고, both A and B 뒤에는 항상 복수동사를 쓴다.
  (2) 사과뿐만 아니라 복숭아도 100칼로리이므로 not only A but also B(A뿐만 아니라 B도)를 쓰고, not only A but also B 뒤에 오는 동사는 B(a peach)에 수일치시킨다.
  (3) 사과도 배도 무게가 300그램이 아니므로 neither A nor B(A도 B도 아닌)를 쓰고, neither A nor B 뒤에 오는 동사는 B(a pear)에 수일치시킨다.

17 • '눈이 많이 왔기 때문에, 모든 항공편들이 취소되었다.'라는 의미이므로 as(~하기 때문에)를 쓴다.
  • '나는 그 박물관에 들어가면서 거대한 조각상을 봤다.'라는 의미이므로 as(~하면서, ~하고 있을 때)를 쓴다.

18 • 'Dave는 초등학교 때부터 규칙적으로 운동을 해왔다.'라는 의미이므로 since(~한 이후로)를 쓴다.
  • '너는 믿을만하기 때문에, 나는 너에게 나의 비밀들 중 하나를 말해줄 것이다.'라는 의미이므로 since(~하기 때문에)를 쓴다.

19 ④ Unless you don't come → Unless you come[If you don't come]

20 ② has → have

21 '비록 나는 해산물을 좋아하지 않지만 이 연어 스파게티 는 좋아한다.'라는 의미이므로 Although[Though/Even though](비록 ~이지만)를 쓴다.

22 • '비록 그 주자는 여느 때보다도 더 빨리 달렸지만 경주에 서 마지막으로 들어왔다.'라는 의미이므로 though(비록 ~ 이지만)를 쓴다.
• '나의 노트북은 집에도 도서관에도 없었다.'라는 의미이므 로 neither A nor B(A도 B도 아닌)를 쓴다.

23 • '나는 휴가로 태국에 갈지 안 갈지 확신하지 못한다.'라는 의미이므로 if나 whether(~인지 아닌지)를 쓴다.
• '만약 네가 더 높은 점수를 받기 원한다면 열심히 공부해 라.'라는 의미이므로 if(만약 ~한다면)를 쓴다.

24 ① will explain → explain
② too → so
④ what is the good news → what the good news is
⑤ Do you suppose who → Who do you suppose

Chapter 09 가정법

UNIT 01 가정법 과거/과거완료, 혼합 가정법

p.50

A 1 could 2 soak 3 would win
4 O

B 1 would have opened
2 were in your situation
3 had planted the flowers
4 could send a letter

C 1 I had checked my pocket
2 would be there now
3 my father weren't busy

D 1 I were a president
2 he had brought his hat
3 I would have called him

UNIT 02 I wish/as if/It's time 가정법

p.51

A 1 had 2 could have met
3 were 4 knew

B 1 were on sale
2 thought about the future
3 were expensive
4 had been much braver

C 1 I hadn't said those words to Justin
2 she had cleaned the kitchen
3 I were as strong as superman

D 1 I wish this actress would star
2 It's time we forgot the mistakes
3 as if he had won first prize

UNIT 03 Without[But for] 가정법, if를 생략 한 가정법

p.52

A 1 Were my feet smaller
2 Without your jacket
3 Were it not for computers
4 Had I played the drums well

B 1 Without a break
2 If it were not for the light
3 But for your advice
4 If it were not for water
5 Had it not been for Tim

C 1 Had it not been for the coach
2 Were it not for my friends
3 Had you told lies before

Chapter Test ✚

p.53

1 ⑤ 2 ④ 3 ③
4 it were not for the roses 5 ③ 6 ⑤
7 ⑤ 8 weren't sold out, I could buy it
9 you had had time to exercise with me
10 brought the ball, we could play soccer now
11 Were it not for flour 12 ② 13 ① 14 ③
15 were → had been
16 released → had released 17 ③
18 he had seen a tiger 19 wish I met the actor
20 Were I you 21 ② 22 ④
23 But for, Were it not for 24 ④

---

1 과거의 사실과 반대되는 일을 가정하고 있으므로 가정법 과 거완료를 쓴다.

2 과거의 사실과 반대되는 일이 현재까지 영향을 미치는 상황 을 가정하고 있으므로 혼합 가정법을 쓴다.

3 주절의 시제(현재시제)보다 앞선 시점의 사실과 반대되는 일 을 가정하고 있으므로 「as if + 가정법 과거완료」를 쓴다.

4 주절이 would + 동사원형인 가정법 과거이므로 「But for + 명사(구)」는 「If it were not for + 명사(구)」로 바꿔 쓸 수 있 다.

5 ③ could have gone → could go

6 ⑤ had been → were

7 첫 번째 빈칸: 과거에 이루지 못한 일에 대한 아쉬움을 나

타내는 「I wish + 가정법 과거완료」를 써야 하므로 had learned를 쓴다.
두 번째 빈칸: 과거의 사실과 반대되는 일이 현재까지 영향을 미치는 상황을 가정하고 있으므로 혼합 가정법을 쓰고, 혼합 가정법에서 if절의 동사는 had p.p.이므로 had learned를 쓴다.

8 현재의 사실과 반대되는 일을 가정하는 가정법 과거 「If + 주어 + 동사의 과거형(be동사는 were) ~, 주어 + would, could, might + 동사원형 …」를 쓴다.

9 과거에 이루지 못한 일에 대한 아쉬움을 나타내는 「I wish + 가정법 과거완료」를 쓴다.

10 과거의 사실과 반대되는 일이 현재까지 영향을 미치는 상황을 가정하는 혼합 가정법 「If + 주어 + had p.p. ~, 주어 + would, could, might + 동사원형 …」를 쓰고, if를 생략하면 주어와 동사의 위치가 바뀐다.

11 가정법에서 if를 생략하면 주어와 동사의 위치가 바뀐다.

12 ② → Had it not been for[If it had not been for]

13 • '안전 요원이 없다면, 많은 목숨들이 구조되지 않았을 텐데.'라는 의미로, 현재의 사실과 반대되는 일을 가정하는 문장이므로 wouldn't be saved를 쓴다.
• 주절의 시제(현재시제)와 같은 시점의 사실과 반대되는 일을 가정하는 「as if + 가정법 과거」를 써야 하므로 were를 쓴다.

14 • 과거의 사실과 반대되는 일이 현재까지 영향을 미치는 상황을 가정하고 있으므로 혼합 가정법을 쓰고, 혼합 가정법에서 주절의 동사는 「would, could, might + 동사원형」이므로 wouldn't be를 쓴다.
• 주절이 「would + have p.p.」인 가정법 과거완료이고 if를 생략하면 주어와 동사의 위치가 바뀌므로 Had she been을 쓴다.

15 과거의 사실과 반대되는 일을 가정하는 가정법 과거완료이므로 if절에는 had been을 쓴다.

16 과거에 이루지 못한 일에 대한 아쉬움을 나타내는 「I wish + 가정법 과거완료」이므로 had released를 쓴다.

17 ③ → As I'm not a cat, I can't sleep all day.

18 '마치 ~이었던 것처럼'의 의미로 주절의 시제(과거시제)보다 앞선 시점의 사실과 반대되는 일을 가정하는 「as if + 가정법 과거완료」를 써야 하므로 he had seen a tiger를 쓴다.

19 '~하면 좋을 텐데'의 의미로 현재 이룰 수 없거나 실현 가능성이 거의 없는 일을 소망하는 「I wish + 가정법 과거」를 써야 하므로 wish I met the actor를 쓴다.

20 '만약 ~한다면 …할 텐데'의 의미로 현재의 사실과 반대되는 일을 가정하는 가정법 과거를 쓰고, if를 생략하면 주어와 동사의 위치가 바뀌므로 Were I you를 쓴다.

21 '만약 ~한다면 …할 텐데'의 의미로 현재의 사실과 반대되는 일을 가정하는 가정법 과거이므로 「If + 주어 + 동사의 과거형(be동사는 were) ~, 주어 + would, could, might + 동사원형 …」를 쓴다.

22 '마치 ~이었던 것처럼'의 의미로 주절의 시제(과거시제)보다 앞선 시점의 사실과 반대되는 일을 가정하는 「as if + 가정법 과거완료」이므로 「주어 + 동사 + as if + 주어 + had p.p.」를 쓴다.

23 주절이 「might + 동사원형」인 가정법 과거이므로

「Without[But for] + 명사(구)」는 「If it were not for + 명사(구)」로 바꿔 쓸 수 있고, if를 생략하면 주어와 동사의 위치가 바뀐다.

24 ① walk → walked
② knew → had known
③ Were Gary at the park → Had Gary been at the park[If Gary had been at the park]
⑤ could have talked → could talk

Chapter 10 비교구문

UNIT 01 원급/비교급/최상급 비교

p.56

A 1 much[even/far/a lot] 2 most diligent
3 O 4 well

B 1 the tallest 2 longer than
3 more often than

C 1 as light as 2 superior to
3 the most relaxing

D 1 as slowly as his brother
2 the best singer of all my friends
3 more popular than strawberry cake

UNIT 02 비교구문을 이용한 표현

p.57

A 1 possible[he can] 2 more and more
3 O 4 the most serious

B 1 better 2 the angrier
3 more cookies 4 the bravest

C 1 important as trust, more important than any other
2 colder, yesterday, colder than all the other

D 1 is getting smarter and smarter
2 the saddest movie I have ever watched
3 The more popular the island got

Chapter Test ✛

p.58

1 ④ 2 ① 3 ⑤ 4 ③
5 worst and worst → worse and worse
6 that → to 7 most → more 8 ④
9 (1) the highest (2) lower than any other
(3) as[so] well 10 ① 11 not as[so] long

12 as[so] cheap as[cheaper than]

13 ① 14 ④ 15 ⑤ 16 ②

17 The more clearly, the better

18 five times heavier than

19 stone, is harder than 20 ③ 21 ②

22 three times as big as[three times bigger than]

23 the most beautiful garden (that) I have (ever) seen

24 one of the healthiest vegetables

---

1 「the + 비교급, the + 비교급」 '~하면 할수록 더 …하다'

2 「as + 원급 + as + possible」 '가능한 한 ~한/하게'

3 '건강은 모든 것들 중에서 가장 중요하다.'라는 의미이므로 최상급 the most valuable을 쓴다.

4 ① very → much[even/far/a lot]
② taller → tallest
④ most big → biggest
⑤ adult → adults

5 「비교급 + and + 비교급」 '점점 더 ~한/하게'

6 inferior(열등한)는 비교급 비교에서 than 대신 to를 쓴다.

7 '좋은 성격을 갖는 것이 성공하는 것보다 더 중요하다.'라는 의미이므로 비교급 more important를 쓴다.

8 ① → sweet   ② → the most
③ → busier   ⑤ → as

9 (1) Betty는 가장 높은 영어 점수를 받았으므로 the highest를 쓴다.
(2) Mark의 과학 점수는 다른 어떤 학생의 것보다 더 낮으므로 lower than any other를 쓴다.
(3) 어떤 학생도 수학 시험에서 Emily만큼 잘하지 않았으므로 as[so] well을 쓴다.

10 빈칸 뒤에 비교급(more exciting)이 있으므로 '훨씬'이라는 의미로 비교급을 강조하는 much/far/even/a lot을 쓸 수 있다. very는 원급을 강조한다.

11 미시시피 강은 나일 강만큼 길지 않으므로 not as[so] long as를 쓴다.

12 다른 어떤 햄버거도 치즈버거만큼 저렴하지 않으므로 「No (other) + 단수명사 ~ as[so] + 원급 + as」 또는 「No (other) + 단수명사 ~ 비교급 + than」을 쓴다.

13 ① warmer → warm

14 ④ wisest → wiser

15 • '…보다 덜 ~한/하게'라는 의미인 「less + 원급 + than」의 than을 쓴다.
• '나는 예상했던 것보다 더 오래 줄 서서 기다렸다.'라는 의미의 비교급 비교이므로 than을 쓴다.

16 • '(다른) 어떤 …도 -만큼 ~하지 않은'이라는 의미인 「No (other) + 단수명사 ~ as + 원급 + as」의 as를 쓴다.
• '가능한 한 ~한/하게'라는 의미인 「as + 원급 + as + 주어 + can」의 as를 쓴다.

17 '네가 명확하게 말하면 말할수록, 듣는 사람은 너를 더 잘 이해한다.'라는 의미의 문장이므로 '~하면 할수록 더 …하다'라

18 「배수사 + as + 원급 + as」는 「배수사 + 비교급 + than」으로 바꿔 쓸 수 있다.

19 「the + 최상급」은 「No (other) + 단수명사 ~ 비교급 + than」으로 바꿔 쓸 수 있다.

20 ③: 「No (other) + 단수명사 ~ as[so] + 원급 + as」는 최상급 표현 「one of the + 최상급 + 복수명사」와 바꿔 쓸 수 없다.

21 ② → Jason is more careful than Karen.

22 '…보다 -배 더 ~한/하게'라는 의미의 「배수사 + as + 원급 + as」 또는 「배수사 + 비교급 + than」을 쓴다.

23 '…한 것 중에서 가장 ~한'이라는 의미의 「the + 최상급 + 명사 + (that) + 주어 + have/has + (ever) + p.p.」를 쓴다.

24 '가장 ~한 것들 중 하나'라는 의미의 「one of the + 최상급 + 복수명사」를 쓴다.

Chapter 11 일치와 화법

UNIT 01 수의 일치

p.61

A 1 is 2 helps 3 O
4 O 5 are

B 1 is 2 are 3 is
4 is 5 are

C 1 Bread and butter is
2 Nobody in the group knows
3 Three kilometers is
4 The number of skyscrapers is increasing

UNIT 02 시제의 일치

p.62

A 1 boils 2 had 3 would
4 O

B 1 said that Laura volunteers every month
2 knew that a bird had built a nest under our roof
3 explained to the kids that the sun rises in the east
4 said that she could help me with my homework
5 learned that dinosaurs existed on earth millions of years ago
6 told me that he had seen a ghost in his dream last night

C 1 we would eat something traditional
2 the pharmacy closes on Mondays
3 the Colosseum was built In AD 80

UNIT 03 화법

p.63

A 1 She asked me when my parents would arrive home
2 The dentist told Mike not to drink too much soda
3 He told me that he had received the package the day before

B 1 said (that) she wanted to order two slices of pizza
2 asked me who had written that novel
3 asked me if[whether] I had been the class president the previous year
4 said (that) I had to come to the hospital the next[the following] day
5 told[asked/ordered/advised] the people not to leave empty boxes there

C 1 asked me if[whether] I could do
2 said (that) it was too late for me
3 told him not to show my photos

Chapter Test ✚

p.64

1 ③ 2 ① 3 ② 4 ④ 5 ④
6 that → if[whether]   7 had ended → ended
8 is → are
9 if[whether] I was going to join the book club the following week
10 to stay calm in any situation
11 Jeff had left three hours before
12 ③, ⑤   13 was 14 ② 15 ④ 16 ④
17 ⑤ 18 ③ 19 ① 20 ② 21 ②
22 makes me happy   23 what my hobby was
24 became the president

---

1 주절이 과거시제이므로 종속절에는 과거시제 was를 쓴다.
2 속담·격언을 말할 때는 주절의 시제와 상관없이 종속절에 항상 현재시제를 쓰므로 현재시제 speak를 쓴다.
3 과학적 사실을 말할 때는 주절의 시제와 상관없이 종속절에 항상 현재시제를 쓰므로 현재시제 are를 쓴다.
4 의문사가 없는 의문문의 간접 화법은 if나 whether로 주절과 종속절을 연결한다.
5 ① are → is

2 will → would
3 had → has
5 have → has

6 의문사가 없는 의문문의 간접 화법은 if나 whether로 주절과 종속절을 연결한다.
7 역사적 사실을 말할 때는 주절의 시제와 상관없이 종속절에 항상 과거시제를 쓰므로 과거시제 ended를 쓴다.
8 「the + 형용사」(~한 사람들) 뒤에는 항상 복수동사를 쓰므로 are를 쓴다.
9 의문사가 없는 의문문의 간접 화법은 「ask (+ 목적어) + if[whether] + 주어 + 동사」의 어순으로 쓴다. 전달동사가 과거시제이므로 현재시제 Are를 과거시제 was로 바꾸고, 전달하는 사람의 입장에 맞게 인칭대명사 you를 I로 바꾸고 부사구 next week를 the following week으로 바꾼다.
10 명령문 Stay를 to부정사 to stay로 바꾼다.
11 전달동사가 과거시제이므로 과거시제 left를 과거완료시제 had left로 바꾼다. 전달하는 사람의 입장에 맞게 부사 ago를 before로 바꾼다.
12 ③ → Lily asked if she could go to the mall with me.
⑤ → I asked Paul when he had cut his hair.
13 역사적 사실을 말할 때는 주절의 시제와 상관없이 종속절에 항상 과거시제를 쓰므로 과거시제 was를 쓴다.
14 부정명령문을 간접 화법으로 쓸 때는 to부정사 앞에 not을 쓰므로 not to run을 쓴다.
15 전달동사 say는 그대로 쓰고, 주절과 종속절을 연결하는 접속사 that은 생략할 수 있다. 전달동사가 과거시제이므로 현재시제 am을 과거시제 was로 바꾼다. 전달하는 사람의 입장에 맞게 인칭대명사 I를 she로 바꾸고 부사 today를 that day로 바꾼다.
16 ④ was → is
17 ⑤ had been → was
18 ③ have → has
19 • 명사절 주어 뒤에는 항상 단수동사를 쓰므로 was를 쓴다.
• 무게 등의 단위 주어 뒤에는 항상 단수동사를 쓰므로 is를 쓴다.
20 • 역사적 사실을 말할 때는 주절의 시제와 상관없이 종속절에 항상 과거시제를 쓰므로 과거시제 was built를 쓴다.
• 과학적 사실을 말할 때는 주절의 시제와 상관없이 종속절에 항상 현재시제를 쓰므로 현재시제 goes를 쓴다.
21 ⓑ Are → Is
ⓓ not make → not to make
ⓔ had → have
22 동명사구 주어 뒤에는 항상 단수동사를 쓰므로 makes me happy를 쓴다.
23 의문사가 있는 의문문의 간접 화법은 「ask (+ 목적어) + 의문사 + 주어 + 동사」의 어순이고, 전달동사가 과거시제이므로 what my hobby was를 쓴다.
24 역사적 사실을 말할 때는 주절의 시제와 상관없이 종속절에 항상 과거시제를 쓰므로 became the president를 쓴다.

Chapter 12 특수구문

UNIT 01 강조, 도치

p.67

A 1 sat a blue bird   2 wait
   3 does Megan go   4 O

B 1 This lemonade does taste sour
   2 It is Mr. Clark that[who] lives in the biggest house in this town
   3 It is on Main Street that[where] the new shopping mall is located

C 1 has Lucy forgotten her promise
   2 was the tunnel
   3 do the rude students show respect for their teachers

D 1 the corner stood a man playing
   2 20 years ago when my parents met
   3 Neither can I

UNIT 02 병렬, 부정, 동격, 생략

p.68

A 1 useful   2 O   3 hand
   4 while[while she was]

B 1 Neither   2 always   3 all

C 1 Martin hurt his arm when he was moving the desk
   2 You don't have to wear suits if you don't want to wear suits
   3 Though she was stressed, she tried to think positively

D 1 can either ride a bicycle or take a walk
   2 may use my towel if you want to
   3 None of the information was helpful

Chapter Test ✛

p.69

1 ③   2 ④   3 ①   4 ⑤
5 I imagined → did I imagine
6 I could → could I   7 ②   8 ④
9 None of the clerks   10 dived the swimmer
11 Not every game   12 did Josh expect
13 ⑤   14 ③   15 ④   16 ①
17 Amy does look tired after taking care of her niece
18 It was Robert that[who(m)] Timmy asked for a favor yesterday
19 It was from the woods that[where] a bear came out
20 ③   21 ②   22 ②
23 Ashley didn't call me because she forgot to call me
24 Unless you are under the age of ten, you can't get a discount

---

1   상관접속사 Both A and B로 연결되는 swimming과 문법적으로 형태가 같아야 하므로 surfing을 쓴다.

2   부정어 Never가 강조되어 문장의 맨 앞으로 올 때, 주어와 동사를 도치시켜 「부정어 + 조동사 + 주어」의 어순으로 쓴다.

3   '~도 그렇다'라는 의미로 so를 사용할 때 주어와 동사를 도치시켜 「so + 동사 + 주어」의 어순으로 쓴다. 앞 절의 동사가 be동사이므로 am을 쓴다.

4   부사구 last weekend를 강조하는 「It is[was] ~ that …」 구문의 that을 쓴다.

5   부정어 Little이 강조되어 문장의 맨 앞으로 올 때, 주어와 동사를 도치시켜 「부정어 + 조동사 + 주어」의 어순으로 쓴다.

6   '~도 아니다'라는 의미로 neither를 사용할 때 주어와 동사를 도치시켜 「neither + 동사 + 주어」의 어순으로 쓴다.

7   • 명사(The rumor)와 절(he ~ test) 사이에 동격의 that을 쓴다.
   • 명사(His ability)와 동명사구(memorizing words) 사이에 동격의 of를 쓴다.

8   ① we could → could we
   ② I do → do I
   ③ That → It
   ⑤ to stay → stay

9   '아무도 ~않다'라는 의미로 전체 부정을 나타내는 none을 쓰고, of와 함께 none of the clerks의 형태로 쓴다.

10   방향의 부사구 Into the water가 강조되어 문장의 맨 앞으로 올 때, 주어와 동사를 도치시켜 「방향의 부사(구) + 동사 + 주어」의 어순으로 쓴다.

11   '모두 ~인 것은 아니다'라는 의미로 부분 부정을 나타내는 「not + every」를 쓴다.

12   부정어 Hardly가 강조되어 문장의 맨 앞으로 올 때, 주어와 동사를 도치시켜 「부정어 + do/does/did + 주어 + 동사원형」의 어순으로 쓴다.

13   '둘 다 ~않다'라는 의미로 전체 부정을 나타내는 neither를 쓴다.

14   '항상 ~인 것은 아니다'라는 의미로 부분 부정을 나타내는 「not + always」를 쓴다.

15   '~도 아니다'라는 의미로 neither를 사용할 때 주어와 동사를 도치시켜 「neither + 동사 + 주어」의 어순으로 쓴다.

16   '우리 중 아무도 야구 경기를 보지 않아.'라는 의미이므로 전체 부정을 나타내는 none을 쓴다.

17 동사 looks를 강조할 때는 동사원형 look 앞에 does를 쓴다.

18 목적어 Robert를 It was와 that 사이에 써서 강조할 수 있다. 강조하는 대상이 사람이므로 that 대신 who(m)을 쓸 수 있다.

19 부사구 from the woods를 It was와 that 사이에 써서 강조할 수 있다. 강조하는 대상이 장소를 나타내므로 that 대신 where를 쓸 수 있다.

20 ⓐ That → It
   ⓓ am → do

21 ② I did → did I

22 ②: 가주어 it
   ①③④⑤: 「It is[was] ~ that …」 강조 구문의 it

23 she forgot to 뒤에 반복되어 생략된 어구 call me를 넣는다.

24 Unless 뒤에 생략된 「부사절의 주어 + be동사」를 넣는다.

HACKERS
GRAMMAR SMART

ANSWERS　LEVEL 3

해커스 그래머 스마트가 특별한 이유!

[Completely master English grammar]

1 누구나 쉽게 이해할 수 있는 **간결한 문법 설명**
2 실생활에서 그대로 사용할 수 있는 **유용한 표현과 예문**
3 '개념 확인' → '연습 문제' → '작문 연습' → '단원 마무리'로 이어지는 **4단계 문제풀이**

[Effectively prepare for middle school English exams]

1 학교 시험 기출경향을 완벽 반영한 문제로 **서술형 포함 내신 완벽 대비**
2 풍부한 문제의 Workbook과 다양한 부가 학습 자료로 학습효과 Up Up!

추가 자료

해커스북(HackersBook.com)에서
본 교재에 대한 다양한 추가 학습 자료를 이용하세요!

절취선